D1239872

THE WHITE HOUSE: THE HISTORY OF AN AMERICAN IDEA

THE WHITE HOUSE

THE HISTORY OF AN AMERICAN IDEA

WILLIAM SEALE

The White House Historical Association

WHITE HOUSE HISTORICAL ASSOCIATION

A nonprofit organization, chartered on November 3, 1961, to enhance understanding, appreciation, and enjoyment of the Executive Mansion. Income from the sale of this book will be used to publish other materials about the White House, as well as for the acquisition of historical furnishings and other objects for the Executive Mansion. Address inquiries to 740 Jackson Place, N.W., Washington, D.C. 20503.

Second Edition

Copyright © 1992, 2001 by William Seale
All rights reserved

ISBN #0-912308-85-0

Printed in the United States of America

Design by Market Sights, Inc., Washington, D.C.

Jacket illustrations:

Front: The White House, North Portico, photograph by William Weems, Woodfin Camp, Inc.

Back: The Burned-Out Shell of the White House (detail), watercolor by George Munger, 1814. White House collection.

The Republican Court in the Days of Lincoln (detail) by Peter F. Rothermel. White House collection.

The White House, South Portico (detail), photograph by Robert Llewellyn.

Digging of the new basement levels during the Truman Renovation, photograph by Abbie Rowe, NPS, The White House.

CONTENTS

TO REX W. SCOUTEN

PREFACE

The idea of the White House began to take shape in the last decade of the eighteenth century, when the house was designed and built for George Washington. But its image was not clear in the public mind until after Lincoln's presidency, the better part of a hundred years later. It achieved its final form in the second century of the house. By the time two hundred years could be measured between the laying of the cornerstone and the year 1992, the White House had become as much a part of America as the presidency itself.

Had the White House been built whole and left that way, it would be less an idea than a venerable piece of architecture. And it probably would not have survived, any more than have the rival presidential residences built at the same time in Philadelphia and New York. They were grand houses, too, and probably better architecture. Excellence of design, however, is not the issue with the White House. Ideas put it up, and ideas have shaped it year by year, until the house itself is a unique and uniquely American place for the presidency.

The White House today is a house that its eighteenth-century builders would recognize; yet, as this book shows, alterations have been nearly constant. Originally the building had no porticoes and no wings of any sort, but stood barren and enormous on its rise of land, surveying the sprawl of swampy bottomlands. Without George Washington, it might never have been; without his ghost it could never have risen again from the flames of the British invasion in 1814, nor survived its first half-century. When it proved inadequate, presidents were willing to tinker with it rather than replace it, and thus a pattern of changes was established; but even by the first decade after the Civil War, the idea itself had become stronger than the impulse to correct it. In a sense the White House was perfect for the job it had to do.

Within the history of the idea lies a mirror of American taste in houses, but with a difference. The White House has always had to accommodate official business as well as ceremonial function. This George Washington understood very well when he set out to build a magnificent house. Jefferson was the first president in residence to impose his architectural tastes on the White House and Harry Truman the most recent. Benjamin Harrison's wife, Caroline, called in an engineer to expand the house to palatial size. Theodore Roosevelt wanted a better house to serve his vibrant presidential image and the needs of his family, and he summoned a master architect to make it happen. In satisfying Roosevelt's wish,

Charles McKim clarified and reaffirmed the idea of the White House.

Not many presidents have been so bold in architecture. But many wanted convenience backstage to better serve their harried public lives. Such alterations left their marks on the fabric of the house, for it was considerably chopped up in their introduction. Jefferson installed waterclosets. Andrew Jackson's Tennessee comrades delighted in the general's east wing shower bath, and they admired the extension of the running water even to a hydrant on each floor. Van Buren was the first to warm himself front and back through the luxury of central heating. Polk set aside oil and candles and lit his chandeliers with gas. Andrew Johnson had a telegraph installed in the office; Hayes brought in a telephone and a typewriter. Electricity came with Benjamin Harrison. President Truman had the first White House television in 1947. The computer made its appearance under Jimmy Carter in the fall of 1980. In between these landmarks of technological advance have come legions of smaller wonders – the elevator, alarm clocks, toasters, electric blankets, remote controls, microwave ovens. Modern improvements have entered in a constant flow. In this way the place is a sort of Everyhouse, beyond its architecture

and the details of its building and rebuilding, a continuing chronicle of changes that affect us all.

The idea of the White House – the image projected by the place where the president lives and works – is summed up in its history as a building. I have found the house more significant, however, as a cultural artifact than as a work of architecture, and the treatment here reflects that viewpoint. This book contains, for example, more reference to the uses of the house by the various presidents than one might find in a more orthodox architectural history. And some of the subjects, such as the various devices for comfort and convenience, might not merit such detail elsewhere. Tracing the White House strictly through American architectural history, on the other hand, makes a spotty story. Its adherence to Anglo-Palladian precedent, it will be seen, had less to do with design than with personal prerogative and politics. The White House was not much of an influence on American architecture, but instead always stood rather aside from the trends, and there is no documentation for the idea that its porticoes inspired the white columns of the South. The White House has been a piece of architecture more or less unto itself. It was always different, from the time it was designed.

In its focus on the White House as a building,

this book differs from my previous book *The President's House: A History* (White House Historical Association, 1986), although it draws similarly on archival research. It differs from the earlier book also in its visual aspect. It was conceived in part as a visual history that would make the subject accessible to readers not necessarily familiar with architecture. It presents a larger selection of historical illustrations of the White House than have appeared in a book before. There are, however, some omissions – for example, part of the incomplete set of competition drawings of 1792, which are readily available elsewhere, and many period photographs of the house that would have become repetitious. Contemporary materials include new documentation in drawings and photographs produced by the Historic American Buildings Survey since 1988 and made available for this book.

In written sources the White House is probably the best documented of American houses, as the consistent detail in this narrative reflects. A note on the sources follows the text, in place of footnotes. These materials cover the building's full two hundred years. Most of the White House construction and domestic documents were, and remain, public information; they were carefully created and assembled and have been carefully preserved, even for portions of the house that are now gone or altered beyond recognition.

Much of this book in fact documents a building that no longer exists, even though it is perceived as unchanging. One looks in vain for an analogy among mansions, palaces, and cathedrals. A whimsical comparison – although it could not be more different in cultural context – is the Shinto shrine at Ise in Japan. This complex of buildings can be traced back more than a thousand years, but by ceremonial tradition the structures are demolished every twenty years and rebuilt exactly as they were. The White House has been pulled apart, rearranged, gutted by fire and renovation, reassembled; yet it is always the same. Its idea has become its essence.

William Seale
February 1992

ACKNOWLEDGMENTS

As with any book this one began as a concept, and making it happen involved the work and devotion of many. I had wanted for some time to write an architectural book on the White House that took advantage of the wealth of illustrative materials. Rex W. Scouten, Hon. AIA, curator of the White House, hoped such a book could be published for the two hundredth anniversary of the cornerstone laying for the White House. At the American Institute of Architects James P. Cramer, Hon. AIA, executive vice president; Steven A. Etkin, group vice president; and Norman Koonce, FAIA, president of the American Architectural Foundation, envisioned this as an AIA book.

The Office of White House Liaison of the National Capital Region, National Park Service, and the AIA were at that time – 1989 – sponsoring extensive recording projects on the White House, inside and out, by the Historic American Buildings Survey of the National Park Service. Robert J. Kapsch, the chief of HABS and its sister branch, the Historic American Engineering Record, agreed that the resulting drawings could be published here for the first time. James I. McDaniel, associate director, National Capital Region, NPS, gave the services and support of his office. The White House Historical Association, a participant in the HABS project with the AIA, gave its help through

Bernard R. Meyer, executive vice president, who has also helped me in many ways with this project. John Ray Hoke, Jr., FAIA, publisher of the AIA Press, added the book to his distinguished list of books about architecture.

Cynthia Ware was editor, and I am grateful for her many insights and tireless efforts in every aspect of the work.

Philip B. Silcott, editor of my earlier book *The President's House*, served as line editor for this volume. At the AIA Press, Janet Rumbarger oversaw production. Pamela James Blumgart provided copyediting assistance, coordinated illustrations and permissions, and helped with production. Elyse Chiland Tipton proofread, prepared the index, and pulled in final, stubborn illustrations. Elizabeth W. Fisher joined in for several months, casting nets over Washington's rich historical archives and other sources for publishable prints of the illustrations.

Marilyn Worseldine designed the book, and I thank her for a beautiful job.

The Office of the Curator of the White House is the best single resource on the history of the house. The office staff, under the direction of Curator Rex W. Scouten, have helped me with this volume in more ways than space permits listing. Betty C. Monkman, associate curator, my longtime colleague on this subject, has read text and made corrections, as well as sharing her wealth of knowledge. William G. Allman likewise has shared his valuable research. Lydia S. Tederick spent many hours gathering illustration materials for the book and assisted the AIA Press in countless ways. Angela G. Horton of the Curator's Office provided additional help.

Gary J. Walters, chief usher of the White House, has given loyal support to this work, including access to parts of the building when firsthand study was required.

Paul D. Dolinsky, chief, and Frederick J. Lindstrom, supervising architect, Historic American Buildings Survey, who directed the interior documentation of the White House, gave time and attention to providing HABS material for the book. The many individual architects and draftsmen who executed the fine ink drawings appear by name in the illustration credits. Jack E. Boucher, HABS staff photographer, extended his documentary coverage of the White House to a number of special shots for this book, including one of the banqueting room at Mount Vernon.

As the source notes and illustration credits suggest, research for this book was far reaching. I owe thanks to too many people and learned institutions to name here, but beyond a general expression of gratitude to all of them, I would like to single out a few. Ierne Grant, Edinburgh, helped by continuing our search for the Scottish stonemasons. Erik Kvalsvik, photographer, Baltimore, whose work appears here both as museum copywork and as original photographs, made himself available on short notice on more than one occasion. I would also like to thank John Dwyer, Cartographic and Architectural Branch, National Archives; Melissa Houghton at the Octagon House in Washington; Donald J. Crump, Ruth Corcoran, and Gloria Hunter at the White House Historical Association; Gilbert Gonzalez, Hayes Presidential Center, Fremont, Ohio; Harbinger, Inc., Washington, D.C.; Michael L. Ainslee, president, Sotheby's Inc.; Pat O'Brien, Denver Service Center, NPS; David Krause, Office of White House Liaison, NPS; W. H. Phillips, Jr., AIA, Mobile, Alabama; Neil W. Horstman, resident director, Mount Vernon Ladies' Association; Sam Daniel, Prints & Photographs Division, Library of Congress; Edward C. Carter II and Jeffrey A. Cohen, Benjamin Henry Latrobe Papers, American Philosophical Society.

Carl A. Ruthstrom helped me in a thousand ways, not inconsiderably in assisting me into the computer age.

Lucinda S. Seale has been a book widow and has climbed with me over ruins, toured musty chateaux and country houses, and remained encouraging throughout.   W. S.

View of the site of the federal city
from Georgetown heights,
engraving by T. Cartwright after
G. Beck, 1801, giving an idea of
the rural landscape where the city
of Washington was built.

1

THE IDEA

OF A PRESIDENT'S HOUSE

George Washington, president from 1789 to 1797. He envisioned a presidential residence, and a capital as well, appropriate to the high ambitions of the new government. His proposed "palace" was reduced in scale in the building of the White House.

T he United States Congress, at the nation's temporary capital in New York, ordered in 1790 that a city be built to house the American government. This new city would, of course, include a hall for Congress and a house for the president. With the Residence Act the architectural history of the White House begins. Not only did the act authorize planning and construction, but it brought the as yet nonexistent building to the attention of many of the minds of the time, raising the controversial and intriguing question of just what sort of house a free people should provide for their chief of state.

President George Washington took charge of building the city, and in no endeavor did he show a greater personal interest. The city was to stand on lands ceded by the states of Virginia and Maryland, country the president had known all his life. At the close of the next year he presented a survey of the site to Congress. He had given the matter time and thought and believed that he had started the ball rolling toward 1800, the year the government was to move to the new capital. But by early winter of 1792 his patience had worn thin. He had been promised much and had received little. Advisers and experts had disappointed him. Speculators had swarmed to

the Potomac River site looking for profits in land deals. These men he had been able to control, but his capital on the Potomac was still no more than a magnificent scheme on paper, for it consisted only of stump-spotted clearings and streets marked by stakes driven in lines through woods and fields.

Thomas Jefferson, the secretary of state, had tried to advise Washington in matters of architecture and city planning but had been largely

1

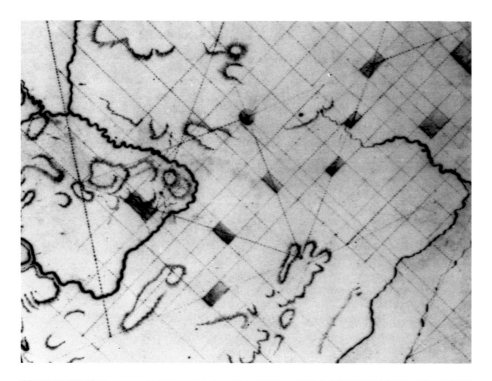

Top:

Detail of one of two so-called dotted-line maps showing sight lines to various public buildings, including the President's House, seen here

Bottom and opposite:

Plan of Washington, 1792 (1800 imprint), and detail, showing foundations of the President's House on the grand scale—four times that of the White House as built— originally approved by George Washington. The configuration of the foundations suggests deep earth terraces and fountains; in scale and siting, the foundations are on axis with Pennsylvania and New York avenues as actually built.

ignored. The president intended to have his own way. The plan he endorsed was for a capital in the European sense, one that would be the financial and cultural center of the country, as well as the political headquarters. He wanted a capital the world would respect and understand, and he meant to build it. The man who had drawn the plan, the unyielding Pierre Charles L'Enfant, perhaps an artist, perhaps an engineer, had already been dismissed because of disagreements with the commissioners appointed to supervise the development of the capital. While Washington would see that the plan was carried out, the schemes the Frenchman had developed for public buildings were now out of the picture. No one knew much about them, anyway. On the elevation where the President's House was to stand, there were only mounds of earth thrown up from what were to be the cellars of the vast "pallace" L'Enfant had envisioned. The cellars revealed little about the design, except that it would be great in scale, and this was confirmed in the city plan L'Enfant had made.

Time was wasting. Eight years remained to make ready for Congress, which by the Residence Act was to occupy the city in 1800. Not a single design had been drawn for the public buildings that would house the government. Jefferson proposed a solution to the standstill: hold a national design competition for the President's House and the Congress house—or "capitol," as it was to be called, the term Virginians used for their statehouse. Washington agreed, and the competition was announced in March 1792.

At the same time, wary of more delays, Washington began his own inquiries to find an architect for the house. Plans were needed, yes, but he also wanted on the scene a competent man who could get the work done. He remembered having met a "practical" man—a builder—introduced to him by prominent friends in Charleston, South Carolina, on his southern tour in 1791. A letter to Henry Laurens in Charleston retrieved James Hoban's name, and soon Washington and Hoban met in Philadelphia, then the capital. It was a successful session, we can assume, for matters between the two developed rapidly. To better understand the challenge, Hoban went to the

The Perpendicular height of the
ground where the Capitol is to
stand is above the tide of Tiber Creek
78 Feet.

Perpendicular height of
branch above the tide in

Tiber Creek.

Branch

President's House

Capitol

POTOMAC

BRANCH

Peter Lacour delin.

A. Doolittle Sculp.

FEDERAL HALL

The Seat of CONGRESS

Printed & Sold by A. Doolittle New Haven 1790

4

building site, drawing instruments in hand.

The commissioners in charge of the federal city gave him every assistance and commented favorably to the president that he had begun his drawings on the spot. Through the late spring and summer competition drawings began arriving at the office of the secretary of state. Some of the entries were reviewed by the president before being forwarded to the commissioners on the scene. Washington wrote to Jefferson, "if none more elegant than these should appear . . . the exhibition will be a dull one indeed."

The president went to the federal city site to make his final judgment on July 16, 1792. He did not pause over the curious assortment of amplified courthouses and town halls and awkward mansions. The winner was Hoban, with an English-style country house that looked like a leaf from one of Washington's architecture books. Given the choice of a medal or a cash prize for his design, Hoban took the medal with the remainder of the value in cash. In many cases in late eighteenth-century architectural work, this

Opposite:
Federal Hall, New York, first seat of the United States Congress under the Constitution. It was through this highly successful building, a neoclassical remodeling of Manhattan's late seventeenth-century city hall, that Pierre Charles L'Enfant gained his reputation as an architectural designer. Emblazoned with neoclassical emblems of the new nation, Federal Hall helped establish the classical ideal in government architecture. Engraving by Amos Dolittle, 1790

Below:
This scheme for a domed house is often but probably incorrectly attributed to Thomas Jefferson, who had earlier envisioned a similar house for the governor's residence at the Virginia capital in Richmond. This may well have been entered, however, at Jefferson's anonymous behest, by John Collins, a Richmond builder who had been involved in public works there. Whatever his connection with this scheme may or may not have been, Collins was awarded second prize by the commissioners for this entry.

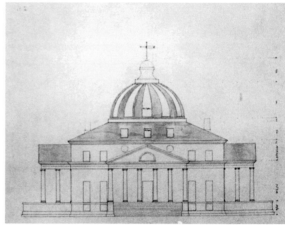

Left:
Andrew Mayfield Carshore, remembered as the "poet of the Hudson River," entered these drawings and notes as part of his competition project for the President's House. The draped canopy shows his awareness that the job of president carried with it ceremonial forms.

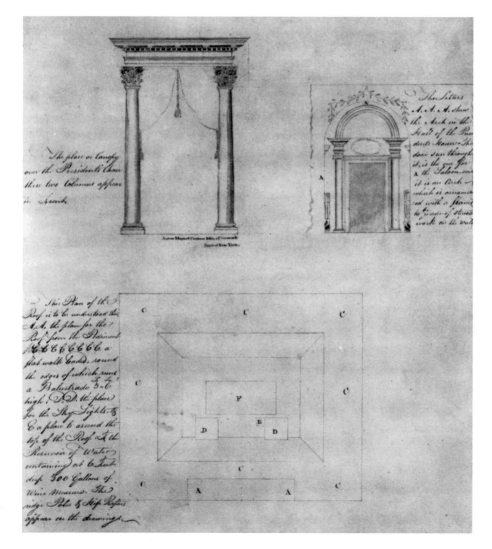

would have been the end of the architect's involvement. Hoban, however, was retained to superintend construction, both because his past experience in Ireland and America recommended him and because he got on well with Washington. The president was pleased with everything for the moment except the size of Hoban's house. It was only a fraction of the scale of the palace for which the cellars had been dug. Before heading back to Philadelphia, he ordered the house enlarged by one-fifth and its stonework greatly enriched with carvings. Washington's participation in the process had only begun.

Hoban's winning project was the first step toward the final design, yet it was close to what the White House would be. The architect had sought to please his pragmatic client with a clear image the president could readily grasp. L'Enfant's model had floated somewhere in the clouds, maybe a French palace, but nothing specific. Hoban's model stood footed in the earth of his native Ireland, the house of the Duke of Leinster in Dublin. Better known for its inhabitants than for its architecture, Leinster House was a familiar rendition of a certain type of neoclassical country house well accepted in both England and Ireland. The style was known to Washington in various more modest buildings and in plates published in architectural pattern books.

It is known that Washington admired the Duke of Leinster's public-spirited Anglo-Irish family, particularly the son Edward Fitzgerald, who, while a prisoner of war in Charleston during the American Revolution, had become a popular figure in that city and close friend to some of Washington's relatives. As a student at the Royal Dublin Society's drawing school, Hoban had known Leinster House, for it was the premier residence of Dublin; since such houses were regularly open to the public he had doubtless toured the state parts of its interior. His master, the Irish-born Thomas Ivory, was a specialist in Georgian neoclassical architecture, then on its last legs in Britain. Ivory had played his part in the eighteenth-century transformation of Dublin. In 1780 two of his earlier students, Robert Poole and John Cash, published *Views of Dublin*, which recorded the architectural monuments of the city through engravings. The view of Leinster House

Hoban's earliest known drawing for the President's House is the plan. The excerpted section (right) shows his scheme for a three-story house. The rusticated raised basement was removed from the plan as an economy measure in the fall of 1793. The plan, with single-story columns probably intended to support a surrounding balcony, suggests a basilican entrance hall, extending up into the second level, as at Leinster House (see page 14). On the left is the space realized as the East Room; across the house on the right is the grand stair, and between the two are the state parlors, climaxed by the Blue Room. This plan was carried on into the revised scheme in 1793, shown (top) in Hoban's elevation, and remains about the same today.

Wax portrait of James Hoban, circa 1800. The portrait, which descended in Hoban's family, was probably made by John Christian Rauschner of New York.

Overleaf:
Detail of Hoban's 1793 elevation

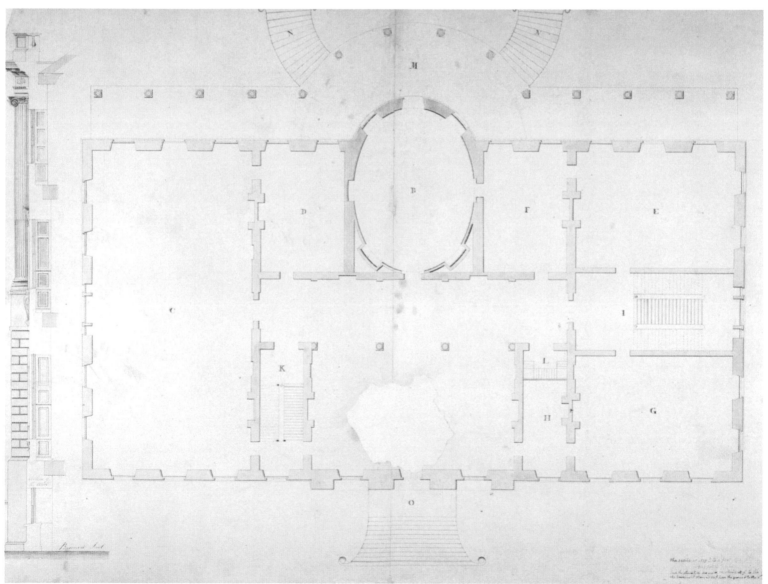

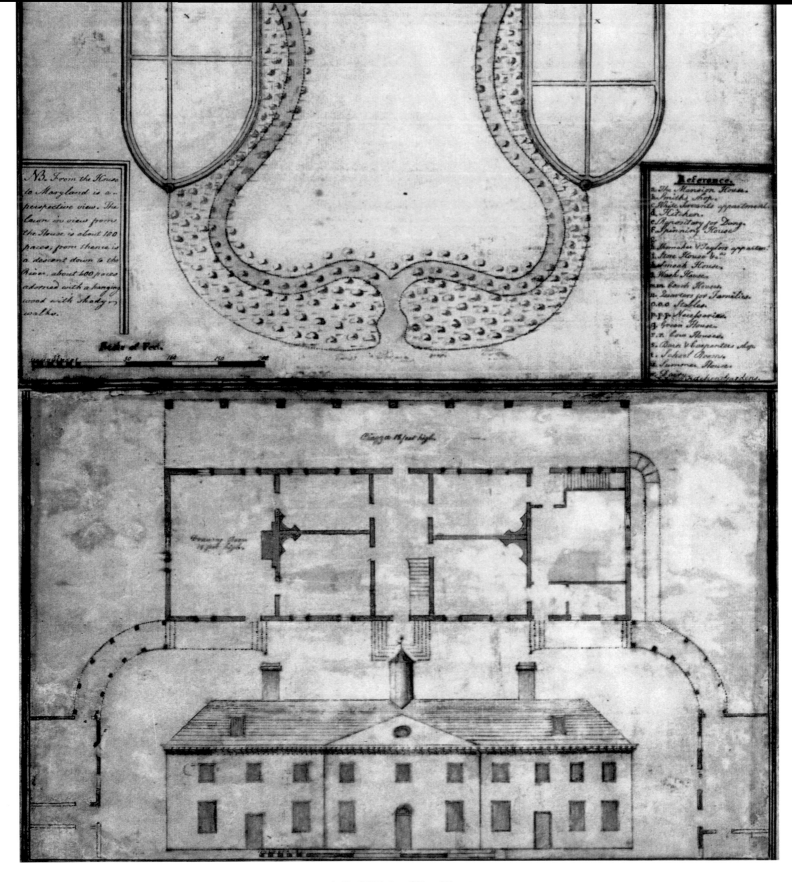

In the 1797 plan of Mount Vernon
by Samuel Vaughan, which George
Washington considered to be
accurate in most particulars, the
placement of the "new room" is
the most striking similarity to the
White House, reflecting as it does
the placement of the East Room.

in this book is the most likely illustration Hoban would have had to show to Washington in selling the idea for his Irish model.

However the inspiration came to be, Hoban's adaptation of Leinster House made sense as a solution to the new architectural challenge of housing a president. Washington realized that he himself enjoyed a singular perspective on the subject, although he often modestly remarked that he had no knowledge of architecture. (Washington in fact had more than a little familiarity with building, and it is believed that his house at Mount Vernon developed in his own imagination – abetted by ideas he had gleaned from pattern books.) Many men had put pencil to paper to suggest the sorts of buildings they thought suitable. Precedent had been presented in the forms of statehouses, palaces, and temples. The cities of New York and Philadelphia had each begun presidential houses in the hope of becoming the nation's permanent capital.

But Hoban's model, a house only some fifty years old, was closer to the target. It was the home of the first gentleman of Ireland, and in the last part of the eighteenth century the Americans and the Irish sensed a strong kinship in political ideals and economic development. Neoclassicism may have had far less to do with the appropriateness of the White House design than with human associations. It seems natural to assume a connection between the arrival of neoclassical architecture in America and the supposed triumph of the philosophical Enlightenment in the Revolution, but it is difficult to find any link of this sort until later on. To Washington's deaf ears Jefferson had promoted his Roman temples as models for the public buildings. The president turned instead to what he perceived as current British precedent. His President's House, approved in the autumn of 1792, is a monument to Washington's vision for the government, and probably also to his limited knowledge of the arts of his time.

The neoclassical Leinster House he admired was one step in stylistic advance from the red-brick William and Mary governor's house – the famous Williamsburg "palace" of colonial Virginia that was certainly the most magnificent house Washington had ever known. Like the palace at Williamsburg, Leinster House was just at the edge of town, an urban palace but also a country house. Hoban's scheme did not entirely depart from the idea of the boxlike mansions colonial Americans had known, but his new house was to be larger and more magnificent than any of these, as befitted the head of a nation. The house probably seemed for those justifications perfectly rational to Washington. If anything, the president wanted the house to be grander, and he was quick to dress it up with more ornamentation than that of the original Leinster House.

Described in terms of architectural history, Hoban's project was for a three-story house in the Anglo-Palladian manner of mid-Georgian England. His original elevation does not survive, but an early revision does, along with a section of the north wall. Between the two it is clear that this is the White House, although not as it was

Washington added his "new room" to the east end of his house at Mount Vernon in the early 1780s as a place for important events. Here he held formal dinners and greeted visitors when large numbers came to call. Here he stood to receive official word that he had been elected president of the United States. If this lofty space was not the sole inspiration for the East Room, it certainly prepared Washington for such a stately interior. Like that of the East Room the ceiling of Mount Vernon's great chamber extends up into the second floor to make the architectural proportions work.

Two American "palaces"—(below top) the governor's palace of Virginia, begun 1704, and (below bottom) that of North Carolina, begun 1770. These were known to George Washington—Virginia's from his youth, the North Carolina palace from his visit during his southern tour in 1791, when it was in use as a statehouse. The American colonies knew no more complete or deliberate expressions of the English country-house form, and the impression they made upon Washington, who had not traveled abroad, must have been great. In arriving at a design for the White House, he agreed upon a style a generation more modern than these stately piles.

Above:
County Courthouse, Charleston, South Carolina, built on the site of an earlier statehouse and completed about 1790. Known from the eighteenth century to the mid–1880s as "the statehouse," this building started out as an effort to lure the state capital back to Charleston from its new inland location at Columbia. It is one of the new public buildings that George Washington could have seen on his southern tour in 1791, at the time he met James Hoban in Charleston. A distinct echo of this building is evident in the White House, although connections between the two cannot be fully substantiated.

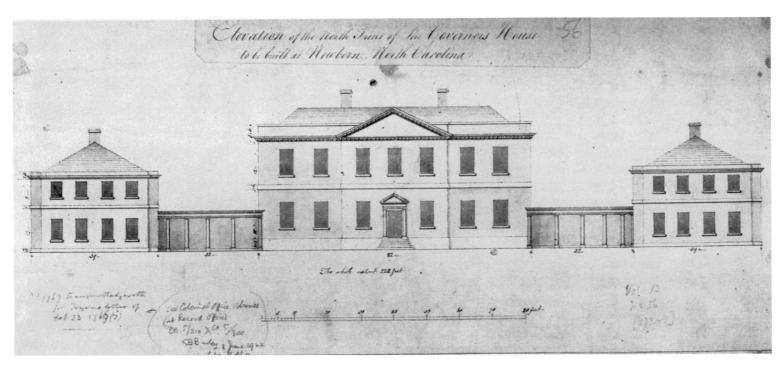

built. The elevation familiar to us is suggested in the section, and the plan is essentially that of the White House. So great is the scale of the proposed building by American standards of the time, and so different from other American houses, that the President's House would have seemed remarkable indeed. The structure, though hardly one-fourth the size Washington and L'Enfant had planned, was to be grand beyond any house or even statehouse or meetinghouse known to have been built in America up until that time and probably larger in scale than any American house before the 1870s.

From the north the place was an imposing rectangular structure two stories high, mounted atop an exposed basement that, as at Leinster House, was rusticated in its center section to form a base for four Ionic columns attached to the smooth ashlar walls of the upper floors. The lines of heroic pilasters in place on the White House today appear in this early drawing. There apparently was no pediment in the scheme prior to the close of 1793, when the basement level was omitted. In his drawing, Hoban detailed with a sure hand the rich stone embellishments ordered by the president. As the project developed further, the carving would be made ever more elaborate.

One would enter the house through the rusticated base of the columned centerpiece. At Leinster House, entrance is made in the same way, and beyond the rather unassuming doorway one finds a lofty saloon that extends up

Two would-be palaces, in (top) New York and (bottom) Philadelphia. Each was constructed in the 1790s during the ten-year waiting period for the completion of the federal city in the hope that the president would forgo his new city and remain. George Washington could not be persuaded even to enter them.

They survived for several decades as state government facilities and, with their splendid rotundas and elaborate English-style neoclassical interiors, were among the most magnificent houses of their respective cities, high-water marks in American architecture in the Federal era. They stood in august contrast to (right) George Washington's official Philadelphia residence, the Robert Morris house on High Street, itself very fine by most standards.

through two floors. Whether this feature was part of the unrealized White House scheme is not known, although it is probable, because the function of the interior spaces is more plausible with the saloon than without it. In any event, the saloon was not possible after the height of the house was reduced when Hoban redrew his project at the close of 1793.

The plan shown in this original version was virtually the same plan as built, with the large entrance hall and transverse corridor off which the principal rooms opened. The most pronounced departure from the Leinster House model was the great bow that projected from the south facade. Leinster House had shallow bows at each end, while at the White House the bow became a deep, three-story bay boldly defined from the outside and containing, on the main floor inside, the room we know as the Blue Room.

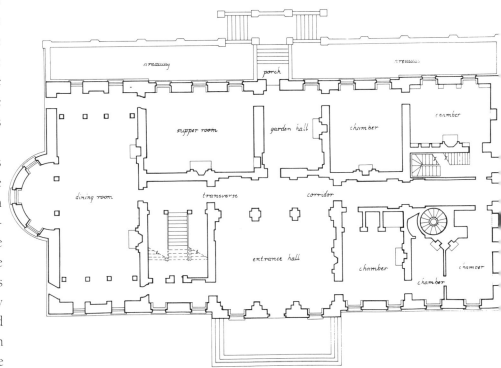

Opposite top:
Leinster House, Dublin, Ireland, from most accounts James Hoban's model for the White House. Although this 1792 view is not the one Hoban would have shown Washington, it is the most descriptive of the eighteenth-century views and gives the best idea of the building Hoban knew. The building survives today, with added wings as the seat of the Irish *dail* or national legislature.

Opposite bottom:
Plan of the main or entrance floor at Leinster House as it is today. Similarities to the White House plan (see page 7) present themselves in the arrangement of halls and stairs, the row of parlors, and the distribution of some of the other rooms. The great state room on the left, situated like George Washington's "new room" and the East Room, was made from three smaller rooms in 1780, while James Hoban was a pupil in the nearby school of the Royal Dublin Society. By comparison, the White House plan is distinctly Americanized by being simplified, with fewer rooms, perhaps showing the direct influence of houses George Washington knew.

Right:
Entrance saloon, Leinster House. This space rises from the ground floor into the first story, an arrangement probably similar to Hoban's original project for the White House.

More cannot be read from the earliest known Hoban drawing. The White House continued to be altered, more by omission than by addition. Washington and Hoban were in frequent contact. Their relationship, traced through correspondence, brings to mind that between a country squire and an able builder as they set out to construct a country house. Washington's acceptance of the genial and hardworking Irishman gave Hoban protection from the commissioners of the city, who interfered constantly, ordering changes in the design of the structure in the guise of doing their job. The president did not hesitate to intervene in controversies to get his way, even to a curt "I require it," to end discussions that, to his thinking, rambled on too long after he had made up his mind.

On one major issue he compromised. From the start he had insisted that the public buildings be built of stone. In part this was an idea emphasized to him by L'Enfant. Washington argued that the "first buildings of Europe" were made of stone, thus making it clear that he included the public architecture of the federal city in his Federalist philosophy that the United States must be a great nation on equal footing with those of the Old World. But he was also personally interested in stone construction. In finishing the external walls of Mount Vernon he used beveled wood to simulate stone blocks, then thickened the paint coating with crushed sandstone to create a stonelike texture.

By 1793 the commissioners were concerned that the local source of sandstone, the Aquia Creek quarry downriver from Mount Vernon, could not provide stone in sufficient quantity to complete both the house and the Capitol. Fearful of reintroducing the subject of changing to brick, they respectfully suggested that the house be reduced in scale.

Washington, annoyed at first, recognized that although the Aquia Creek quarry had provided material for some houses, it had been used mainly for architectural trim, gravestones, and odds and ends such as the Mount Vernon cornerstone, probably set by his father in the late seventeenth century. There was no way to gauge the capacity of a stone quarry, so he listened to the commissioners.

At the close of the working season in 1793, he agreed to a major reduction in scale, but he insisted on keeping the ground dimensions of the enlarged plan, which apparently could have been altered even at this late date. The lower or base floor was eliminated. On the north side this placed the two stories of smooth stone and the four columns visually on a level with the ground, while on the south the basement, with its areaway, was wholly exposed and rusticated all around with massively articulated blocks. To add importance to the now smaller north facade, a pediment was placed over the four columns,

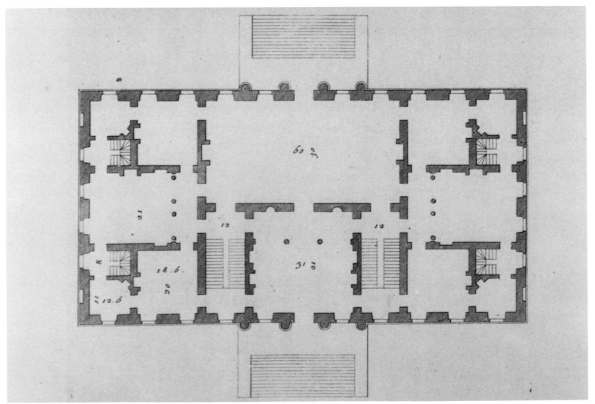

Top:

Plate 57, James Gibbs, *Book of Architecture* (London, 1728). Gibbs's architectural pattern book was one of the most influential of its time, and Hoban almost certainly owned a copy. The book was a stock item in the libraries of many eighteenth-century Americans interested in studying English neoclassical architecture. Early in this century the architectural historian Fiske Kimball argued, in an article published in *Century Magazine*, that this Gibbs design was the inspiration for the White House ("The Genesis of the White House"; vol. 95, February 1918), and the idea was current for more than sixty years. While the Gibbs elevation bears some resemblance to the White House as it was built, it is not like the elevation in Hoban's original three-story project. The entrance hall and adjacent back stairs in Hoban's original plan are very like the corresponding space in Gibbs's design (right), but otherwise there is no similarity between the plans.

forming what Washington and the commissioners called the "frontispiece." Hoban rendered the pediment elaborately, with sun rays and a noble eagle, all to be carved in stone in the sort of French-influenced Federal style L'Enfant had introduced at Federal Hall, where Congress had met in New York.

The White House was now in a sense Americanized. It had lost its most obvious reference to Leinster House in the removal of the high base. Because Washington had kept the ground dimensions of the enlarged plan, the house remained very large for an American house, yet it was modified enough that it no longer suggested so strongly an English mansion. Oddly enough,

there was something evocative of French architecture in the way the house hugged the ground on the north instead of being set up high on a base.

There were to be few other changes. The marble pavement intended for the principal floors was abandoned in favor of wooden floors, in the interest of trimming costs. By that time the groin vaulting in the basement was so far advanced that the decision was made to retain it but to complete it in brick instead of stone. This magnificent feature of the White House, once hidden in utilitarian hallways, now forms a major architectural element. The long back porch in the plan was never built, although the doorways cut for it

Aquia Creek Quarry, about 1800, sketch by Benjamin Latrobe. Opened by the Brent family in 1699, this quarry was the principal supplier of stone for buildings and tombstones in the Chesapeake Bay region and also had a market eastward along the Atlantic seaboard. Limited use of Aquia sandstone was made at Mount Vernon, a short distance up the Potomac River. L'Enfant arranged a ten-year lease of the quarry in 1791 for the government.

still pierce the south wall. In most other particulars the house was built as planned and revised by the close of 1793.

The cornerstone was laid October 13, 1792, and work went on each year from about mid-April to mid-October, until the occupation of the federal city in 1800. The White House progressed well ahead of the Capitol. Workmen and craftsmen were engaged by various means, often through newspaper advertisements, but more often by word of mouth – the way in which Washington had found Hoban. The chief stonemason, Collen Williamson, was located in New York through his cousin John Suter, who kept the tavern where the commissioners met and thus had heard them complain of the stone problem.

The stone shell of the White House is of great interest today because it is about all that survives of the original building. Williamson was stonemason until the time of his dismissal in 1795.

His White House work was revealed in the 1980s during a joint National Park Service/White House conservation project that involved removing nearly 200 years' accumulation of white paint from the stone.

Williamson, a country builder, probably came to America from Scotland no earlier than the close of the Revolution. Like Hoban and other immigrants in the building trades, he seems to have anticipated a reborn career in the new United States. Williamson is found first at work in the Highlands of Scotland, in the late 1760s on Castle Grant, seat of the powerful Grant family, and after that on a country place called Moy House, a tall, rambling residence for Sir Ludlow Grant, who owned extensive lands. Williamson planned the house and built it almost to completion, before he was replaced by John Adam.

Moy is one of those erratic, strangely proportioned Scottish gentry houses found throughout

Detail from a watercolor by William Birch. Stonecutters at work at the Capitol, cutting smooth-faced ashlar building stones with a copper wire as a blade and sand for grit. The same method was used on the White House.

Stone cutters in the different branches are most wanted, Masons and bricklayers are also though not so much wanted — Those who pay their own passage will be immediately employed at the same rates given to such workmen in the Country —

Signed Th Johnson D Stuart

Dan Carroll

Above:
Detail of a resolution in the
Proceedings of the
Commissioners of the District of
Columbia, dated January 3, 1793,
about terms of employment for
"workmen & Mechanics" who
came to work in the federal city.

Below:
White House watertable, laid
originally under the supervision of
stonemason Collen Williamson

the Highlands in the eighteenth century. Its look, in part that of an enlarged farmhouse, shows the situation in Scottish country house architecture before the Adam brothers, native sons, made their neoclassical impact. Georgian detailing at Moy, generally following Williamson's extant elevation, is heavy and sometimes awkward. Nevertheless, the house in its way foreshadows the change that came during the second half of the century, because John Adam, the Edinburgh-based one of the brothers Adam, was eventually called to the work to replace Williamson. Under his direction, not Williamson's, Moy House was completed and the new version of neoclassicism forced on the old pile.

Williamson turned up in New York in the 1780s. Of his work there—if any—we know nothing. Moy House extends the context for studying Williamson's work beyond the White House. At the two places the touch of the stone-masons is in some respects not dissimilar, although the scale of the White House as a structure is far greater than that of Moy. Williamson's stone construction at the White House,

executed from 1792 to 1795, extended from the basement level up to the top of the first or principal floor.

The American work does suggest, at the basement level, the walls of Moy House in the rustication of its ashlar blocks with the tooth tool—the tooling or striation at Moy diagonal and that at the White House vertical—and the general smoothness of its trim stone. Quoins framing the basement windows of the White House are rather like the quoins on the corners of Moy House, and some of the exterior moldings, though typical of the age, are the same in both places. The setting of the stone at Moy and at the White House has excellence that has stood the test of time. But in an overall sense the naïveté in most of the stonework at Moy House sets it quite apart from that at the White House. The White House carving, in particular, although marred somewhat by the grainy Aquia stone, is of high quality.

Credit for the carving at the White House belongs principally to two groups of Edinburgh stonemasons recruited by the commissioners in

Examples of stonemasonry at Moy House, in Scotland, circa 1765, probably superintended by Collen Williamson nearly thirty years before his work on the White House

the fall of 1793. The first group consisted of members of Lodge No. 8, operative stonemasons attached to the local Masonic order, and the second, two brothers, John and James Williamson – of no known relation to Collen. Six members of Lodge No. 8 agreed to travel: George Thomson, James White, Alexander Wilson, Alexander Scott, James McIntosh, and Robert Brown. The Williamson brothers came at the same time and probably brought others with them.

In New Town, Edinburgh, there are still houses from the early 1790s that are known to be the work of these men and that show their skill at stone carving in the neoclassical mode of the Adam brothers. One example, at 64 Queen Street, is particularly fine. Here, a sharply rusticated floor at street level forms a bold base for two upper floors lightened by smooth ashlar blocks. Details – trim, molded window openings and hoods, and the delicate stone surround of a fan-transformed doorway – are all carefully planned and masterfully executed.

By 1794 the stonemasons faced a moratorium on building in Britain as a result of the war with revolutionary France. To flee, though unlawful, was for some an economic necessity. Many went to America, departing quietly from the western coast. The Williamson brothers' party and the stonemasons from Lodge No. 8 were ready for work on the White House when the construction season opened in April 1794.

After working so much within the classical simplicity of the Adamesque architecture of Edinburgh, the Scots must have looked in wonder at the lush carvings proposed for the President's House. The roses, garlands, leaves, griffins, acorns, ribbons and bows, and great acanthus leaves were for the most part of the older Anglo-Palladianism that fashion in Scotland had long since laid aside. Rich carving, however, was what Washington wanted, and he would have his way, particularly on this house. The Aquia Creek blocks were brought by boat from the quarry downriver, drained of their sap in the stoneyard, then brought to the cutting shed to be transformed.

The typical process of construction at the time

Moy House,
principal elevation,
Collen Williamson,
circa 1765

Details of the house at 64 Queen Street, Edinburgh, built for the earl of Wemyss by the stonemasons of Operative Lodge No. 8, who later completed the upper walls of the White House and executed its stone carvings. The house, completed in 1790, was considered one of the finest residences in New Town, Edinburgh. The architect's name is lost, but the possibility of John Adam's involvement cannot be discounted.

was to supply the various building trades with a general set of architectural drawings – elevations, plans, a few details – and let the masters themselves generate the working or shop drawings needed to secure the details. This creative role had always belonged to stonemasons. Few buildings in America were finished with dressed and carved stone, while in Europe and the British Isles they were numerous; on many projects even as late as the 1790s the stone ornaments were devised by the masons in counsel with the client. This was no longer the case with major works, where the architect designed every feature. Taking his elevations, the masons would make full-scale shop drawings for the architect's approval. In this sense Hoban was the architect of the White House, not merely the master builder as he is sometimes described. Perhaps this was at the root of the intense dislike Williamson developed toward him; that he, like John Adam in Scotland, had usurped the mason's traditional role. Hoban had no known collaborator on the White House other than Washington.

Hoban in fact had extensive knowledge of stone construction, gained in Ireland. There Thomas Ivory, his teacher and sometime employer, designed important buildings in stone. Hoban worked for Ivory on Dublin's Newcomen Bank and on the Royal Exchange. The stonework on both buildings was very fine, especially on the bank, where the smooth surfaces and embellished openings display particular delicacy and harmony.

Thus the White House was plagued by the problem of having two experts in charge from the moment the first stones were set. Hoban and Williamson battled frequently. Opening the building season of 1795, when the walls of the second floor were begun, Williamson at last lost the respect of the commissioners and was dismissed. Taking his place as master and supervisor was the English mason George Blagdin, master of the Capitol. He was not full time, but at certain junctures he inspected the White House work for the government. No trouble came from the Edinburgh masons, however. They seem to have worked largely on their own, with their own organizational structure, doubtless of the kind familiar to them in Scotland. Most of the stonework was completed by the summer of 1797.

The presidential mansion was unrivaled in the United States for the quality of its carving, setting it apart as one of the most remarkable buildings in the country. Because the house is set back so far on the site that the carving is not visible from the street, and because the image the White House projects is so familiar as to be seldom studied, the fine carving has been generally overlooked in works on American architecture.

The Aquia Creek stone is arkose sandstone of the Lower Cretaceous period. Highly porous, it is a poor building material that must be sealed almost as soon as it is set. The Scots were used to a harder stone, which they believed also needed sealing. Traditionally they sealed stone with a dense lime-base whitewash, which was forced into every crack and joint. Sometimes the initial coating was refreshed and sometimes it was not. The weather eventually wore away what it could reach, leaving the whitewash in the crevices as a sealer and filler.

First painted with whitewash in 1798, the White House was to be continually repainted and is painted still today. When the Park Service/White House conservation work began and some forty-two layers of paint were stripped away, it was found that the Scotsmen's whitewash was the most difficult to remove. The original recipe for the whitewash survives, a curious concoction with portions of salt, ground rice, and glue added to the usual mixture of water and lime. In America, whitewash was applied to fences and barns with brooms or broom-like brushes. At the White House the situation seems to have been different. The whitewash was applied like paint, for original orders for finer brushes survive in the papers of the day.

So the cold, grayish color of the Aquia stone in the walls was to be known only to the builders and to those who saw it before it was whitewashed. Not until the cleaning in the 1980s were the walls exposed once again for a brief time. Like all stone, that of the walls varied in color and texture, and the intense and often conflicting movement in the grain of the blocks is reminiscent of the effect produced by stone in many buildings in Scotland. White paint brought the

Below:
Detail of the main floor walls, White House, during the process of cleaning and repainting, 1990. By autumn 1795, before his dismissal, Collen Williamson had completed the building up to the top of the main story, excluding perhaps most of the carved work.

Overleaf:
Transom and swag over the north entrance to the White House shown in 1985 while it was being cleaned of generations of paint. The richly carved door surround survives from the eighteenth-century construction of the White House, representing not only the skills of the Edinburgh stonemasons but the finest stone carving seen in this country up until that time.

Below:

Stonemason's marks on an eighteenth-century White House building stone. The masons, following age-old custom, were paid not in wages but by the task and identified their work for payment with personal "banker marks" such as these. Typically the fee was based on the cubic volume of the work as determined and priced by a professional "measurer." Some thirty different marks are preserved on White House stones.

Opposite:

Detail of the south facade of the White House, showing stone construction remaining intact from the eighteenth century. The richly detailed quoins, fish-scale and acanthus-leaf decorations, pediments, and pilasters are more typical of English architecture in the mid-eighteenth century than forty years later, when the White House was built.

stone walls to a serene calm, emphasizing Washington's carved ornamentation, which the liveliness of the uncovered stone would have rivaled.

The sides or ends of the building were twins, but the north and south fronts were different, united only by the richly detailed cornice, the window hoods and trim, and the rusticated basement that banded the house, forming a base on the south but sinking out of sight into the areaway on the north. By the early 1800s the north was being considered the business side, while the south was the residence front. Whether Washington intended this is not known.

At the outset the question of where to position the house on the site troubled the commissioners. In scale the building as finally approved was swallowed in the cellars of L'Enfant's palace. Apprehensive about making the decision themselves, the commissioners argued about where the smaller house might be placed in the large space – to the north, to the south – and then turned to Washington. He went to the scene and personally drove the stakes siting Hoban's house in the northern extremity of L'Enfant's ambitious rectangle. In making this decision the president renounced the axis of Pennsylvania Avenue in favor of the park on the north, which the avenue at that time did not cross as it does today. This marked an important departure from L'Enfant's idea that the President's House and the Capitol should be visible to each other at opposite ends of the avenue. (For many years Andrew Jackson has been accused of blocking the Pennsylvania Avenue view with the Treasury Building, begun during the 1830s. This was not the case. The White House was never in the line of vision from the Capitol.)

On the south the house was lofty and detailed, almost frothy with ornament; and it presents itself today as a superb garden front. Had the proposed one-story south porch been built, it would have crossed the main floor, probably with an uncovered terrace on its roof. Without the porch the south front became a serene curtain of neoclassic architecture facing a long sprawl of landscape.

The appearance on the north was wholly different. By design this front was meant to feature the main doorway. Central to the north front

were four attached Ionic columns – at Leinster House they were Corinthian – crowned by the pediment, which never got its carvings. The doorway was highly embellished with pilasters and carved borders and splendidly draped above by a swagged garland, representing the best stone carving on the building and the first truly fine representation of that art applied to architecture in the United States. Window hoods in the form of rounded and pointed pediments alternated along the smooth walls of the principal floor. Together with the modillioned cornice and molded water table with its drip molding, they formed the only decorative stone elements that linked all four sides of the building.

In scale the stone carving is bold, following traditional classical themes, with a mid-Georgian use of leaves and flowers. The window hoods, much like those at Leinster House, are supported on consoles of long, slim, staid acanthus leaves, in contrast to the considerable animation of the brackets and elegant guilloches beneath the windows. All of the carvings give deep shadowed

effects that change throughout the day and with each season. The plain ashlar walls – laid in rectangular blocks of slightly varying sizes – are the perfect foil for the carvings that embellish them. Nor is the ashlar so flat that it provides an unbroken surface; indeed, the slight irregularity, so evident with the paint removed, gives the impression in places of a pavement with gentle differences of position among the stones. Ornaments on the column capitals are lushly rendered with roses set between the rich Ionic ram's horn scrolls and tilted downward to be seen despite the columns' great height. This motif is carried around to all four fronts in column and pilaster alike.

Despite the Aquia stone's shortcomings, the stonemasons did their job well. The roses and leaves, the griffins, medallions, and classical chains are dramatically carved, and the details are excellent, from the rustic blocks of the basement to the tooth-tooling of corner and running borders, which is characteristic of the early stonework in the federal city.

Opposite:

Detail of an eighteenth-century White House pilaster, carved with the rose characteristic of all the pilasters, engaged columns, and nineteenth-century full columns of the house

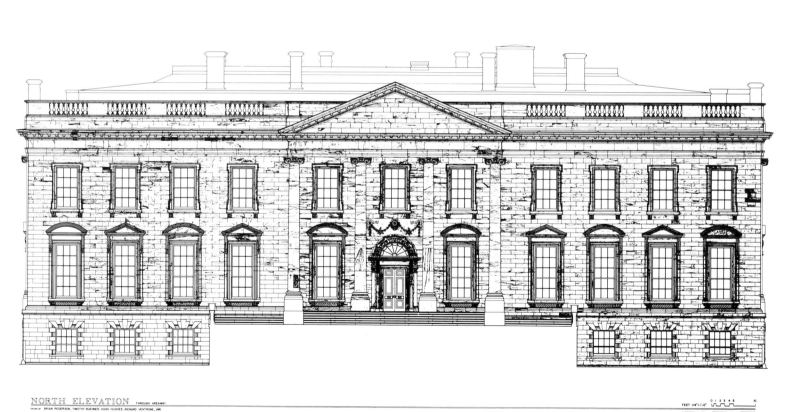

NORTH ELEVATION THROUGH AREAWAY
DRAWN BY: BRIAN PEDERSON, TIMOTHY BUEHNER, HUGH HUGHES, RICHARD VENTRONE, JNR.

FEET 1/4"=1'-0"
METERS 1:48

North elevation of the White House, as recorded by the Historic American Buildings Survey, 1991, and (overleaf) detail

This drawing is one of a set based on photogrammetric documentation and careful measurements. The work was done while the walls were stripped of paint, allowing a record to be made that includes details of weathering and damage.

30

31

Of the trades other than stonemasonry we know very little, for the original work is gone. The only evidence is archival. From written records we know that the site was a hive of activity, with unpainted shanty buildings serving carpenters, joiners, stonemasons, brickmasons, and, later, plasterers. Food was prepared in a central kitchen house. Pay was weekly, minus fines imposed by Hoban and Williamson for any imaginable infringement, from being late for work to refusing to work high up on the building to being drunk or insolent. The roll was called army style every morning just after daybreak. On Sunday, the only day off, the workmen sometimes walked to Baltimore and back.

The brickmason, Jeremiah Kale, had an enormous job and, like Hoban, was a survivor. He reported for work with his crew in the fall of 1793. At that point the height of the walls had been reduced, and the use of stone was limited to the exterior of the house. The walls were to be lined with a good two feet of brick and the interior partitions were all to be of brick, comprising a system of arches that sprang from the ground to the attic. Kale built two kilns, which were in operation that October producing soft white house bricks that measured 9 inches by 4.5 inches with a 2.5-inch thickness. The kilns remained in full operation until the close of the building season in October 1797.

Carpenter's Hall was the name used both for the long wooden building erected in 1797 approximately where Andrew Jackson's statue now stands in Lafayette Park and for the carpentry crew itself. The rough, unpainted structure stood up on piers and was fitted with workbenches to serve the various needs of joinery and finish carpentry. On Sundays it doubled as a church, as sometimes did the stonecutters' lodge.

Two carpentry crews labored at different tasks. The first, under Peter Lennox, fashioned with axes and saws the large timber framing that

would support the floor and roof structure. Joseph Middleton led the second crew, which commenced the cutting and building of window sash, doors, and other finish details for the interior. Through 1798 Carpenter's Hall stayed in operation producing wooden parts, which were stacked away, for nothing else was done on the house that year. Early in 1798 Lennox framed the hip roof, and by October the Philadelphia slater Orlando Cooke and his partner, John Emory, a plumber, had installed the slate roof, an immense structure cut through by dormer windows on each face and topped by a platform.

The building season for masonry work usually stopped in October before the first frost and resumed when the trees began to leaf in April. No one can predict a season in Washington, however, so there were variables, such as an occasional frost in September. Freshly laid walls and newly cut stone were packed in sand and straw for protection through the winter. The stonecutters, unpaid when they could not work, set themselves to making gravestones, doorsteps, and milk troughs.

For the carpenters, work could go on year-round, so the pace of their job increased. At the time Washington's presidency ended in 1797, the house was an open shell. At the close of 1798 it looked finished from the outside. The head plasterer, Hugh Densley, began nailing lath in April 1799, and by the fall closing he had plastered the basement's groin-vaulted corridor and several adjacent rooms. On the main floor he had plastered the parlors we know as the Red, Blue, and Green rooms.

President John Adams inspected the public buildings in June 1800 and complained to the commissioners, who now included Dr. William Thornton, architect of the Capitol; Gustavus Scott, businessman; and Alexander White, politician, that he was certain the work could not be completed by the time the government arrived November 1. Adams ordered composition reliefs incorporating nude figures removed from the mantelpieces; he ordered a bell system installed for summoning servants—so he could employ fewer of them; he ordered wallpaper; and he ordered a garden planted, not surprisingly, as all the Adamses were ardent gardeners.

Through the summer the work continued, now

Sketches of (above) the north and (left) the west sides of the White House, circa 1800, by Samuel Blodget, a Washington merchant, entrepreneur, and amateur artist. Taking license only on the north, where he added carved laurel branches to the entablature's plaque, which was in fact blank, Blodget has provided a faithful rendering of the President's House in its very earliest years. The grand stair, not yet built, was to rise behind the great central lunette window, which appears in the west view.

John Adams to his wife, Abigail, November 2, 1800, written on the day after his first night in the President's House: "I pray Heaven to bestow the best of blessings on this house, and on all that shall hereafter inhabit it. May none but honest and wise men ever rule under this roof." First published in 1841, the letter became so much a part of White House history that President Franklin D. Roosevelt ordered this benediction carved on the stone fireplace of the State Dining Room.

in haste. In the house big log fires burned night and day in many of the thirty-nine fireplaces to hurry the drying of the plaster walls. About one-third of the rooms were not to be plastered until later, including the great "audience chamber" we know as the East Room. The grounds were littered with debris and with construction shacks not yet removed. On the east and west, tall, red-brick government office buildings were rising at a steady pace, having been hurriedly approved and sited by Washington just before he left office.

There had been pressure in Congress to locate these government offices near the Capitol to put the public employees in close proximity to the legislators who paid them. Washington felt the employees belonged next to the executive and he feared that his successor, the New Englander Adams, who had seemed at first to care so little about the new city, would yield to Congress.

Already Adams had said publicly that he would as soon occupy a row house as the President's House. Washington had been particular enough about the public office buildings that he finally sited them himself, just as he had sited the White House. He knew with reasonable certainty that his wishes would be honored, but his faith was strengthened perhaps by the assurances offered by bricks and mortar. This work was pushed to be as far along as possible by the time Washington left office in 1797.

If in the blaze of autumn 1800 the commissioners thought they would make a last-minute finish, they were mistaken. Adams arrived November 1 to find a house only partially complete, smelling of new plaster (mixed with hog hair and horse hair) and wallpaper paste (made with white flour and beer), of raw unfinished mahogany flooring, and of lead paint and varnish. A perilous chasm yet awaited the grand staircase

Before I end my Letter I pray Heaven to bestow the best of Blessings on this House and all that shall hereafter inhabit it. May none but honest and wise men ever rule under this . roof.

John Adams, president from 1797 to 1801. He would as soon have occupied a row house on Capitol Hill as the new President's House but moved in anyway and gave it his blessing. Both he and his party fell from power within three months of his move.

Washington had approved. Planks formed a narrow bridge from the front door on the north over the deep areaway to the rude gravel road that led to that side of the house. Furniture that had served the former presidential mansions in New York and Philadelphia had been brought across the stormy sea, then towed upriver to be scattered like doll furniture in the large chambers.

On the outside the house looked finished. Hoban had done his job well. His august client had lived to see what the President's House would look like and to be pleased with it. Washington had pronounced it a house that would expand to serve the needs of ages yet unborn. The exterior is not so different today from what it was in 1800. Remove the porticoes and the wings and it is about the same great, heavy house, thick and tall of wall and wider and deeper than probably any private house or public building then standing in the United States. East to west it measured 168 feet, and north to south 85 feet. The walls rose 45 feet to the eaves.

The tremendous mass of the edifice might have made it seem fortresslike and even awkward had Hoban not taken architectural measures to lighten it. One understands this when viewing the structure at close range. It is a large building, and it rests solidly on its site. Hoban made his windows expansive, far beyond those of Leinster House and in proportion greater than those usually found in such Georgian houses. They are emphasized by broad, handsome moldings and carved stone ornament. Along the south, east, and west walls the tall pilasters help lighten the effect. Washington, who liked this architectural style, called the range of piers, or pilasters, "pilastrades," anticipating K. F. von Schinkel in Germany thirty years later. All the stone carvings are exaggerated in size to suit the scale of the building, giving the house a delicate frosting that tends to bring the mass under control, especially when seen from a perspective distant enough to permit a full-facade view.

Today the great scale of the White House is subjugated by that of the city around it. When it was new it commanded its majestic pedestal of an elevation. Its chimneys, indeed for the most part its parapet, reached higher than the highest trees. The sweeping views southward took in woods, fields, and the broad, shimmering river and made the house seem to hover above the earth, instead of being sunk, as it actually was, into the hillside.

So grandly did it rise over the nascent city, so supremely complete did it seem compared with the Capitol, which was long yet to be finished, that it was the prize statement that Washington the city would prevail. The President's House dazzled the eye with the coat of whitewash the Scotsmen had brushed over the stone walls. It seemed less of stone than one monolithic, bright stone itself. Very early, perhaps even before John Adams moved in, but certainly within two years of his arrival, it gained its sobriquet, the White House.

The City of Washington in 1800,
drawn by George Isham Parkyns

2

THE IMAGE CHANGES

T he White House, tailored to serve a dynasty of Federalists, housed only one of them, John Adams, who was defeated in the month he moved in, November 1800. George Washington, nearly a year in his grave, was not there for the "revolution," as it was called.

The election of Thomas Jefferson in the fall of 1800 delivered both a crushing defeat and a mighty victory. The tone of the government was profoundly changed. Jefferson's Anti-Federalists sought republican simplicity, not the grandeur espoused by the Federalists. The capital city, with its Anglophile public buildings, was perhaps the most immovable Federalist symbol, being its prime physical manifestation. To one of republican beliefs, buildings that symbolized England were despicable. (A notable example of this attitude was the desecration of the Georgian buildings in Virginia that housed its Episcopal churches.) Styles from ancient architecture seemed more appropriate for a democratic society. But it was too late now to reduce Washington's great city to a compact Roman forum. Jefferson intended to do what he could, however, and as the new decision maker he assumed a role no less than that taken by Washington. He reorganized the city government and, unlike Wash-

ington, lived there and took part in its operations every day.

The quarrelsome capital city commission was disbanded in favor of a single surveyor of public buildings, a government architect answerable to the president. This architect was to oversee the public buildings in the federal city and hurry the Capitol project along. James Hoban was passed over for the job in favor of English-born Benjamin Henry Latrobe. Although Latrobe's main

Thomas Jefferson, president from 1801 to 1809. Jefferson was the first full-term occupant of the White House. Such a mansion was not his choice, but he took an interest in improving it.

work was to complete the Capitol, he was also to consult with Jefferson on all improvements in Washington and to pay special attention to plans that came from Jefferson's drafting table. He would also make plans of his own that might interest the president. Latrobe's relationship with the White House would continue off and on from 1803 until 1817.

The architect did not always admire the designs of his patron. History remembers Jefferson as a more important architect than he was considered in his own time. He drew hundreds of

Above:

Benjamin Henry Latrobe, portrait by Charles Willson Peale, circa 1804. Born and trained in England, Latrobe was made surveyor of public buildings by President Jefferson in 1803 and served until 1812, well into Madison's administration, to return briefly from 1815 to 1817. His most significant Washington work was on the Capitol. In the history of the White House he is usually credited with the idea for the north and south porticoes, which may have been presented as early as 1807.

Right:

Latrobe's 1803 drawing of the principal floor of the White House with the rooms designated as Jefferson used them. A comparison of this to Hoban's plan shows that the original scheme was faithfully followed. The wooden steps and balcony on the south, outside the Blue Room, were built by John Adams, who considered the south the main entrance. These were eventually removed and the entrance returned to the north.

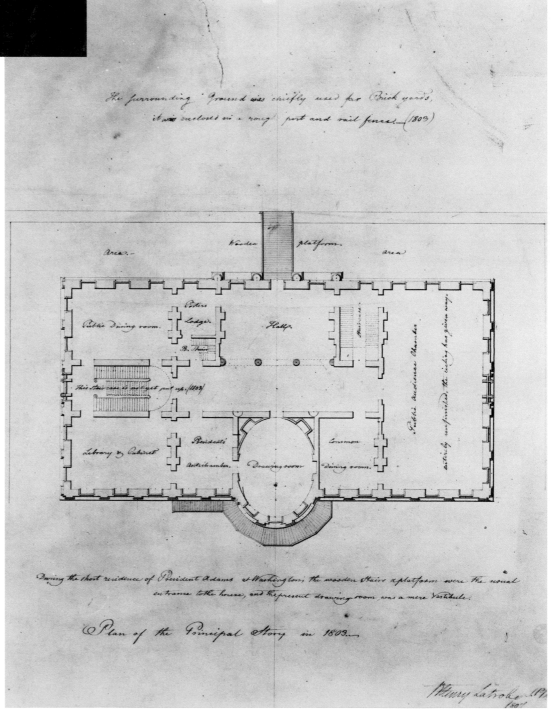

plans and details, working out each mathematically, making extensive notes, and adapting ideas of all kinds to his own uses. Because Latrobe did not have a high opinion of Jefferson's architectural ability, he was frustrated that Jefferson stuck so close to his "old French books" on architecture, "out of which he fishes everything." Still, the president provided Latrobe with the opportunity to design important projects for the republic, and, as one impassioned with republican philosophy, the erratic Latrobe was devoted to him.

Latrobe was an adherent of the classical plain style then current in England, most notably in the work of Sir John Soane, and in France to a lesser extent in the public works of Claude-Nicolas Ledoux. This stripped-down neoclassicism was in part a reaction against the decorative Anglo-Palladian style found in buildings like the White House and the Capitol. Jefferson's taste was not especially English, although he did have an affection for red brick and there is something generically Anglo-American about the execution of his buildings. His ideas came originally from

The earliest published view of the White House, frontispiece to a travel book, was drawn during Jefferson's administration, prior to the construction of Latrobe's stone platform at the north door. It shows the temporary wooden porch and steps of 1800.

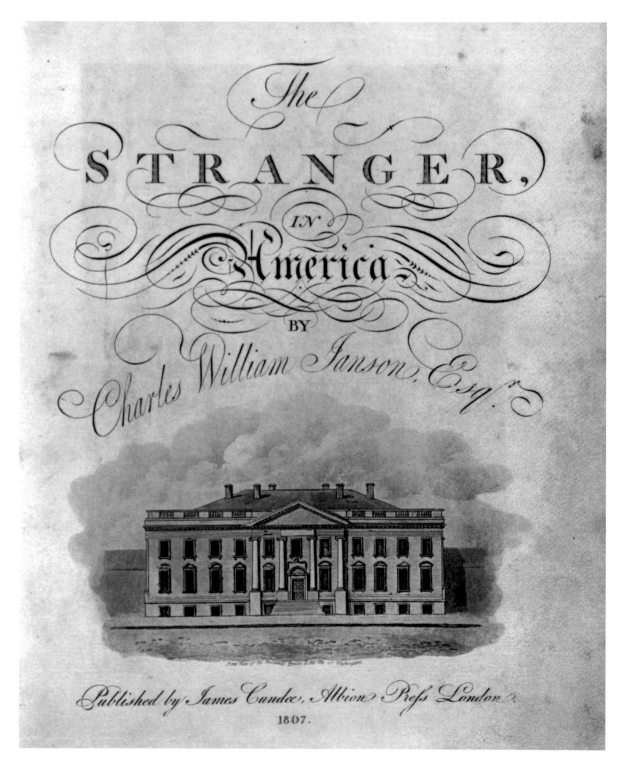

The
STRANGER,
IN
America
BY
Charles William Janson, Esq.

Published by James Cundee, Albion Press London.
1807.

the Renaissance architect Palladio – whom he mistakenly believed accurately represented ancient Roman architecture. Actually, several years abroad had exposed him to eighteenth-century French architecture, itself adapted from Palladian, and this made an enduring impression.

Jefferson and Latrobe were intellectually immersed in architecture and spurred by republican purposes that were practical as well as visionary. The two worked constantly at both new designs and remodeling existing buildings. They were often together in Jefferson's southwest corner office, which is incorporated into today's State Dining Room, planning and conferring on the White House and other public projects, including the Capitol. (Just one wing of that edifice stood even partially finished, and the design was being questioned.) Drawings, notes, and letters only hint at the conversations that must have gone on between them. The imagination is teased by sketches in the margins and penciled modifications made on their plans.

Latrobe, a professional, was, of course, the master of the two. Jefferson, who was first of all an amateur, could not match Latrobe's knowledge of engineering. Yet the president's broad

philosophical context for architectural design must have kept Latrobe on his toes, for with Jefferson's taste came deep convictions about appropriateness, particularly for the United States. He had tried to sell George Washington on the idea he had earlier sold to Virginia for its seat of government in Richmond. The group of temples he had proposed for the hilltop at Richmond had been reduced by the politicians to one temple, the capitol, which still stands. Washington saw the Richmond building, but did not record his views. One suspects that he reacted with a shrug at such an odd contrivance. Jefferson had the plans sent to the commissioners of the federal city, hoping that they, if not the president, would see the good in his idea. He was unsuccessful in persuading the governor of Virginia to send the plaster model of the temple he had commissioned. It was just as well, for the city and its first public buildings were to be Washington's.

Jefferson, who had opposed the first president's Old World style, must have sensed the irony of his moving into the Anglophile White House. It was the only one of the public buildings that had appeared complete when the govern-

This drawing, probably by or in part by Jefferson, was for the expansion of the house as well as the landscaping and fencing of the White House grounds, circa 1804. By this plan Jefferson reduced the approximately sixty-acre White House grounds to a high-walled yard of some five acres, leaving a public common on the north and meadows and abandoned marshes on the south. On the north he has proposed allées of trees, suggesting the unrealized avenues L'Enfant had proposed to focus on the house. With the sweeping driveway, shown in the bottom lefthand corner, accompanied by screens of trees and rhododendron bushes, Jefferson compensates for the awkward placement of the house off-axis from the vista down Pennsylvania Avenue to the Capitol. The east and west wings, or "terraces," are outlined as he intended them, extending to the executive office buildings, with large structures interrupting them midway; that on the east was an arch of triumph through which the driveway passed. While most of the scheme was not realized, the skeleton it formed for the layout of the grounds remained in use until the late 1850s.

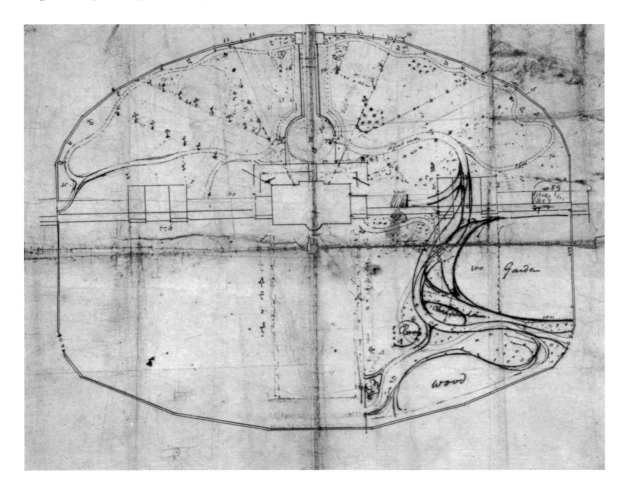

The presidents house in the City of Washington, Sept 1811

The President's House, probably by Latrobe, 1811, during Madison's administration, showing Jefferson's east and west wings and the platform over the areaways. This was the north or public front of the White House, and the scene is probably idealized. Whether the eagle ornaments were ever installed is uncertain; there is no documentation other than this drawing. The high stone wall was built on the south but never put up on the north.

ment moved to the new city. It was too big and too British for Jefferson. Perhaps it amused him, for in its way it was a mockery of the ambitions of the Federalists. A bitter John Adams, the second and last Federalist president, had left the house after only four months there. Jefferson would fill the great interior by the close of his eight years. He began ordering changes before he moved in, about March 20, 1801, and continued adding and subtracting, mostly in small ways, for as long as he lived there. The "levee room" of the deposed Federalists became his office. It developed into a wondrous sanctum filled with books, official papers, his drafting tools, potted plants, and pets—all of them the signature of the many-faceted president.

What we know as the Green Room Jefferson made into a breakfast room. The family dining room we know today—and which he knew as a larger space—became his formal dining room. For large dinners he used the great entrance hall. The unpolished mahogany floors were carpeted in some rooms; elsewhere he covered them wall to wall with canvas, which was painted green and varnished, providing the practical attributes of modern linoleum. Two water closets were purchased in Baltimore and installed upstairs, one in the southeast corner room and one in the southwest corner room. Tin reservoirs in the attic collected rainwater, which flushed through the bowls and on outside through pipes into a temporary roadway behind the south yard.

Jefferson ordered the house enclosed in an approximately five-acre yard bounded on the south by a high, plain stone wall and by simple rail fencing on the other three sides. In this way he excluded from his domain the larger part of the President's Park, the original sixty acres or so that Washington had approved for the park and gardens. This park was to remain intact and is under National Park Service jurisdiction today, but intrusions upon it began early, with Washington's decision of 1796-97 to build executive offices at its edges. He put them there for the simple reason that he could build on his presidential grounds without consulting anyone, and because he was in a hurry to get the buildings started. Expansions of these facilities were to be nearly continual, and they would crowd the grounds on the east and west extremes. The President's Park was also used for other pur-

Treasury fireproof, sections and plans by Latrobe. Intended as the eastward conclusion of the east wing, attached to the Treasury Building, the structure was isolated by the abandonment of the intervening carriageway. It seems to have been finished and to have had a handsome interior, with special fittings. Although work was done toward a partial restoration of a surviving section of it after the British burned the Treasury on August 25, 1814, the fireproof was not reused, and by 1825 it was a tool house for the White House gardener. Made into an orangery in 1833 and central to a greenhouse sometime after that, it was demolished in 1859 to make way for the Treasury's south wing.

Opposite:

The west colonnade, facing the Rose Garden, is the only one of Jefferson's terrace porches to survive.

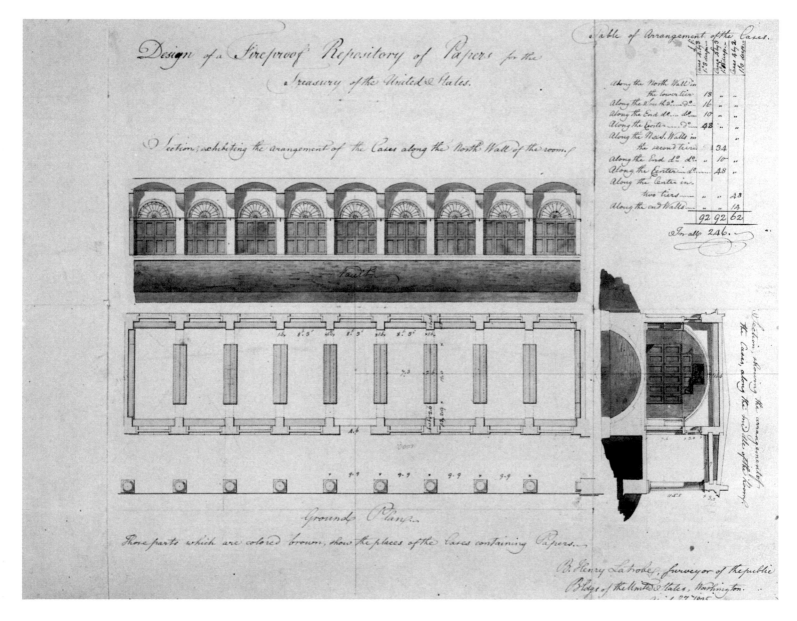

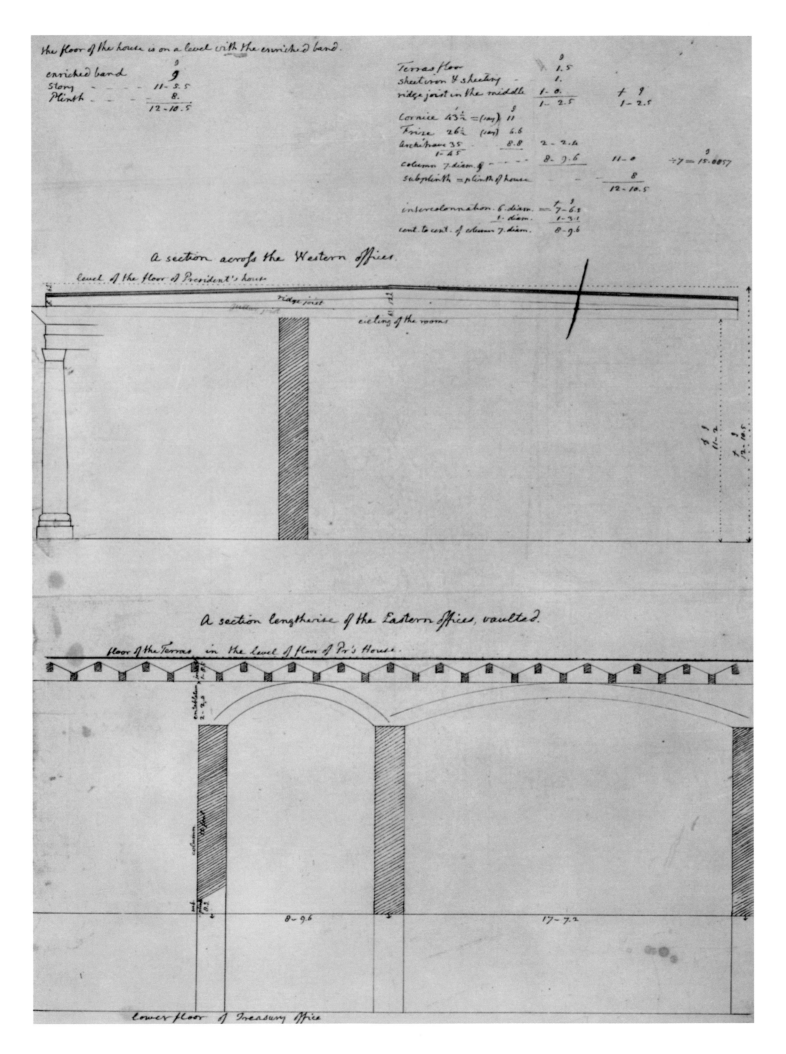

the floor of the house is on a level with the enriched band.

enriched band   9
Story   - - -   11 - 5.5
Plinth - - -   8.
           12 - 10.5

Terras floor   1.5
sheet iron & sheeting   -   1.
ridge joist in the middle   1 - 0.   ÷ 9
                     1 - 2.5   1 - 2.5

Cornice 43½ = (say) 11
Frize 26½ (say) 6.6
Architrave 35   8.8   2 - 2.4
      1 - 45
column 7. diam. of - - - 8 - 9.6   11 - 0   ÷ 7 = 15.6857
subplinth = plinth of house - -   8
                                 12 - 10.5

intercolonnation. 6. diam. = 7 - 6.1
                1. diam.   1 - 3.1
cent. to cent. of column 7. diam.   8 - 9.6

A section across the Western offices.

level of the floor of President's house

ridge joist

ceiling of the rooms

A section lengthwise of the Eastern offices, vaulted.

floor of the Terras   in the level of floor of Pr's House

8 - 9.6   17 - 7.2

lower floor of Treasury office

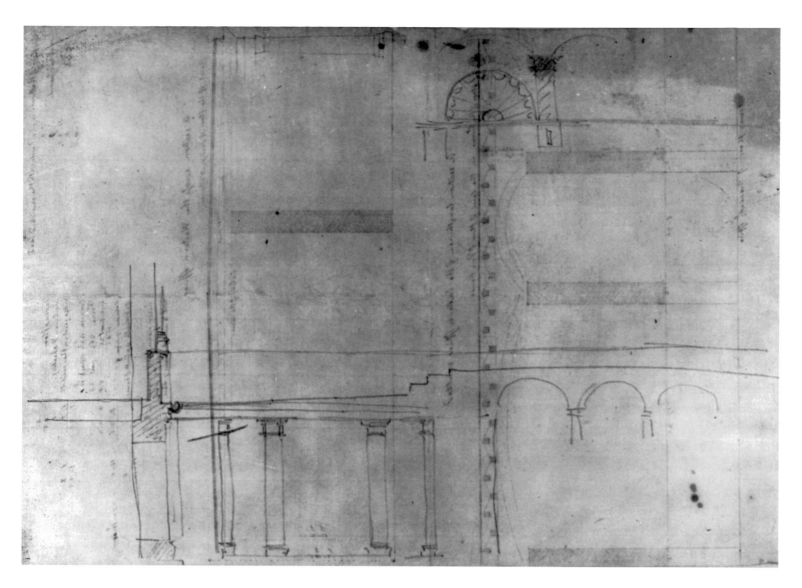

Jefferson's sketches for the east
and west terraces, circa 1803.
He wanted the roofs of the White
House wings as nearly flat as
possible and gave much attention
to the issue of drainage.
The upper drawing hints of
proposed details for the driveway
arch of the east wing.

poses. Jefferson knew the north part simply as the market common. This eventually became Lafayette Square, and then Lafayette Park. Pennsylvania Avenue was not cut across in front of the White House until about twelve years after Jefferson left office. His north gates opened directly onto the meadowlike common.

Beyond the stone fence on the south, across the country road that crossed the park at that point, was a long, broad marshy area that would one day incorporate the Ellipse. These southern reaches of the President's Park were avoided as unhealthful. Jefferson himself feared the marsh and used to stand in his office windows early in the morning watching the fog rise from it, fog that many generations of White House occupants were to consider poisonous.

Latrobe built the grand stair from the main floor to the second floor, abandoning the original scheme in which Hoban had called for a broad, free-standing center run that divided two ways at

a landing. The new design was for a horseshoe-shaped pair of stairs that rose along the walls and from a central landing completed the trip by a single short, wide flight to the second floor.

The immediacy and certainty with which he had the grand stair redesigned shows that Jefferson probably had ideas for east and west wings by the time Latrobe arrived in 1803. Jefferson hoped to achieve a long east-west cross-axis view through the house by the addition of one-story wings with rooftop promenades opening off the main floor. Hoban's design for the stairs would have blocked this. With the horseshoe stairs Latrobe arched the axis or central line, and thus visually the transverse hall of the house swept beyond the walls out along the roofs of the wings.

Planning for the east and west wings probably began as soon as Jefferson moved into the White House, but perhaps even before. It can be said with certainty that the planning was mainly

Jefferson's. Surviving drawings, most of them by Jefferson, some by Latrobe, only hint at the extensive scheme the third president had in mind. The east and west wings of the White House as built were only part of a much larger plan to unite the residence with the executive buildings to each side.

In Jefferson's time there were two executive buildings. After the rebuilding of Washington following the War of 1812, there would be four. (Today there are again two, Treasury and old State, War and Navy—now the Old Executive Office Building—but they are far larger than was ever imagined in the early nineteenth century.) The first executive office buildings were designed by George Hadfield, who was for a time the architect of the Capitol and more successfully the architect of Arlington House, known today for its later association with Robert E. Lee. He had intended to dress the utilitarian office buildings by adding flat-roofed porches with heavy, smooth-surfaced Doric columns not unlike those at Arlington House. The columns were never put up, so Hadfield's executive offices were plain, three-story, rectangular structures of red brick trimmed simply with keystones, lintels, and door surrounds of Aquia sandstone.

Jefferson's full concept for the wings is not entirely clear, but the general idea presents itself through drawings and sketches. He obviously wished to achieve several things: to refine the towering, hulking White House by giving it a strong horizontal base; to provide convenient communication between the executive departments through new covered ways linked by the vaulted corridor in the basement of the central house; to remove the domestic services or "offices"—laundry, servants' quarters, storage rooms—from the plantation-like cluster of shanties in the yard and put the functions in rows of rooms out of sight beneath the new terraces, as he was doing at Monticello; and to break out of the confining box of the house with the open-air rooftop promenades. The promenades must have been an obvious need, for the only exits from the main floor were the front door on the north and a set of gallowslike wooden stairs on the south that led down from the Blue Room—an unnerving distance of nearly twenty feet—to the ground.

The wings were to have no areaway on the north. They rose only to the height of the basement, or rustic, level of the house and had visible transom-like lunette windows lighting the interior from that direction. On the south they were to present fully revealed one-story colonnades of the Tuscan order, shading the same style of lunettes as on the north, with double doors to the rooms. Besides domestic service rooms near the house, these wings were to provide, at their extremities, fireproof record rooms for the post office on the west (which occupied part of the building called War and Navy) and the Treasury on the east (which shared a single building with the State Department).

Central to the wings were to be great architectural pieces, structures put there more for form than use, vertical thrusts that were to break the horizontal monotony of the long wings yet be in themselves powerful enough to hold their own between the White House and the executive offices. The character of these unrealized structures is vague, but the design for the one on the east is not totally obscure. This was apparently to be an arch of triumph—a triple-arched affair, in any case—containing a gatekeeper's lodge. An inclined driveway was to pass through it from one side of the house to the other, from the high elevation on the north to the south, which was an entire story below that. We know nothing of the appearance of the archway in the east wing except for the fair idea we can gain of its footprint in a sketch Jefferson made of his ideas for the grounds.

The character of the west structure is not actually known. It would have balanced the archway on the east, so the two were obviously intended to relate. In Jefferson's architectural papers is a drawing for a building that would have worked in this situation, an orangery, or greenhouse. The context for the design is not known, but Jefferson seems almost certainly to have drawn it himself. For lack of any apparent designation it has been attributed to Monticello's high garden slope. Such a building would have worked well as the centerpiece of the west terrace. It was to have been two stories on one side, with a large amount of glass

Southeast entrance gate to the White House grounds, painted circa 1820 by the Baroness Hyde de Neuville. Built by Latrobe for Jefferson, the gate stood until 1859, when it was demolished during the expansion of the Treasury.

filled into a tall arch, and of a single story on the other. Applied to the White House, the single-story face would have been presented on the north. The pedestrian, entering from the north into this pavilion, would descend a stair to the lower level, where large windows admitted light into the southward-looking orangery. This kind of building, to serve as a greenhouse or even a coach house, is probably what Jefferson had in mind for the west wing.

Work on the two wings began in the summer of 1805, while Jefferson was out of town. As it turned out, the issue of connecting the wings to the office buildings, as well as the matter of the centerpieces, is academic, because Jefferson's wings were built only in part. The east wing was nearly completed, but its centerpiece was not quite done by the close of the building season in the fall of 1806. In an effort to finish at least the skeleton of it, work was pushed too late into the season, and, because of the cold, mortar for the great arch did not set. When the supporting forms were pulled away the arch tumbled.

Practically everyone had an opinion about this disaster, and it was an unhappy reflection on Jefferson, for all presidential efforts at the White House must appear flawless. The ruin was qui-

etly torn away and the space left vacant. The east wing therefore survived in two parts, the one adjoining the house, and the second attached to the Treasury Building and containing the Treasury's fireproof records rooms. A possible echo of the doomed arch was built by Latrobe, along with the wings, as an entrance gate, designed as an arch of triumph, on Pennsylvania Avenue southeast of the White House. It stood for fifty years. At the time the earlier arch fell, the west wing had been built out from the house only to the point where the centerpiece was to stand. The post office facility had not been commenced, nor was it to be.

Latrobe put down a broad stone pavement in place of the wooden bridge that crossed the north areaway to facilitate access and to beautify the north entrance. The four-columned frontispiece now had a terrace before it, which was accessible by broad steps. The main structural element of this terrace, a mighty groin vault of stone, still survives, intact and in use, supporting part of the floor of the north portico. In the early days of the White House this sheltered section of the lower areaway was where kitchen deliveries were made, the grocery sellers' carts entering at Jefferson's arch of triumph on Pennsylvania Avenue and rolling through the breezeway of the east wing into the areaway. At the kitchen door, immediately below the principal entrance of the house and screened from view by Latrobe's terrace, daily dickering took place between farmers, butchers, soapmakers, and other tradesmen and the steward, who kept close watch on the presidential pocketbook.

Except for the addition of the wings, the north vault, and the gate, Jefferson's changes were few. However, his utter fascination for remodeling and building made it inevitable that he would make his mark on the White House. What he did to the building was paid for directly by the government, often charged as repair. The unsatisfactory roof of slates, set like pavers in mortar, was replaced in 1804 by a new roof of sheet iron. The president elaborated the interior doorways of the main floor with neoclassical overdoors or crowns of some kind. Stoves were placed in two great niches in the transverse hall, visible from the front door through the screen of King of Prussia blue marble columns. Since the niches

do not appear in Hoban's plan, they may have been added by Jefferson to hold the ordinary metal stoves that Latrobe made magnificent by encasing them in plaster molded to represent classical urns. The designs for the north and south porticoes are usually attributed to Jefferson, but this conclusion is by no means certain and is probably even unlikely. No reference to either portico appears in his papers, or in Latrobe's at this early date. This will be discussed later.

Jefferson departed at the close of his second term in 1809. The extensive inventory of the house he ordered made before he left described more elaborate interiors than he had found in 1801. Some of the rooms remained unfinished, notably the bare-brick East Room and several upstairs bedrooms. Jefferson's servants had lived in the shadowy basement, rejecting the sunny attic, which had ample servants' rooms lighted by dormer windows. They probably made their choice through fear of entrapment by fire in so high a place.

Opposite and overleaf: Latrobe's working drawings for the "platform" and accompanying vault system over the areaway to the north entrance of the White House, 1807-08. The heavy stone floor of the platform is supported by a groin vault, a vault composed of intersecting arches, carrying much of the weight from above to the supporting walls, themselves strengthened by structural arches. This construction survives today.

Left:
Latrobe's vault over the north areaway today

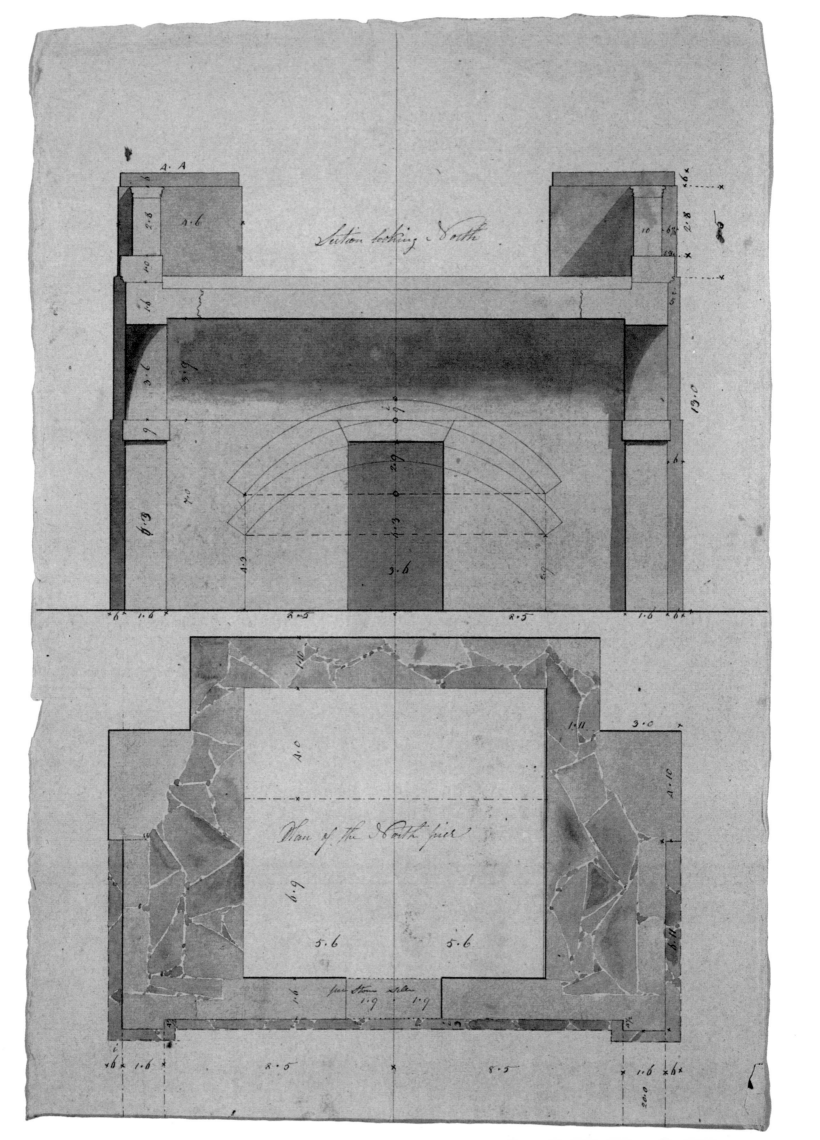

Section looking North

Plan of the North pier

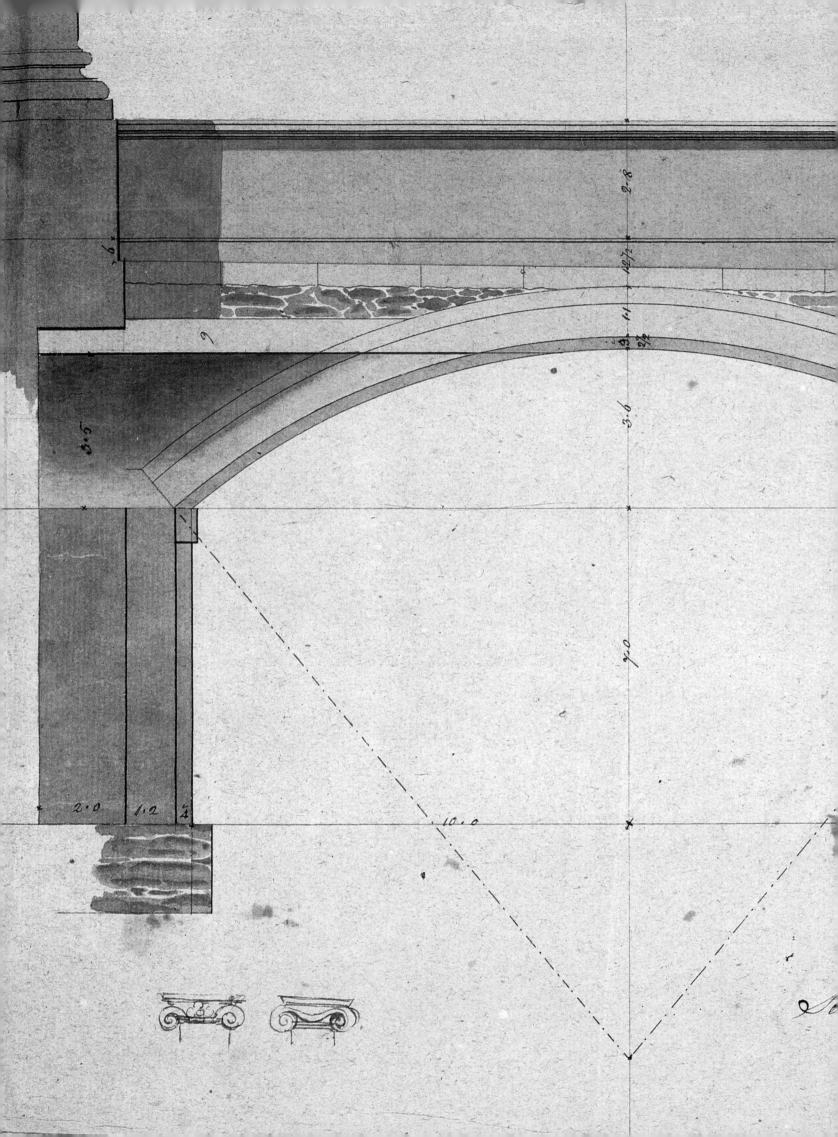

2.8

2.0

9

9

3.5

12.7/2

1.1

3.6

2.7

7.0

2.0   1.2   2/4

10.0

looking West

Section looking South

Plan

James Madison, president from 1809 to 1817. Madison moved to the White House to face an approaching war with England and made good political use of the President's House. He and Mrs. Madison fled ahead of British invaders, who burned the mansion. The president ordered it rebuilt exactly as it had been.

Dolley Madison, painted by Gilbert Stuart in 1804 in the first month of her thirty-sixth year. At this time she served often as Jefferson's hostess in the White House. In five years she would begin her own reign there.

James Madison, Jefferson's successor, had Latrobe poised to start a partial redecoration of the main floor even before Jefferson moved out. This renovation was to serve as background for a political strategy of Madison's by which he sought to attract a quarreling Congress to his doorstep in a social way, so that its members could be observed and cultivated. The politicians, who seldom brought their wives to Washington, occupied political party boardinghouses, where they ate and drank and swam in politics. Only at the occasional events of social life among the residents of Washington, Georgetown, or Alexandria did they enjoy the company of genteel women and conversation that was not necessarily political. Jefferson's restricted social life had centered on small dinners, where he dominated the conversation. He had scorned formality, sometimes dramatically, to illustrate his republican sentiments.

With war clouds gathering from across the Atlantic, Madison's administration could not be so exclusive. He intended to make the White House a gala place. The active social life proved politically useful to Madison, even though it was not ostensibly political. He revived the weekly salons, or drawing rooms, of the Federalists but without the stuffy ceremony, a republican touch.

Latrobe redecorated the rooms we know as the Blue Room and Red Room and changed Jefferson's office into a dining room, which it has remained ever since. He was solicitous of Dolley Madison; in the course of preparing designs for the rooms, he wrote long letters to her describing his often fruitless inquiries in New York, Philadelphia, and Baltimore for large mirror plate, glass chandeliers, and rich fabrics, particularly damask, which he never found. He was enthralled with the work. Mrs. Madison respected him and usually trusted his judgment on what was fashionable in England and France. "I consider it my duty," he wrote, "to follow her directions in all things relative to the Pr. House." She could be opinionated, however, and had a hearty bourgeois taste for fancy things. In trying gently to restrain her, Latrobe sometimes lost his patience, of which he had little to begin with. When at last he was forced to hang red velvet in the oval drawing room he groaned, "The curtains! Oh the terrible velvet curtains! Their effect will ruin me entirely, so brilliant will they be."

The suite was Anglophile indeed for a presidency haunted by a threat of war with England. While this might have troubled Jefferson, James Madison it bothered not at all. From all accounts, the rooms were quite theatrical. In the two parlors the decor of Regency London made its appearance in colorful flamboyance. The Red Room was then the yellow parlor, sumptuously done up in fabrics of sunflower brightness fashioned into sunbursts and festoons. Crimson was the drapery color of the "elliptical saloon," not

Copy delivered to Mr. Leng
Oct. 3d 1809

Looking Glass frame
Presidents house.

Left and opposite: Latrobe's decorating and furniture details for the oval drawing room of the White House, 1809. The interior we know as the Blue Room was decorated by Latrobe for President and Mrs. Madison in the latest British taste, including the whimsical, almost Brightonesque embellishment of the simple mantel with a giant "French plate" mirror, marbleized frame, and lambrequin crown, edged in gilt balls. The forty-two-piece suite of "Grecian" furniture was japanned or lacquered in Baltimore by Hugh and John Findlay, who may also have made the suite to Latrobe's designs, shown here, which featured the American shield in color.

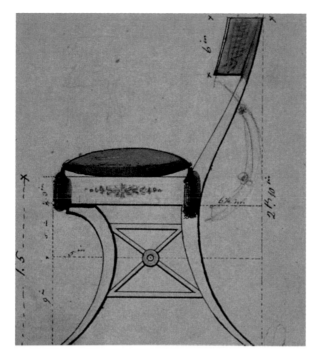

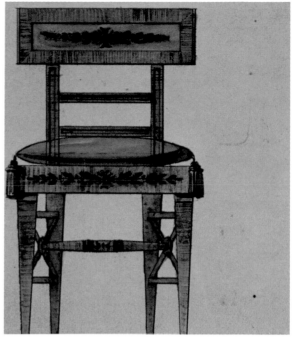

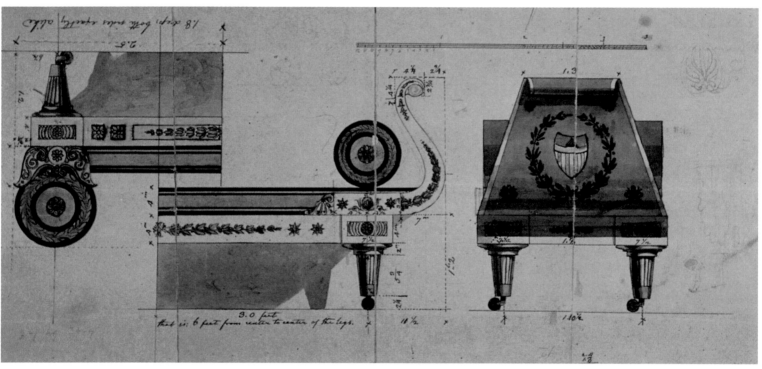

only at the windows, but also in mirrored niches that, set across from the windows, made the room seem to spin, carousel-like, in air.

Some drawings by Latrobe survive, as do many of the accounts for this work. They comprise the most complete record that exists of his decoration of a domestic interior. Most of what we know of Latrobe comes from his public works, so his 1809 White House decorating reveals a little-known facet of his taste. He designed for the oval parlor a suite of movable furniture in the classical mode, light, graceful painted chairs and sofas that looked rather like the furniture pictured on

ancient Greek vases; they were painted with the presidential shield and the ancient honeysuckle motif. Hugh Findlay of Baltimore provided the furniture to the government. He practiced the art of the chair japanners Latrobe had recalled as fashionable in London. Judging from Findlay's surviving work, he was capable of carrying out Latrobe's designs masterfully.

George Bridport, a London decorative painter who had relocated in Philadelphia and occasionally worked in Baltimore, was employed to adorn the Blue Room's plaster ceiling and perhaps the plaster walls. What he did is now

forgotten, but Bridport had decorated houses and public buildings and had painted ceilings for Latrobe in the Capitol. He had the ability to create figural decorations, maidens in togas, warriors in helmets and armor. Latrobe's brief reference to his work in the oval room suggests that he shaded the ceiling from dark blue at the outer edges into a paler blue toward the center, evoking sky and clouds in an atrium. There was no chandelier, so the effect of the ceiling, a full eighteen feet from the floor, must have been magical in the luminous nuances of the oil lamps that ringed the walls.

A sheet of mirror surmounted at least one of the fireplace mantels, and Latrobe draped it elegantly with a lambrequin valance. Mary Sweeney, a Georgetown seamstress, did the sewing under Latrobe's direction, and a large quantity of fabric was used in the parlors in window hangings, upholstery, and cushions. The effect was opulent and festive. Both parlors seem to have been crowded with furniture, mostly chairs, all placed in orderly rows over wall-to-wall carpeting. These rooms were in turn a contrast to the relatively sparse dining room, with its two fireplaces and mahogany furniture. Dining rooms are finished only when their tables are set, and Latrobe knew this, envisioning the dining room of the White House as a picture gallery when not in use, as in an English house, with the table probably kept in the hall outside. To begin the gallery he hung in the dining room Gilbert Stuart's full-length portrait of George Washington.

By 1810 the Madisons needed no more assistance at the White House. Madison himself took little interest in the Capitol building project and, preoccupied as he was with international danger, wearied of the temperamental Latrobe. When the two wings of the Capitol were finished, Latrobe moved on to Pittsburgh to pursue private business. The decidedly English rooms of the White House were filled with anti-British war talk among crowds invited first once a week, then twice a week, and sometimes more often. Dolley Madison filled out cards of invitation every day. Dinners were numerous, usually for forty. Wizened Madison was a good politician as well as a sound thinker, and Dolley Madison was a bubbly

hostess. They kept the political company coming from both sides of the aisles.

The British marched at last on Washington in August 1814. Madison was at the White House on the day of the invasion, August 24. In the afternoon he went out to inspect the military preparations. Dolley Madison ordered the French steward, Jean-Pierre Sioussat, to set the dining room for the customary four o'clock dinner. Forty were to be served. In the great kitchen below, the cooks commenced work. Distant cannonades, however, soon sapped the bravery Dolley Madison had mustered, and she fled in terror, with her pet macaw in tow. We have her dramatic letter, written and rewritten through the balance of her long life, justifying her flight, placing her at the center of things. When Madison returned to the house in late afternoon he found almost everyone gone. Of Stuart's portrait of Washington in the dining room, only the

A VIEW of the PRESIDENT'S HOUSE in the CITY of WASHINGTON after the Conflagration of the 24th August 1814.

frame remained, for Mrs. Madison had ordered the painting cut out and taken to safety. A storm was brewing. Madison and his aides departed.

The British troops arrived in the city about 7:30 in the evening, and some three hours later, with the Capitol in flames behind them, British Rear Admiral George Cockburn and Major General Robert Ross, with 150 sailors, made their way down Pennsylvania Avenue to the President's House. They entered and toured the house, finding the dining table still set and the food

William Strickland, brilliant pupil of Latrobe, made this engraving of the White House ruins in 1815. It is the truest representation of the pre-fire house known to exist. The drawing is based on a watercolor by George Munger, but, comparing the two, it is clear that the young architect also went to the site to render his subject more accurately. The details can be compared rather minutely to the existing stone walls and their carved decorations, showing that although replacements were made in the reconstruction of 1815-17 no change was made in the original design; it was copied exactly, as President Madison ordered.

Opposite:
Scars from the 1814 fire appeared 176 years later, in 1990, when white paint was removed from the walls in the course of restoration.

Opposite:

Detail of Strickland engraving

on page 57

ready in the kitchen. In Madison's dressing room they found disarray from Dolley Madison's hasty departure. The officers paused to change into the clean underwear they found.

Orders were given to burn the house. While the officers ate the repast in the dining room — recalling later the excellent Madeira — windows were broken out and lamp oil was sprinkled on furniture, bedding, and other materials the sailors piled in the rooms. At about half past twelve midnight of August 25, the house was ceremoniously ignited when javelinlike torches of "hellfire" were hurled through the windows. Fierce storm winds whipped the flames. By daybreak rain was pouring on the fire-blackened shell.

Months passed. The immense ruin was a topic of both shame and wonder. Through the fire the exterior remained white except for great licks of soot that scarred the sockets that had been windows. The blackened masonry interior walls rose arch over arch like Roman aqueduct remains. The steward Sioussat recovered the kitchen range, stewpots, and many skillets and pans buried in the ashes and debris but usable still. The basement's groin vaulting held, and what a terrible dungeon it must have seemed, it and Latrobe's north areaway vault being the only covered areas in a roofless place open to the sky.

The ragged tree of heaven, a tree that likes desolation, took over the White House grounds while Congress debated building a new capital elsewhere. Cincinnati was a front runner, but after the great victory at New Orleans on January 8, 1815, the city of Washington won out. Its adherents, including Madison, insisted that only a repair of the public buildings was necessary for a resumption of business as usual. The idea of rebuilding in the same place became in itself symbolic of winning the war. "In carrying into execution the law for rebuilding the public Edifices," wrote James Madison on May 23, 1815, "it will best comport with its object & its provisions not to deviate from the models destroyed. . . ."

Through the influence of Dolley Madison, the president brought Latrobe back to Washington to restore and complete the Capitol. A friend of Latrobe's wife, Mary, Mrs. Madison had learned of the failure of his Pittsburgh projects and of the family's near destitution. Latrobe set to work. He

assembled an office of assistants and students. Stonemasons, brickmasons, and carpenters were put on the payroll. For Latrobe it was a great chance to start again. But controversy soon surrounded him once more, and he did not last long as the rebuilder of Washington.

Of his influence on the rebuilding of the White House it can be said that he may have contributed at some point to the idea for the porticoes, but whether or not he had invented them earlier is unknown. There was some controversy on this subject, for Hoban claimed he had designed the porticoes for George Washington. He may have meant the long south porch Washington wanted on the original project; perhaps not, for at the time he made his claim, the present porticoes

State portrait of George Washington, painted by Gilbert Stuart in 1797. Moved into the White House probably in 1801, the portrait was hanging in the State Dining Room when Dolley Madison saw to its safety only hours before the White House was burned. Since 1930 it has hung in the East Room.

were under way. Notations on Latrobe's drawings for a drastic remodeling of the house indicate the design of the porticoes more or less as built was developed as early as 1807. If the dates are inaccurate, they join notable company among both White House drawings and Latrobe's drawings in general.

Latrobe's 1817 elevation of the south front showing a half-round porch is labeled as a copy of a drawing made in 1807. Another drawing bearing only the date 1807 shows the house from the east, with both south and north porticoes. On the north the arrangement of columns is slightly different from what was built. The third drawing is a plan clearly meant to accompany the other two, for it shows the porticoes; it calls for remodeling the principal floor of the house, probably a reconstruction project Latrobe pre-

sented, unluckily, to Madison. The plan casts suspicion on the 1807 date of the elevation, for it proposes a rebuilding so radical that the president would have had to move out to allow the work. This step was taken by only four presidents in 200 years—Madison, Theodore Roosevelt, Coolidge, and Truman—and then only as an emergency measure, with the president demanding a return to the house as soon as possible.

Latrobe's plan, if applied to the standing house, called for piercing many brick partitions and cutting out the north end of the Blue Room entirely. The project would have transformed Hoban's grid of large rooms into a much subdivided Regency interior, with column screens, anterooms, alcove beds, toilet closets, and other elegances and preferences for comfort familiar in

Above and opposite: Latrobe's drawings for porticoes to the White House, excerpted here, may have begun as ideas during Jefferson's administration, but probably date from early in the rebuilding process under Madison. With the plan (see page 62) they probably describe the extensive improvements he proposed to a president who wanted for political reasons as near a reconstruction of the original as possible.

Authorship of the idea of porticoes was a sensitive issue during the rebuilding and for some years after, with Hoban claiming the house was always to have had them. The columned additions shown in Latrobe's drawings are somewhat as built, notable exceptions being the broad, central south stair and the high elevation and column arrangement on the north. The actual porticoes built in 1824 and 1829 were designed by Hoban.

stylish English houses of the time. In the new scheme, the central part of the original plan was broken down, cut through, and rearranged in almost every way. There were to have been twice the individual spaces once featured in the White House. The plan was plausible for the house during the reconstruction, when all that was left were some of the walls, but such a remodeling for Jefferson, when the house was adequately serving his purpose, was unlikely.

All three drawings show the north and south porticoes, with entablatures as built, but differences in the steps. Clearly the three drawings are a set, and they appear to show a new White House, keeping the shell of the old. The historical context for these seems obvious. Latrobe proposed an appealing, indeed an exciting revised house for Madison, but his plan did not reflect

the "repair" politics demanded in Madison's rebuilding. The drawings provide a small glimpse of the greater difficulties Latrobe caused. Soon he was on the grill politically, and soon after that, in 1817, he was gone, to New Orleans, this time for good.

James Hoban, meanwhile, had been hired in March 1815 to rebuild the White House. He incorporated the two porticoes into his plan, although he proposed to build only the bases of them to begin with. Substantial portions of the walls had to come down. The rain that followed the fire had saturated the hot stones and caused splitting. What remained, however, was more than had to be replaced. Most of the basement survived; all of the south front could be saved; the four-columned frontispiece on the north was saved for the most part. What was lost were the

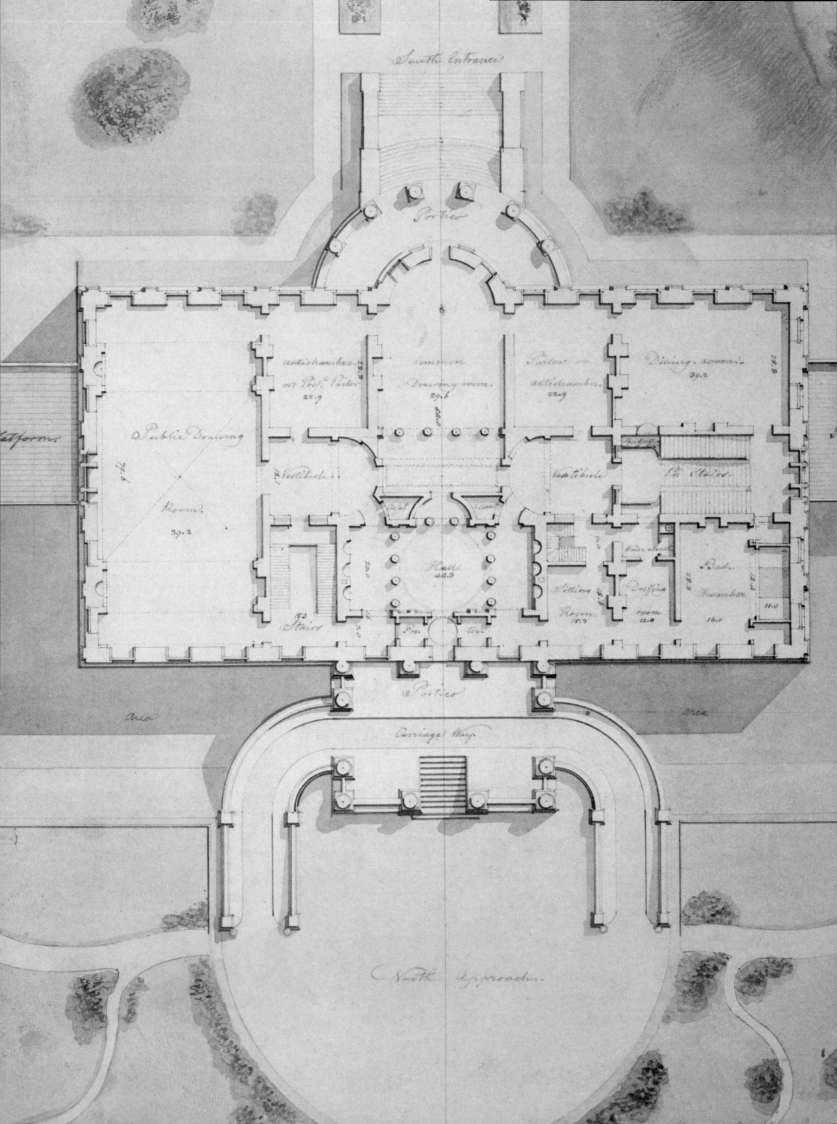

South Entrance

Portico

Platform

Public Drawing

Room.
39.2

antichamber.
or Prof. Parlor
22.9

Common
Drawing room.
29.6

Parlor or
antichamber.
22.9

Dining room.
39.2

Vestibule

Vestibule

Pr. Stairs

Hall.
44.3

Stairs

Sitting
Room.
15.3

Dressing
room.
12.0

Bed
Chamber.
16.0

Portico

Area

Area

Carriage Way.

North Approach.

James Monroe, president from 1817 to 1825. Eager to move into the rebuilt White House, Monroe urged the work on personally. He wanted to make the presidency a symbol of the unity of the American people, as it had not seemed since Washington's tenure, and a splendid restored White House was a feature of his plan.

Opposite:

Latrobe's plan for remodeling the interior arrangements of the White House is clearly a set with the two exterior elevations shown on the preceding page. This drawing, too, is often associated with Jefferson's tenure. The alterations it proposes would have involved so radical and costly an intrusion into the masonry structure that the plan makes more sense for rebuilding the burnt-out house. In this plan Latrobe has converted the barn-like interior of the mansion into a stylish ensemble of colonnaded spaces, bow-ended antechambers, and secluded drawing rooms.

Right:

Field note from the 1816 survey by F. C. de Krafft, with a sketch of the proposed north portico, apparently taken from Latrobe's drawings

two ends, east and west, down to the tops of the rusticated walls of the basement, and the north front up to each side of the frontispiece.

The actual repair and restoration of the stone-work was undertaken by Scots and Italians. Some of the Scots had migrated to the federal city in the 1790s, notably James McIntosh and Robert Brown, both formerly of Lodge No. 8 in Edinburgh. Brown had set up his own stoneyard in Georgetown, and he would live to do work for Andrew Jackson. He was put in charge of the lodge of eleven stonecutters and carvers on the reconstruction. The Italians were borrowed from the Capitol project, primarily for carving. Carlo Franzoni had come over from Leghorn with good recommendations from British merchants there. Giuseppe Valaperta, a sculptor, made the column capitals, repairing and replacing the lush roses that are trademarks of the White House pilasters and column capitals. Peter Bonanni produced working drawings from which the carvings were made. The main effort of the stoneworkers was to restore what had been there before. No new carving designs appear to have been added. Because of the porticoes to come, the elaborate tympanum approved by Washington vanished from the scheme of things.

Most of what we know about the actual appearance of the White House before and just after the fire comes from a superb engraving probably made in the summer of 1815 by Latrobe's bril-

liant pupil, William Strickland, later architect of the Exchange in Philadelphia and the Tennessee Capitol building at Nashville. The engraving is based on a watercolor by George Munger, undoubtedly made at the scene, but so superior in detail to Munger's painting that it is certain Strickland went himself to the site and adapted Munger's view into a perfectly detailed rendering. It is the only really readable document of the house as it stood before it was rebuilt. In fine detail Strickland shows the stone carvings, window moldings, and the rustication and even suggests the interior system of arching. Comparing the Strickland engraving with the walls today, we know that the exterior of the original house was reproduced to the letter, just as James Madison wanted.

Finishing of the interior was different. Perhaps Latrobe's project had stirred the waters, for, while it was not copied, it may have paved the way for more up-to-date interior detailing than was in the house before. A new president was by then on the scene. James Monroe was a man of striking appearance—he looked to many like a young George Washington—and he had an inter-

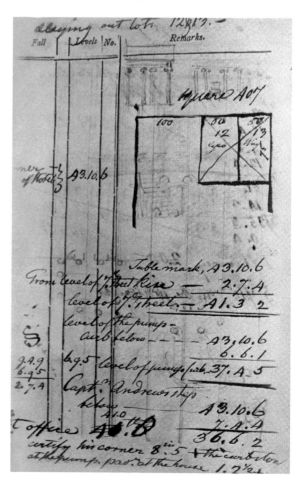

Below:

This fine "statuary marble" mantelpiece in the Green Room was in the highest category of the twenty-five marble mantels President Monroe purchased from Italy through Baring Brothers and Company in London. The piece was delivered to the White House in the winter of 1819.

Opposite:

Detail of the marble mantel in the Red Room

Right:

Door trim, Blue Room. This style, adopted for the rebuilt house, is probably different from the trim found in the pre-fire house. Written sources such as bills, orders, and receipts suggest the original may have been of the mid-Georgian type, with pediments over the doors. Corner blocks, however, are shown in Latrobe's 1809 mantel design for Madison (see page 54).

est in elegant, fashionable living. His wife, Elizabeth, a rose-petal sort of beauty, was enchanting in her costume and her manner, if to the public a bit too queenly. That the Monroes might have been inclined to change things a little is not surprising, for they loved houses and furniture. Hoban got on well with them and was to build their fine neoclassical country house, Oak Hill, which still stands in Loudoun County, Virginia.

We have only hints as to the detailing of the state rooms before the fire. There were wooden mantels at the fireplaces, and composition ornaments were glued to them. The ornaments were of fruit and flowers, as specified by John Adams, to replace the original nudes. From a distance the mantels could probably have passed for stone or marble. Some of the doors may have had pediments, giving an eighteenth-century Georgian flavor more consistent with the exterior than the neoclassical trimmings installed after the fire. The window sash were mahogany, as were all the doors. These were probably varnished, rather than painted, but the surrounds were all painted white. The barren neoclassical strain of the restored interior seems to have been very different from what had burned. Hoban introduced to the doors at this time the richly embellished corner blocks that were among the earliest, if not the earliest, in the country. Set at the upper corners of the doors of the first and second floors, these square elements, with their elaborately carved circular mounds of acanthus leaves, climax a restrained trim molding of sharp verticals that frames the door openings in delicate shadow lines. The mahogany of the doors on the state

The White House, watercolor by the Baroness Hyde de Neuville, 1820, showing the house after the reconstruction of 1815-18. Fences and walls are completed. To the east (left in the painting) are the departments of State and Treasury. On the west are the War Department and the Navy Department. Note the east wing, where the ruins of Jefferson and Latrobe's failed archway survive between the east wing against the house and the Treasury fireproof east of that. Pennsylvania Avenue is soon to be cut through, before the White House fence.

floor was highly figured, reeded along the edges and inlaid in the panels with fans and stripes made of light colored satinwood, presumably copying the inlaid mahogany doors that were there before.

A wooden wainscoting, inset with panels, banded the rooms of the two floors, for they were to be busy spaces and the plaster walls and wallpaper needed protection. Chair rails alone might have been considered more fashionable. Some of the ceilings were enhanced with plaster centerpieces, sunbursts, or floral ornaments that surrounded the pulley devices that moved the chandeliers up and down for cleaning and lighting. English merchants at Leghorn provided Italian marble mantels, custom-carved by "our first artists." Two of these survive in the White House, ones that were originally at the east and west ends of the State Dining Room and in 1902 were moved to the Red and Green rooms, where they remain. They feature the popular statuary marble polished finish, carved as terms, or figures supporting a shelf adorned with Grecian devices.

Since the East Room had never been plastered, its decorations were entirely new. The most elab-orate in the house, the ornamental plaster featured a heroic frieze of Grecian anthemia, which formed a heavy band around the top of the walls. From old photographs it can be estimated that each anthemion was about thirty inches tall and at least twenty-two inches at the broadest width. Hoban highlighted the anthemion band with gold leaf and backed it with black flocking. This rather sumptuous conceit was to be the sole decoration of the room for eleven years. Otherwise the walls were bare plaster, awaiting paper. The tall and unadorned windows presented many-paned grids of watery-looking crown glass; the mantels were of painted wood, the floor of raw boards, and the ceiling equipped only with three plaster centerpieces where chandeliers would one day hang. President Monroe and later his successor, John Quincy Adams, used the East Room as an overflow room for great receptions. In this curious setting the Marquis de Lafayette was entertained on a state visit in 1824.

The president moved into the house late in 1817 and first opened its doors to the public on New Year's Day 1818. About 3,000 callers walked

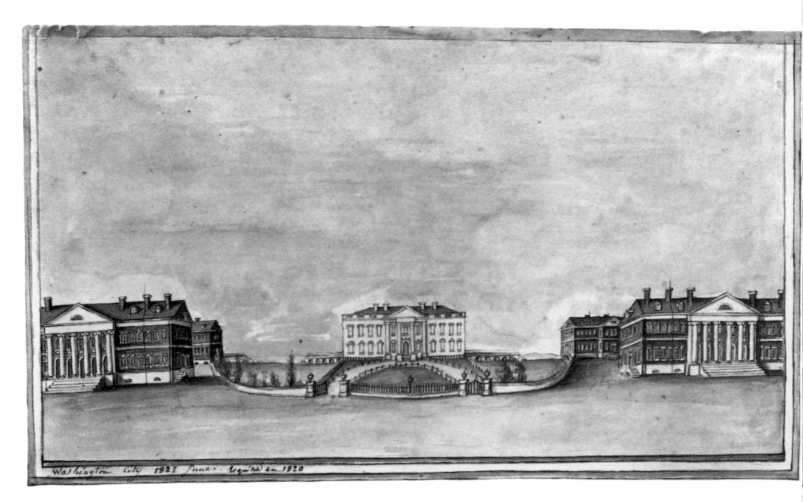

the carpet-covered board floors of the state rooms; below, the workmen who had rebuilt the house were thanked with the "best old whiskey" and cheese and crackers. Six years passed with constant small innovations and corrections. Since Jefferson's wings had been rebuilt as Jefferson had left them, the issue of connecting them to the office buildings was silenced forever. When Monroe ordered a stable appended to the west wing in 1818, it was decided not to extend it west but instead to turn its sixty-foot length to the south, so that from the north the balance of the east and west wings would be preserved as they were. This stable formed, with the White House and the existing west wing, a brick-paved courtyard, but though in use until the early 1830s it was never in much favor because of its location beneath the dining room windows. The Oval Office today is built at what was the end of the added stable's colonnade.

Also during 1818 Paulus Hedl brought from his forge in New York City several sets of iron en-

trance gates for the north side. Tall and heavy, decorated with Gothic motifs and spears, the gates followed into a long, at first partially serpentine fence of closely placed spears, foreboding of purpose but very delicate and harplike to see. Hedl painted his fencing black, the record shows. The new fencing was mounted on a parapet wall, and great stone piers were provided for the gates. Not for some three years, in about 1821, was Pennsylvania Avenue made to detour around Fifteenth Street and pass in front of this fence. As for who designed the fence and gates, it is not certain. Hoban may have done it; or the designer could have been Hedl himself. The design has endured through the years, although the originals are no longer in use. Most of the fencing at the White House today is identical to Hedl's, and the last of his original gates survived at the northwest entrance until sent to museum storage and replaced in 1976 by President Ford.

Monroe was intensely interested in the White House. As a former diplomat he admired the

The White House triumphant, attributed to Rufus Porter, circa 1820, originally in Prescott Tavern, East Jaffrey, New Hampshire, and devised after the engraving of 1819 by George Catlin

social form and gentility of the diplomatic community, and he had ambitions for a setting suitably splendid for social events. His receptions were popular. His dinners were wholly French and followed every formality, with, however, some lapses—once he had to disarm an infuriated guest who drew a sword and challenged another guest from across the table. He did so with grace. Monroe imported rich gilded furniture from France, as well as bronze clocks, a table plateau, and silver. Much of this is still in the house today. In March 1819 he entertained a proposal from the painter John Vanderlyn to supervise the decoration of the plaster walls of the East Room. This project never came to fruition.

The most enduring of James Monroe's marks on the White House was his last one, the building of the south portico in 1824. Whatever the concept for this addition, the final design and execution were Hoban's. He had first planned the work in 1816. It was laid aside. When federal

Group portrait before the White House commemorating the visit of General Lafayette in 1824. He was the first guest of state to stay at the White House, and President Monroe named the new square north of the house in his honor.

officials were considering reviving the project in 1824, they could find no drawings to study. Hoban offered his original set for both porticoes, which he had framed and hung on his sitting room wall. The Capitol architect, Charles Bulfinch, traced the essentials of these for the commissioner of public buildings. The originals,

Forged in New York by Paulus Hedl, probably after designs by James Hoban or Charles Bulfinch, these gates on the northwest of the White House grounds served from 1819 to 1976, when they were placed in museum storage.

returned to Hoban, were apparently lost when his house burned a decade later. Of Bulfinch's tracings, only that for the north portico remains.

The south portico is built entirely of Seneca stone, which is somewhat pinker than Aquia but is also a local sandstone, quarried upriver from Washington on the Maryland side of the Potomac. Richard Holdsworth was paid $260 "For carving 2 Ionic caps for the south portico" under the direction of George Blagdin, who was still employed on the Capitol work. The rest of the carving for the south portico appears to have been carried out by Giovanni Andrei. The "portico"—it is called, when in reality, without a pediment, it is a porch—opened off the three state parlors. From the ground the high stone

Top:
This drawing, made by the Historic American Buildings Survey in 1990, shows the south side of the White House today but without the south portico, added in 1824; it shows the house about as it appeared between the administrations of Adams and Monroe.

Bottom:
The south front as it appears today, with portico (including the Truman balcony) and double stairs

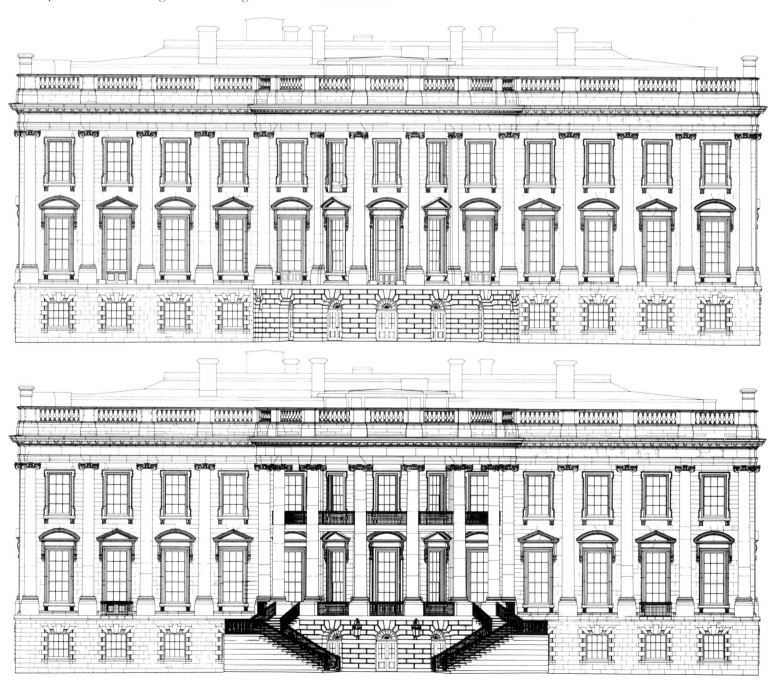

70

South elevation of the White House, an illustration provided by James Hoban for Robert King, Jr.'s 1818 map of the federal city. Oddly, the character of the window hoods on the main floor has been rendered incorrectly. In designing his stairs Hoban may have opened his 1728 edition of Gibbs's *Book of Architecture* and paused on plate 51, adapting that model to ensure an easier descent. This facade of the White House was the least disturbed by the fire, and the walls are about as they were when completed for George Washington.

porch is approached by leisurely double arms of stairs, each with generous landings midway. Possibly Hoban's, they are among the most successful architectural solutions in the rebuilding of the house, for they are at once ceremonial and practical, making a broad base for a portico of slightly awkward proportions.

No second floor balcony then encumbered the tall sweep of the Ionic columns from their high arcaded and rusticated base. The sense of scale and elevation was dramatic when experienced on leaving the parlors. From a distance the White House gained new importance on the south. The portico took some significance away from the frothy effect of the heroic pilasters and the window hoods, which it decidedly crowds out, but it gave the White House an individuality.

Overleaf:

White House and Capitol, about 1827. The Capitol was at last completed in 1821, three years after the rebuilding of the White House was accomplished. This small, anonymous watercolor, expanded here to some sixteen times its original size, shows a setting of muddy streets, wooden fences, clusters of houses—dwarfed by the two white-painted edifices of stone—and open pastures. Shown with the White House are Jefferson's stone wall; the orchard and vegetable garden, fenced in rails; and several workmen's shanties left over from the reconstruction.

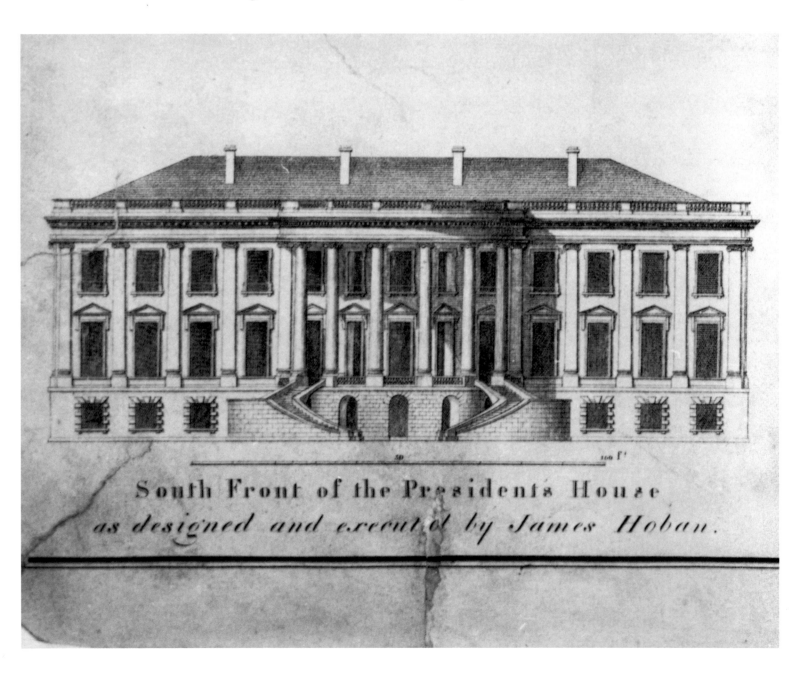

South Front of the President's House as designed and executed by James Hoban.

It made the place seem somehow more generically American, a touch not lessened by its faint cast of clumsiness. Except for the unfounded attribution of a model in the roughly contemporary Château de Rastignac at Périgord in central France, whose porch is, from a distance, strikingly similar, no model has been put forth. The south portico seems an obvious solution to access to the outside from the south side of the main floor and, because it lends verticality, is a great improvement over the long one-story porch Washington had in mind. It provided the necessary porch, while giving a monumental architectural presence appropriate to the house of the chief of state.

The portico on the north, begun by Hoban five years later, was authorized by Congress at the end of the administration of John Quincy Adams and completed by Andrew Jackson. It had been planned probably in 1815 or 1816, and the surviving Bulfinch tracing was made from one of Hoban's original drawings. At the time construction began in the early spring of 1829, an unsightly wooden mask covered the open attic where the pediment had been before the fire and where the portico was to be built out from the body of the house. The funding of this project must have irked John Quincy Adams, for it was approved by the House Committee on Appropriations only after Jackson's election and his own defeat in the hate-ridden campaign of 1828. It seemed a rising monument to the new order of Old Hickory.

Built also of Seneca stone, from the bases of its columns to its pediment, the north portico made less of an impact on the north facade than the south portico made on the other side. But it likewise made the old walls and carvings recede. The swagged garland of roses and acorns, once the focus of that front, lost the punch it had delivered from a distance and was thereafter to be enjoyed at its best from under the shelter of the portico.

In general the effect of the new portico was that it had simply popped out from the body of the house. It seemed a natural projection of the frontispiece that was already there, the same pediment and four columns, now with return rows of columns as well, extending back to the

Château de Rastignac, near Périgord, France, built at about the same time as the White House. It has often been speculated that the design of the south portico of the White House was inspired by the semicircular porch of the château, but though the design is similar no connection can be found.

Opposite:
The south portico, showing the neoclassical detailing of the Seneca stone carved in 1824 by Richard Holdsworth, from England, and Giovanni Andrei, a native of Italy, both hired from the Capitol building project.

house. Within the portico one is contained in a lofty square of columns. The north portico served not the functions of a porch but rather of a porte-cochère, for it extended beyond the existing platform and steps and covered the driveway. Visually the north portico so dominated the scale of the house that the White House was always to seem smaller from the outside than it really is.

In 1833, three years after the completion of the north portico, as a feature of improvement Andrew Jackson ordered further separation of the two pairs of stone gate piers at the Pennsylvania Avenue entrance. He seems to have found the graveled carriage circle too tight. The great piers were accordingly cut from their foundations, tilted onto a bed of logs, and rolled to new foundations at the preferred location some fifty

Top:

North elevation of the White House, a 1990 scale rendering showing the facade today, without the portico, as it must have appeared before the fire. (The pediment was not rebuilt after the fire, for the portico was to be built there.)

Bottom:

The north front as it is today

Opposite:

The north front as it appeared with years of paint removed from the portico

feet to the east and west, where they remain today. Paulus Hedl's wrought-iron gates were re-mounted and his fences put back, this time to parallel the street without the earlier serpentine design. A new fence was added to enclose the ground between the two arms of the driveway and atop the parapet wall of the north areaway. Designed after the anthemion band cornice of the East Room, this lacy confection in iron controlled public access and framed a tapestry-like garden of gravel paths and flower beds inset into a lawn that was cut with a mower and rolled with a stone to carpet smoothness.

With the re-siting of the gates, the White House can be said to have been complete. The general image – the exterior – that would carry through time was now established. Those who

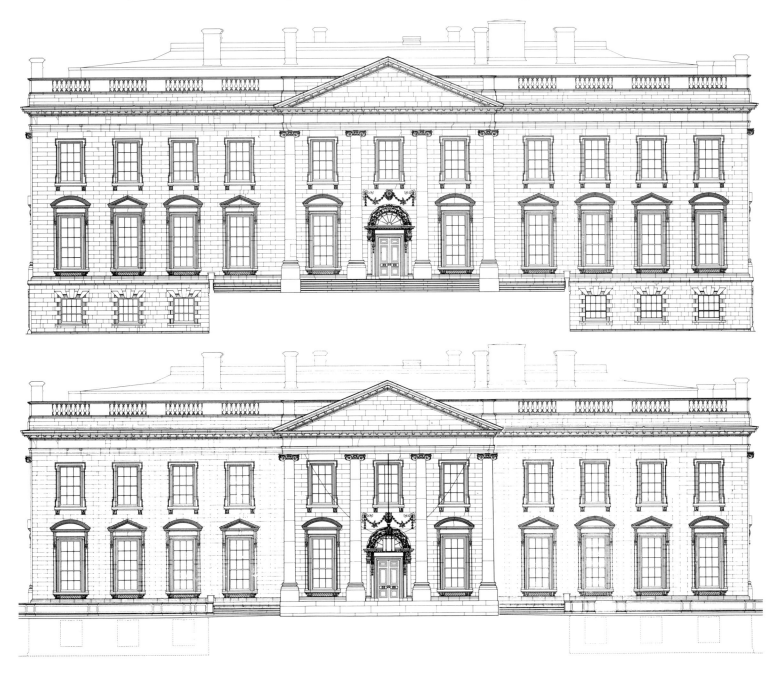

saw it during these early years were for the most part pleased. "It is a magnificent mansion," wrote a visitor in 1830, "or rather it will be when finished. It stands near the center of one of the largest squares in the city, on an eminence, nearly a mile and a half west of the Capitol. The building is of the Ionic order, with a southern and a northern front. It is one hundred and seventy five feet long [168 feet in fact], and eighty-five in width; it has two lofty stories above a basement. There are thirty-one rooms [probably 34, not counting those in the attic] of considerable size within the walls. . . . The site of the house is elevated about sixty feet above the river, and the descent is quite gradual to it."

Another visitor, about four years later, found the White House "very much in external appearance like the Capitol excepting the domes – and excepting that, although an immensely large house, it is small compared to the Capitol – it is a Capitol in miniature – and all that I can say of it is, that in the inside it seems to a stranger to be curiously arranged, so much so that he might with ease get lost in it. It is most richly and elegantly furnished, and comes up to my idea of a Royal Palace. On the outside it is commanding and magnificently grand. . . . The whole concern together looks as if it might be the Manor of some Nabob as Uncle Sam."

Hoban's north portico had not been completed long when *The People's Magazine* reviewed both the White House and the accusations that it was too grand for the president of a republic: "Some persons, under every administration, have objected to the style of the President's mansion, as bordering on unnecessary state and parade – but we are of a different opinion. It is the house provided by the people for the residence of the chief magistrate of their choice, and he is the tenant at certain seasons for four or at most eight years; it hardly equals the seats of many of the nobility and wealthy commoners of England, and bears no comparison with the residences of the petty princes of Germany or the grand dukes of Italy. . . . It is what the mansion of the head of this Republic should be, large enough for public and family purposes, and should be finished and maintained in a style to gratify every wish for convenience and pleasure."

Opposite:
Detail of a north portico column
capital, carved by the Italian
Francisco Jardella, 1829-30

City of Washington from Beyond
the Navy Yard, painted by George
Cooke, 1833. The federal city in
Jackson's time, from the south

3

HOUSE PORTRAITS

n the four decades after its reconstruction, the White House enjoyed what might be called the second period in its architectural history. From the late 1820s to the late 1860s the White House sheltered a succession of thirteen presidents, from Monroe to Lincoln. These were the leaders who saw the United States through years of territorial expansion, western conquest, and a climax of national history in the Civil War. At the close of this span of forty years the presidency itself was tried in the impeachment of Andrew Johnson—and it survived. In such times the White House naturally underwent change.

Yet, architecturally, the building's external appearance changed hardly at all from 1833, the year Andrew Jackson moved the gates, until 1857, when President James Buchanan added a greenhouse on the roof of the west terrace. His addition was only a flimsy wooden concession to privacy and winter sunshine, riding the terrace like a howdah on an elephant. Otherwise the history of the President's House from the early 1830s until the Civil War period concerns not actual building construction, but rather a continual introduction of technical innovations in comfort and convenience and a series of redecorations.

Andrew Jackson, president from 1829 to 1837. Old Hickory, hero of the War of 1812, arrived at the White House in a cloud of glory, with thousands in adoring pursuit. He decorated the East Room in splendid gold stars and piped the house for running water.

The house of Washington and Hoban was a giant of a place, but beyond the snug plaster walls, which insulated well, and the tall spaces, which were cool in hot weather, the comforts offered by the house were not much greater than those of a barn. Heating, for example, was difficult with such large windows and high ceilings. The interiors of the White House were originally warmed somewhat by log-burning fireplaces with fireboxes deep enough to hold big fires, yet sufficiently shallow to reflect their heat, and

Left:

The heroic Jackson: Clark Mills's equestrian statue in bronze was unveiled in Lafayette Square on January 8, 1853, and maintains its powerful presence at the north end of the President's Park. The inscription, though originally planned for the pedestal, was not applied until 1909; presumably the order was canceled when the statue was new by the chairman of the Senate public buildings committee, Jefferson Davis.

Opposite top:

Idyllic view of the White House during the Jacksonian age, circa 1834. This may be a reversed view made from a daguerreotype, for it does not show the L shape of the west wing and the ornamental garden presented here was on the east side. In any case, it probably presents a fairly accurate idea of the appearance of the White House in its pastoral period.

Opposite bottom:

Plan of the White House in use by Andrew Jackson. Alexander Jackson Davis drew several views of the house and this plan while in Washington in 1834. At that time he and his New York partners were preparing a book on American public buildings that was never realized. While Davis's exterior dimensions are somewhat off, the plan suggests he had more than ordinary access to the interiors of the state floor. Some of the room labels have been added to this plan, for neither the Blue Room nor the Red Room were so called at this time.

chimneys with sharp curves or rolls where their throats began, above the fireboxes, after the Rumford principle of draft efficiency. White House chimneys tend to smoke today, surrounded as they are by taller buildings, but no complaints survive from the early times, when most chimneys smoked and those at the White House, rising over the city, worked well. Insulation was provided by the plaster, as well as by wallpaper, curtains, and floor coverings. Every floor in the first and second stories was covered wall to wall with carpeting, painted canvas, or straw matting laid over a newspaper or tobacco-cloth pad.

The fireplace heat was not adequate, cooking a person on one side, while freezing the other, and by about 1804 some of the fireplaces had been adapted to coal. Apparently the change was not made for Virginia coal, which had nearly always been available along the eastern seaboard, but for the more recently abundant coal from western Pennsylvania. In adapting a wood-burning fireplace to coal, one had to install brick blocks, or hobs, in the sides of the firebox, about half as high as the opening. Between the hobs a coal fire

burned in an iron basket. Some of the White House coal fixtures were finer than others. Jefferson had his made of steel or brass, which seem to have comprised an entire fixture with hobs and baskets that fit into the fireplace opening. How well coal heated the big rooms is questionable, though probably it did not do a good job.

The Madisons' receptions were uniquely warm, however, thanks to the central heating system Latrobe supplied for the dining room, using the hot air furnace patented by Daniel Pettibone. This design called for a cluster of "kettles," or air chambers, which were heated externally, and as the air rose up from them through a funnel insert in the chimney it was drafted off through clay pipes, or ducts, to the various rooms. Fireplace fires hurried the movement of air from the furnace by heightening the draft action of the chimney. The Pettibone furnace, with its air chambers enclosed in a brick outer structure, seems to have been located in the present medical office on the southwest corner of the basement floor.

Destroyed in the fire in 1814, the Pettibone

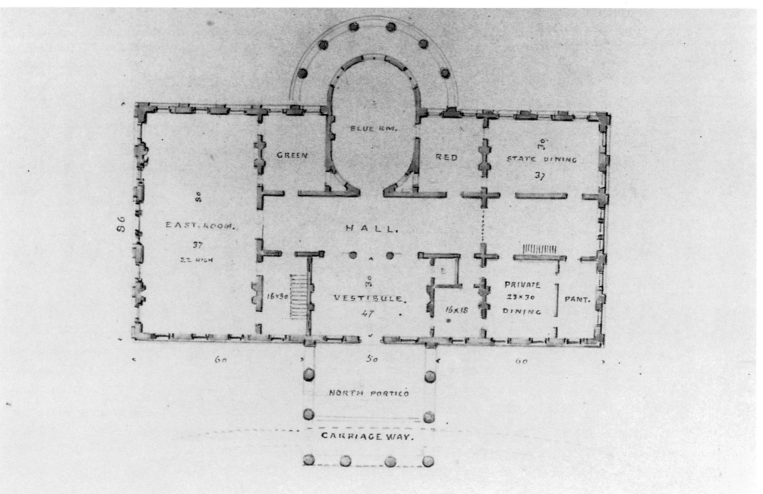

James K. Polk's Cabinet in the State Dining Room, May or June 1846, the earliest photograph taken in the White House. Although vague the photograph does show certain features of the interior, from the wallpaper to the chandelier and the large mantel glass, all elements of decor that might be found in expensive houses of the time.

furnace was not replaced in the rebuilding of 1818. James Monroe, John Quincy Adams, and Andrew Jackson warmed themselves by wood and coal fires. Martin Van Buren, accustomed to the luxuries of city life, altered the situation by ordering a central heating system in 1837. The realization of a system took awhile, and it was not fired up until the winter of 1840. Preparations proved complicated. The ducts had to be built from the basement furnace room, which usurped the oval servants' hall, today's diplomatic reception room. Channels were found in the dead spaces on each side of the fireplaces for the round ducts, with their neat, white-coat interiors. For the two oval rooms above the furnace chamber, duct space was more plentiful than in rooms with corners.

To function properly, the system required the admittance of as much fresh air as possible to the furnace room and as little as possible to the heated rooms above. A glass vestibule was built inside the north door, containing a second entrance door to the hall. Window sash and french

doors were installed between the columns in the hall, separating the entrance hall from the transverse hall, off which the state parlors opened. Not every room benefited from the heating system, but the parlors and some bedrooms were included. A fireman was employed to manage and feed the new convenience. He was on duty twenty-four hours a day, with summers off, and resided comfortably in the room we know as the china room.

The heating system was continually enlarged. By 1848 the furnace was a cumbersome thing that thumped and groaned and processed nature's air into a dusty, stale source of widely proclaimed luxury. Built of metal encased in a great superstructure of brick, it had fuel and draft doors of cast iron. Ducts extended spiderlike from its arched top into walls and floors, threading up into the rooms two stories above. Coal was shoveled in as needed from storage bins beneath the outside stairs to the south portico. In the continued absence of fans, or other mechanical means of pushing or pulling the hot air from the heat chambers of the furnace through the ducts, fireplace fires and draft chimneys were still necessary to make the system function.

Joseph Nason of Walworth & Nason, Boston, converted the furnace to a more efficient hot water system for Franklin Pierce in 1853. The air was still moved by gravity, but it tended to be hotter, because it was warmed in the furnace by water-filled copper coils, which could be maintained at almost 212 degrees Fahrenheit. This is the system that warmed the Civil War White House and was in operation for some years after. Its advantage was that the furnace used less coal than before. The warm air was more moist and not so stale as it had been. But when the rooms were crowded it could be stifling; given space, the heat seemed to roll about in gusts.

James Hoban built the house to be lighted in the simple ways known in the world of his time. Natural light provided the main illumination. It entered the house through tall, broad windows that rose a full fourteen feet and were five feet across, glazed with Boston crown glass that had

the surface beauty of a clear pond. Life centered on these windows during the day. Tables were pulled close to them, as was President William Henry Harrison's bed, as he lay dying in 1841. Chairs were arranged for tea where the light fell, and the pastry cook's marble-top table was kept in the kitchen window.

At night the White House was lighted by lamps and candles. Lard oil, made from animal and vegetable fats, was purchased in large quantity. Foul-smelling but cheap, it fueled lamps mainly in bedrooms, family living rooms, and service rooms. Some lard oil was undoubtedly made from fats in the kitchen, stored in earthenware jars that were glazed inside and kept, sour and obnoxious, at the basement lamp station, where all the lamps were cleaned and refreshed every day. Candles were purchased in lesser numbers than might be imagined, and there were several classes of them. The tall tapers one associates with the age of candlelight were reserved for special occasions in the most formal rooms.

Lighting entire rooms was a weekly obligation

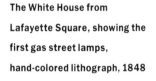

The White House from Lafayette Square, showing the first gas street lamps, hand-colored lithograph, 1848

View of the Capitol from atop the south portico of the White House, engraving, 1839. Beyond the arched gate, the avenue leads straight to Capitol Hill.
In the foreground is the stone balustrade that fences the edge of the White House roof—this portion of it built in 1824 for the portico.

at the White House because of the regular social schedule, but such a degree of light was rarely necessary in private houses. There people normally lighted only what was necessary – the pages of a book, sewing, a circle of soup plates. Before the era of gaslight, chandeliers were more familiar – and safer – in public or quasi-public places because table lamps were at peril in rooms filled with people. All of the main floor rooms of the White House had chandeliers that burned candles, and the large lanterns of the halls were equipped with oil lamps. The earliest view of a White House chandelier appears in a photograph of President Polk and his Cabinet taken in the dining room in June 1846. Purchased by James Monroe in 1818 as one of a pair, it was a vertical, basketlike fixture made of long, reflective strands of cut glass beads draped on a thin bronze frame that supported a ring of candles. Large mirrors furthered the luminous effect of the candlelight.

The Argand burner, a great innovation in artificial lighting, appeared in Europe just after the close of the American Revolution. It was known to Hoban, of course, but it could not be called a common means of light until well after the White House was built. The remarkable Argand lamp made its presidential debut in George Washington's drawing room in New York at the republic's beginning. Two wonderful features set the lamp apart: it gave bright light and consumed its own smoke, thanks to a vertical chimneylike arrangement that introduced an abundance of oxygen to the flame. Adams and Jefferson had used Argand lamps at the White House. Madison's oval saloon had featured them in the form of silver wall brackets that dripped oil on the carpet and upholstery through the air holes beneath the wick. Strangely enough the Argand burner, invented to hang overhead, was never used in the White House except in hall lanterns. Candles were the rule in hanging fixtures until Jackson installed small glass lard-oil lamps in the East Room chandeliers in their stead.

Gaslighting made its appearance at the White House in 1848 during the administration of James K. Polk. The chandeliers of the state floor were piped for the new light, except for the one in the Blue Room, which, on Sarah Polk's orders, remained a candle fixture. She enjoyed sweet vindication for her backwardness when the gas ran out during its White House debut, leaving a state reception in darkness. Most of the upstairs rooms had wall brackets or elbows, one to each room, usually installed beside a chimney or near a window to take advantage of dead spaces for the gas pipes. To fuel a table lamp, hoses of India rubber could be attached to a chandelier burner or a wall bracket by means of a special nozzle.

The public buildings commissioner laid gas pipes down Pennsylvania Avenue from the Capitol to the White House and placed streetlamps along the way. Some merchants on the avenue piped gas from the central flow, and only after repeated blackouts at the White House was this thievery found out and stopped. So successful was the White House gas service otherwise that it was extended frequently, room after room.

A significant feature of gaslight was that it was a stationary source of illumination, curiously enough the first known to mankind. All artificial lighting mechanisms in the past had been portable; lamps could be carried, chandeliers unhooked and moved. Thus the eternal shifting of chairs and tables into the light could finally stop, and furnishings could remain in place, attrac-

View northwest down Pennsylvania Avenue from the high grounds of the U.S. Capitol to the White House. During the time of Polk the avenue first glowed with gas lamps, the pipes being buried in the center of the street. (Note that the White House is off-axis with the avenue. Pierre L'Enfant's "palace" would have filled the vista.) The image has been reversed from the natural daguerreotype rendering to better serve documentary purposes here.

tively arranged. By the time of the Civil War gaslight had overtaken all other artificial light in use in the White House. Extra light, small scale, was provided by candles and by kerosene, the new petroleum oil, which was not really to come into its own until the Civil War.

The introduction of conveniences for this period climaxed in Jackson's 1833 installation of a running water system. Hoban had proposed running water for the White House in 1816, but was turned down as being too visionary. When Jackson came to office, water was drawn from a deep well in the columned breezeway between the house and the west wing. It was distributed from that point in buckets, which were hauled to the kitchen on the same floor level but had to be carried up the small service stairs to a dozen or more washbowls and pitchers. The convenience

east of the White House. When work began in earnest on the water system in 1833, the first step was to provide a pond or reservoir between the State Department and Treasury buildings, east of the White House. This was carefully excavated, perhaps round in shape, its sides rubbed with clay, like a grave of the time, to help seal them. A deep bed of white sand was introduced and the entire pond covered by a tin roof.

Meanwhile, from Franklin Square, an underground pipe, or trunk, made of hollowed-out tree trunks was extended south down the middle of Fourteenth Street. It turned southwest along New York Avenue, then south again on present day Madison Place to the White House grounds, where the water fell five or six feet into the pond. The water flowed easily, for the pipe sloped the full distance. The rippling disturbance made by

Opposite:
In this Seneca stone column of the north portico the patch reveals the channel made in 1858 to receive a gas pipe for column-mounted porch lamps (see below). Here the stone has been cleaned, and the scar revealed, before being covered again with white paint.

of the well to the laundry in the west wing was important, for the greatest amount of water was needed there; after it was used it was dashed into the courtyard outside the L-shaped colonnade. There it soaked away between the brick pavers, cleaning what was then a horse yard and today is the Rose Garden.

Major William B. Lewis, one of Jackson's several resident friends, seems to have encouraged new conveniences wherever he could, and he activated Hoban's plan to install running water. Work took place in the summer of 1833, while Jackson was at home in Tennessee. The system, though not unique, was ingenious. Several years earlier, the government had purchased a spring on a lot at Franklin Square, several blocks north-

Sketches of the north portico railings and similar ones at the Capitol, Alexander Jackson Davis, 1835. Railings much like these can still be seen at William Strickland's 1818-24 Bank of the United States in Philadelphia.

Looking north from the shelter of the portico, circa 1873, this view shows the iron anthemion railing installed circa 1818–20 and removed in 1902. It repeats the anthemion motif Hoban had used in his plaster frieze in the East Room.

the splashing stream was part of the genius of the system, for the continual filtering of the water through the white sand discouraged algae. Mounted over the "fountain" was a hand pump of iron and brass contained within a highly architectural wooden pump house, which looked like a courthouse steeple, complete with neoclassical detailing, a clock, and louvered blinds that ventilated the stove used there in the winter. The pump itself was a hand-operated contrivance that had heavy counterweights that rose into the tall interior of the pump house.

The pump was activated when necessary by a wheel turned by the full-time pump keeper. The wheel pushed water through a small pipe to fill a single reservoir, or bulb, in the basement of the White House and another in the whitewashed, brick-floored bathing room in the east wing. Single hydrants were provided for each of the reservoirs, somewhat like office water coolers; the same arrangement was made in the ground floors of each of the four departmental buildings flanking the White House. As the appetite for convenience is never satisfied, so this wonderful system was expanded yearly. Pipes were extended to the second floor in 1835 to serve a hydrant in the hall. Apparently no particular effort was made to hide them. Pipes may have run along the walls from the basement up through the main floor to the second floor. Upstairs, individual hand pumps raised the water to the reservoir from a ground-level holding tank.

In 1853 a more comprehensive plumbing system was introduced by President Franklin Pierce, when he ordered a bathtub put in his dressing room on the southwest corner upstairs. It was the first stationary bathtub in the White House, notwithstanding that H. L. Mencken in jest gave the honor to Millard Fillmore. The dressing room had contained a water closet since 1801, but heretofore the only bathing facilities outside the bathing room in the east wing – used only by men – had been portable, in the form of sitz or hip tubs and the shoe-shaped bathtubs made of tin. Pierce's new tub was made of copper encased in wood. The water was heated as the bath was prepared by a gas burner set beneath a cylindrical copper water heater mounted on the wall beside the tub.

Pierce also built a water closet in the passage beside the service stair on the main floor, but, while such a facility was to last there until the twentieth century, for lack of space no such way station serves the main floor today. The system of plumbing was to remain about the same until 1861, when President James Buchanan ordered marble-slab shelves inset with round lavatory bowls for each of the bedrooms. Replacing the old bowl-and-pitcher washstands, the new bowls were served by pivot-mounted, nickel-plated faucets, one to each, pumping Potomac River water that flowed when the spout was turned. These were in place about a month before Lincoln moved to the White House.

The conveniences added through the 1830s, '40s, and '50s were by the standards of the time luxuries, not necessities, and there were those who, for various perfectly sensible reasons, wanted no part of them. Privies, after all, could

Drawn from a daguerreotype and published in *United States Magazine* in 1856, this view of Franklin Pierce's office shows the room we know today as the Lincoln bedroom, in the southeast part of the second floor of the White House. Andrew Jackson's standup desk is seen covering the door in the far righthand corner, while his portrait hangs over the black marble mantelpiece; Jefferson's simple worktable, with drawers along each side, serves as the cabinet table and simple bookcases line the east wall.

be clean and sanitary and were normally outside, not inside. Gaslighting entailed the risk of asphyxiation. When the gas plant closed down at nine or ten at night, the gas valves on each light fixture had better be closed, lest deadly gas fill the sleeping house when the gas company resumed service the next morning.

Central gravity heating was bone dry, drafty, and uneven. Heat reached the backside as well as the front, but it was not pleasant heat like that from a wood fire. Even when Pierce introduced the hot water coil apparatus to the furnace in 1853, it made the air that came from the registers only less stale and unwholesome than before. Of all the comforts and conveniences introduced in those years between the rebuilding of the White House in 1818 and Lincoln's time, the only one universally approved was running water. The appearance of the hydrant indoors was the knell of the bucket, even though the death of bucket hauling was yet a long way off for most Americans. Everyone could relate joyously to that.

In the eighteenth and early nineteenth centuries the presidents maintained offices at home, a custom begun by Washington. By the mid-1820s the president had set aside two rooms upstairs as his office – a bedroom and the adjacent southeast corner dressing room. Here he worked with a single assistant, his secretary, usually a relative paid by him personally. In 1848 James K. Polk

(Experts can usually tell the difference.)

There being no real office furniture in the earliest times, the presidential offices always represented a mix of domestic-style desks and long tables covered with baize; storage was in pigeonholes and in rows of clothing wardrobes, as well as in trunks. Andrew Jackson, whose health required that he stand a lot, made use of a stand-up clerk's desk when he established himself in the White House in 1829. That later Tennessean, Andrew Johnson, stopped remodelers nearly forty years later from removing this desk, but it was gone by 1875.

Presidential papers left the White House with departing presidents, who took letterpress copy books and any correspondence received that was not passed on to the departments for action. The papers also included hundreds and perhaps thousands of small notes carried about the city by messengers. These were scattered like fall

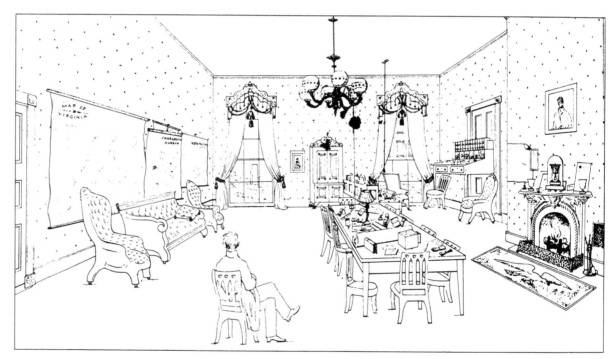

Lincoln's office in 1864 in a sketch by C. K. Stellwagen. The wallpaper is recorded as having been dark green, and the mantel is different from the one in the earlier views. A rubber hose from the chandelier fuels a gas table lamp, while a cord toward the rear of the room activated a bell in the outer office. Through a door to the left was a small corner room that served as a secretarial office; the hallway outside was the reception room. Eventually a room to the right would be added and that suite would serve the presidents until 1902, when the office function was moved to the west wing. The unfinished Washington Monument is visible through the lefthand window.

created the salaried federal job of secretary to the president as part of his office management reorganization. Lincoln was to have two secretaries, then three. But until that time the president had only one, and when he needed help, as when there were many duplicate papers to write, clerks were borrowed from the departments. Before Polk's time, however, the president's signature was rarely affixed to a document by anyone other than him or his secretary, imitating his signature.

leaves and appear occasionally tucked away in manuscript collections of every imaginable sort. The telegraph was to curtail this practice, and the telephone ended it almost entirely.

During the pre-Civil War period the second-floor cross corridor, running from end to end of the house, was not used as three sitting rooms, as it is today, but merely as a passage divided by three broad, arched doorways with fan-shaped glass transoms. In the second and third or easternmost of these arches, glass doors separated the office part of the house from the living quarters. The back stair landed in the area between these two arches, and when the doors were shut the resulting space made a vestibule. To the right of it was the private area, and on the left several steps led up into the office section. This office area was raised above the floor level of the remainder of the second story to accommodate the unusually high ceilings of the East Room below. The office stair was thus the back stair – designed by Hoban for family use – now become the means of public access from the entrance hall to the office. After the addition in 1837 of the glass screen in the hall below, the north entrance seemed more like an office hall than one in a house, its floor covered with oilcloth, chairs lining the walls, and doormen presiding over callers, who lounged about awaiting word that the president or his secretary would see them.

**North passage, second floor.
This small corridor was
partitioned through the center of
the large state bedroom during
the Pierce administration in 1853,
allowing the president access to
the window over the north
entrance for impromptu
speeches. Lincoln made frequent
use of this window, where candles
were held to light his notes.
The purpose of this confining
perch was to assure security. It
became a permanent part of the
White House.**

By 1860 the office function filled the entire east end of the second floor. Civil War demands would see it crowded with work space and sleeping quarters for the president's principal secretaries, George Nicolay and John Hay. The hallway that divided the rooms was outfitted as a

waiting room and an overflow place in which office tasks could be performed. In 1862 Lincoln annexed a nearby southside bedroom – known for awhile as the Treaty Room and today as the president's office in the residence – for use as a reception room. Across the south end he had a temporary partition constructed, forming a passage through which he could go unseen from his office into the oval room of the family quarters.

Private life was concentrated in the balance of the second floor, the west and central part of the house. Principal among those nine rooms was the oval room over the Blue Room. This has been called by many names but usually has been known as the library. It was shaded by the south portico, and the windows were left open except in the coldest weather because the deep overhang of the porch protected them. Inventories list bookcases and comfortable sofas and armchairs here for the years 1829 to 1869. In the earlier years of this period the room tended to be more formal than later on, when it was a cherished sanctum for the presidents and their families.

Across the hall was a large room, which no longer exists, located over the entrance hall and shaded by the north portico. It had fireplaces at each end and was the grandest bedchamber in the house, reserved for honored guests and for the use of women as a powder room after dinner parties. Lafayette almost certainly slept there on his visit in 1824. Jackson had the room done up elegantly in yellow and pink. But in 1853 Franklin Pierce effectively did away with it by cutting a narrow passage through the middle to give access from the hall to the window over the north door. Now when crowds marched on the White House to serenade or celebrate some event, or register protest, and he was "called out," he could make his speech from the protection of the window, instead of following the tradition of appearing unprotected on the gaslit porch. Lincoln made his last speech from this window, three days before the fatal visit to Ford's Theater.

By 1853 the family quarters boasted seven bedrooms, counting the room east of the oval room, the one Lincoln was to take into the office space. West of the oval room was the bedroom for the president's wife, then the president's bedroom and the corner dressing room. The grand

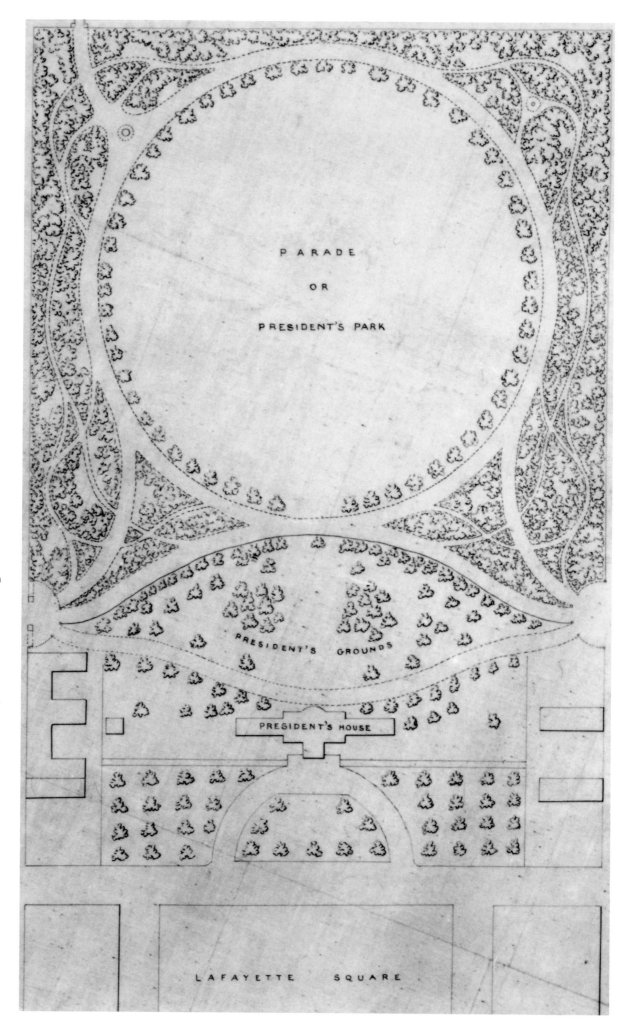

Detail, the White House grounds, from Andrew Jackson Downing's 1851 plan for redesigning the public spaces of Washington. Brought to Washington by Millard and Abigail Fillmore, who had read his works on landscape architecture, Downing did his plan as a somewhat detailed schematic, but died before his ideas were completely expressed on paper. Security was a major consideration at the White House in the troubled years of the 1850s, as can be seen in Downing's careful placement of trees, where sharpshooters might be stationed.

PARADE

OR

PRESIDENT'S PARK

PRESIDENT'S GROUNDS

PRESIDENT'S HOUSE

LAFAYETTE SQUARE

stair descended in the center of the west end of the corridor, against a tall, round-headed expanse of window glass that gave a dramatic view when a fiery sunset possessed the western sky. At the beginning of state dinners and large receptions, the president and his lady stood here, awaiting the signal to descend to their guests, who stood crowded into the transverse hall below. The great window was equipped with small, movable louvered shutters that shielded it from the hot afternoon sun in summer and allowed the window to be opened at any time.

From the family quarters the most direct route to the lower floors or to the outdoors was by way of the small service stair that linked all the floors, attic to basement. It landed twice between each level, seeming to twist over and over itself as it rounded the small chamber that contained it. This was the stair so familiar to Lincoln, by which he escaped the legions of business callers to go to the telegraph office next door in the war department or out for a drive in his carriage.

For all of the nineteenth century the basement was a utilitarian area, but it had architectural merit because of the magnificence of its stone-and-brick structure, particularly the groin vaulting of the central corridor and the arching of the various rooms. This beauty gained no special notice at the time, at least as far as the written word was concerned, nor to present knowledge was it ever photographed. The basement's architectural possibilities were not to be identified until Charles McKim's renovations in 1902.

In the first half of the nineteenth century the basement was a workplace. Servants' bedrooms, meat room, cold and warm pantries, and various work spaces occupied its fourteen rooms, including the great kitchen below the entrance hall with its stone fireplaces, which were a good eight feet wide. Normally this kitchen was used only to cook for large events. As with everything else, Washington had approved its design fully aware of the crowds that had to be fed. And presidents personally watched kitchen economy, realizing at the outset, or soon learning, that warm hospitality, though essential to the job, could lead to ruin if not controlled.

Jefferson installed the kitchen's first cooking range—so-called because it held a range of pots;

it probably burned coal. This was bricked into one of the fireplaces. Large numbers of implements for cooking furnished the kitchen, more than inventories of the time show in private houses, and many more for preparing sweets and desserts. Mrs. Madison's celebrated ice cream balls in hot pastry were made here, as was the charlotte russe served by Sarah Polk thirty-five years later. A second smaller kitchen in the corner room on the northwest was used by the everyday cook.

The remainder of the basement rooms were servants' living quarters. When not cleaning, cooking, or serving, the household staff gathered in the servants' hall, the oval room beneath the

Milk trough carved for Andrew Jackson in 1834 by Robert Brown, one of the original Edinburgh stonemasons who built the White House in the 1790s. Brown stayed in Washington and worked in the stonecutting business in Georgetown for the rest of his life. The trough is in use today as a garden ornament.

Blue Room. When this room became the furnace room in Martin Van Buren's time, the servants' hall was moved to the storeroom between the great and small kitchens on the north side. The servants' hall had a large table and many chairs, and the staff gathered there during slack times to do odd jobs, such as polishing silver and making repairs, and to plan for further chores. There was a fireplace, and a floor of brick pavers, which, because it was clammy and blamed for rheumatism and because it was hard on the feet, was covered with wood about 1840. On the wall was a row of wire-line bells, each with a label identifying the room it served. These were activated to summon servants by cords or by cranks connected to a system of taut wires and springs artfully threaded through dead spaces in the walls and converging in the servants' hall. Such bells appeared in Europe in the second half of the eighteenth century as a means of ensuring privacy for the employer and economy in numbers of servants. The first Mrs. Adams had pleaded for them in the unfinished house, but they were to be installed later by Jefferson, who with some difficulty found a bell-hanger from Baltimore to do the work.

Voters seem not to have complained about so many people in residence at the White House. It was an enormous place and in numbers there was a certain security for the president and his family. A steward managed domestic operations, keeping watch over the costs of entertaining, for which the president paid personally out of his annual salary of $25,000. There was usually a female housekeeper. Both she and the steward had "closets," or "offices," in the basement. The steward slept in his office, which stood between the corridor door and an inner chamber where the silver was kept in trunks fitted to its storage. Shelves and cupboards in the housekeeper's office held valuable linens, and her bed and bureau were also in that room.

The basement's massive groin-vaulted corridor was lime-washed, sometimes white, sometimes yellow. There are few descriptions of it, but the invoices for work done there are revealing. This corridor was only a passage, but it often contained storage, and at least once housed a small fire engine (James Monroe) and again a rowboat

(John Quincy Adams). All the basement windows were fitted with wrought iron bars, installed on order of the security-conscious James Monroe, who must have been concerned about theft of foodstuffs as well as the safety of the household. The bars remain in place. Service and storage rooms and sleeping quarters extended into the colonnaded wings. A large privy shared the west wing with the icehouse and the laundry. This last was a long, brick-floored room lighted by the lunette windows high on the walls. After Jackson moved the stable out of the west wing, Monroe's old stable became a storage place. Besides the bathing room, the east wing contained a privy and an apartment for the gardener.

Beyond the east wing, just on the other side of the foundations of the ill-fated triumphal arch, was the old Treasury fireproof built by Jefferson and Latrobe. It may have survived the ravages of the British, or it may have been damaged by the fire. Whatever its fate, the Treasury never used it after the new Treasury Building was completed in 1818, and it was soon turned into a storage house for the White House grounds. When

Bars have guarded the basement windows of the White House from at least the 1820s, to protect the house as well as the many storerooms that held silver, liquor, and food and shared the ground-level basement with kitchens, pantries, and servants' rooms.

James Monroe, and later John Quincy Adams, laid out the flower garden in the place Jefferson had selected southeast of the house, the fireproof became a tool shed. Andrew Jackson had it remodeled into an orangery about 1833, and it served until it was demolished in 1857 to make room for the south wing of the Treasury.

The state floor was the only part of the White House most outsiders ever saw. It was maintained as stylishly as the money available allowed. From the late 1820s until the late 1860s the Congress appropriated $20,000 every four years for repairing and improving the house, something of a no-questions-asked grant, which was nevertheless sometimes questioned anyway. Now and then the Congress increased the figure to fund a special project, such as the building of the north portico or the repainting and papering of the parlors. The state floor was usually more than presentable, while the family quarters were as often seedy, with faded reused matting and carpeting and tattered curtains brought up from downstairs. Presidents were more willing to spend on the areas the public saw than on their private rooms.

James Monroe had brought the state parlors back from the fire in style, and during most of the forty years in question here the furnishings formed the basis for the interior decoration of the White House. Washington's portrait and silver candelabra, rescued by a slave named Rhodes, were the only formal furnishings known to have survived the fire. The drawing room furniture Monroe's agents sent from Paris was made by Pierre Antoine Bellangé, who had risen to become one of the premier cabinetmakers of Napoleonic France and continued under the *restauration* of Louis XVIII, wnen Monroe made his purchases. This suite, typical of Bellangé's distinctive and reserved Empire style, was finished in gold leaf and covered in crimson silk. Its upright parts looked a bit like cannon barrels, and it was decorated with carved laurel leaves. Monroe's agents also purchased a gilded bronze chandelier, which was gathering dust, having been ordered during Napoleon's reign but not called for after the Empire collapsed. This elegant *lustre*, fitted to hold thirty candles, brought its history along, with exaggeration: For as long as it

hung in the Blue Room – about thirty-five years – visitors to the White House were delighted to be able to stand beneath a chandelier that had belonged to Napoleon.

In Monroe's barrels and crates from France were table silver, porcelain urns, bronze clocks that stood beneath glass domes, a magnificent

The East Room, circa 1861, lithograph.
With the exception of the painted ceiling
and the marble mantelpieces, added by
Franklin Pierce in 1854, the room seems
to be much as it was when Jackson
decorated it in 1829 and gave it the
first of its great chandeliers.

bronze plateau for the dining room table, and other costly and elegant decorations for the state rooms. While the gold furniture was sold at auction in 1860 by James Buchanan, most of the rest of the furnishings continued in use, and many are cherished components of the White House today.

Andrew Jackson completed the East Room. The decoration and furnishing were handled in a matter-of-fact way made possible by modern commerce as it was known at the time. Jackson sent his friend Major William B. Lewis to Louis Veron's Philadelphia warehouse – that day's equivalent of a furniture and house-fittings store combined – where he selected, apparently in one stop, the contents of America's first room of state. Grand it was to be, in the best taste the American market could produce; for this, one would have thought first of Philadelphia in 1829; two decades later it would be New York.

Veron saw to the installation of the decorations. The walls were papered in lemon yellow, the windows draped in royal blue and yellow, and the upholstery and carpeting were predominantly blue. Hoban's mighty band of anthemia

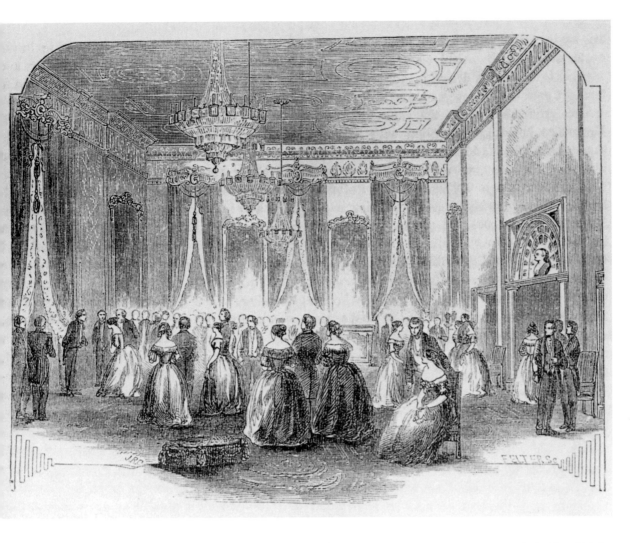

The most accurate picture of the White House state floor in the 1850s is provided in a set of views published in 1856 in the *United States Magazine*.

Opposite, clockwise from top: The Green Room was a comfortable parlor given its name by the early 1820s. The Blue Room was made blue for Van Buren at the beginning of his administration, and the Red Room became red about 1845. Following the modes of the time, the interiors were elegantly "French," with florid wallpapers—sumptuous in brilliant color against white; heavy gas chandeliers enriched with cast foliation and glass globes; marble mantelpieces; and deeply gathered draperies pulled back to reveal powdery lace undercurtains.

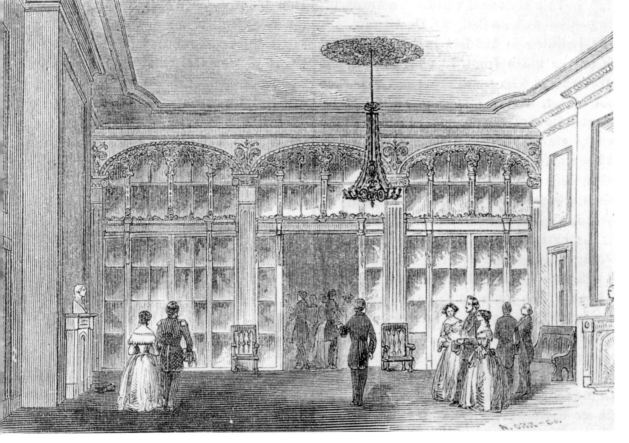

Top: Reception in the East Room, an artist's idea based on a daguerreotype of the room. The East Room sometimes welcomed as many as 6,000 reception callers on New Year's Day or January 8, the anniversary of the War of 1812 victory over the British at the Battle of New Orleans. On weekdays visitors to the city could wander through the room and admire its great oil-fueled chandeliers and extravagant floral carpeting.

Bottom: The entrance hall, with its two fireplaces; the glass screen was installed in 1837 to accommodate the gravity heating system. Originally of wood, it was replaced in 1853 with ground glass in an iron frame.

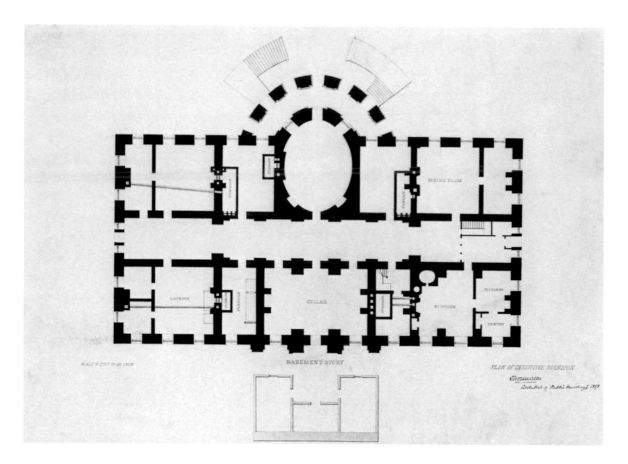

Plan of the basement of the White House, Thomas U. Walter, circa 1856. This floor, wholly exposed on the south and lighted by a deep, broad areaway on the north, contained the service areas. Information about it, apart from that found in household inventories, is scant. This plan is very rare and shows the familiar layout of rooms, spreading east and west from the oval on the south and the long room on the north. The oval room—since 1902 the diplomatic reception room—was originally a servants' hall but became a furnace room in 1837; at that time the hall was moved to the southwest part of the basement. On the northwest were the family kitchen and the great central kitchen used for banquets. East of the large kitchen was the meat room. Other rooms were divided between steward's pantries and servants' bedrooms. Originally paved with square bricks the basement by the 1830s had wood floors, preferred because they were drier.

crowned the room in gold, emphasized by the black background flocking. The ceiling was whitewashed, and this was repeated every year to clean it of soot. Over the archway to the transverse hall Veron pasted gilded stars on the yellow paper, dramatizing the entrance to the room Masonic-hall style. Twenty-one spittoons, as if in military formation, stood in lines east and west, each centered reassuringly on a square of oilcloth.

Most enduring as a theme in this room were the three large glass chandeliers. Plain ones of iron had been put there temporarily in the 1820s, probably the chain-and-rod-suspended hoops found in many public places, made by blacksmiths and holding twelve or so candles. Jackson's were the first glass chandeliers in the East Room; Grant's were second in 1873, and Theodore Roosevelt's, in use today, were installed in 1902. The chandeliers of 1829 measured some eight feet from the place where the chain attached at the top to the bottom of the lowest cut-glass prism, and they hung about nine feet from the floor. Hundreds of square-cut glass pieces reflected the light and made rainbows from the sunlight in daytime and from fifty-four candles during receptions at night. The East Room's

shine was increased by wall lamps, monumental table lamps in the solar form of the Argand burner, and great sheets of mirror, which topped the four black marble mantelpieces and filled the piers between the windows at the south and north ends of the room.

At first Jackson burned candles in his fixtures. When this proved too costly, he changed to oil lamps, which consisted simply of small, bulb-shaped fonts equipped with string wicks. Pegs, or "stems," on the bottom fitted them in the candle sockets. Polk was to pipe the chandeliers for gas in 1848, and it was beneath these, in the gaslight glow, that Lincoln's guests waltzed in the years of the Civil War.

The "color" parlors—Green Room, Blue Room, and Red Room—arrived at their permanent definitions at various times. Monroe introduced the Green Room at his New Year's reception in 1818. A glimpse of the inventory of its furnishings when he left office reveals "1 Elegant Chandelier, glass and gilt," mantel mirrors, "14 Elegant silk bottomed Chairs," one "Large Mahogany writing table, green cloth cover....," and that it was called the Green Drawing Room. While it was to retain its green color for all time—such longevity would have pleased Monroe, for permanence was what

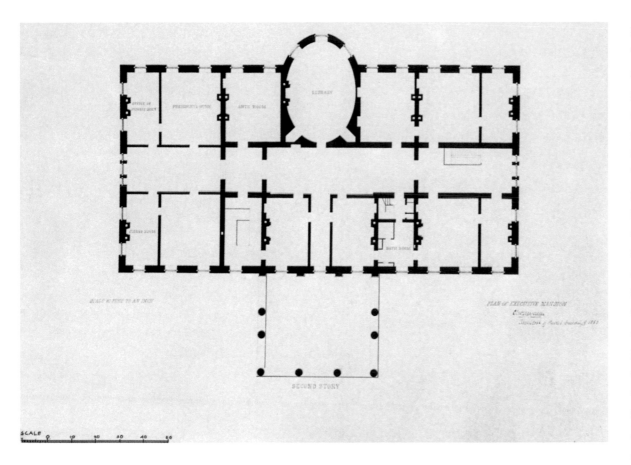

Second floor of the White House, Thomas U. Walter. This floor was approached by three stairs, the grand stair on the west, the small service stair nearby, and the back stair, off the entrance hall, which served the offices in the east end. The central hall was only a passage in the family quarters; now and then, when an important document was required in duplicate, long trestle tables were set up in the hall and clerks copied the documents for the president to sign. Most families used the oval room for a library, and the presidential bedrooms were on the southwest. Water closets were provided, beginning in 1801, in the southwest and southeast corner rooms. A second water closet was installed on the north, off the small hall, probably in 1860 for the Prince of Wales, who occupied the northwest corner suite during a visit.

he hoped to give his country—its survival for the first several decades was coincidental. By the time of Lincoln it was well established as the Green Room.

Van Buren selected blue in 1837 for the "Elliptical Saloon," which Monroe had made crimson and Jackson green. Blue satin was hung at the windows, blue and gilt wallpaper on the walls, and Monroe's gilded French furniture was upholstered in blue satin. When the Washington-based upholsterer, the French-born Charles Alexandre, removed the curtains, replaced the Brussels carpet with straw matting and put on the slipcovers in June 1838 his bill identified the "Bleu Room," first mention of the name that was to prevail.

In this setting of blue satin, at New Year's 1839, Van Buren's daughter-in-law, Angelica Singleton Van Buren, married to the president's eldest son, Abraham, was first presented as hostess for her widower father-in-law. She was dimpled and teasing, a southern belle from the Santee in South Carolina, who was nevertheless somewhat formidable in height in an age of short people. She towered over the president and is remembered in a delightful portrait in the White House collection today, floating in white gauze and silk, her

Thomas U. Walter, Architect of the United States Capitol from 1851 to 1865, was frequently called upon to design work gratis at the White House, notably in the times of Pierce and Lincoln.

101

head crowned with three white plumes to show that she had been presented at court.

Angelica and Abraham made a highly successful goodwill tour of the courts of Europe in 1839, representing the president, whose interest lay particularly in pleasing the British in the light of border difficulties with Canada. Being of about

James K. Polk, president from 1845 to 1849. Polk was not a well-known figure when he entered the White House, but he rode in on a Jacksonian wave whipped up by imperialist ambitions. He saw the nation expanded to the Pacific. Gaslighting was installed during Polk's tenure, and insofar as is known the White House was photographed then for the first time.

Sarah Polk presided over the wartime White House with strict formality. It was she who banned hard liquor from presidential entertainment, though she permitted the use of wine. She purchased rich, gilded furniture for some of the state rooms in the stylish "French" modes.

the same age as the young Queen Victoria, Angelica returned with some strong new ideas about entertaining and presentation gained at the Court of St. James. Denouncing the receiving line at the Blue Room door as passé, she ordered a platform built in the southward bow. Callers at the reception, entering the oval room, found the

president in his traditional place at the right of the door—but at the end of the room appeared an apparition, a tableau with Angelica at the center in a colored ball gown, surrounded by her young female friends all in white. This program quickly fell before harsh criticism that reflected on the president, and the Blue Room soon smelled the powder of a political war.

The Red Room was yellow until the Polks changed it to red in 1845 and 1846. It was described then as crimson, but one suspects it was a darker red with a more subtle fire, the sort of color that pleased and flattered the dark-eyed beauty Sarah Polk. W. W. Corcoran, the banker and founder of the art museum, advised in this work of redecoration. In New York he selected the Polks' furniture in the French Antique style, so-called for its evocation of old days at Versailles. Curvilinear and richly carved, the rosewood and mahogany chairs and sofas were deeply upholstered in silk velvet buttoned to articulate the springs inside the seats. Ruby carpeting with flowers and leaves, fine wallpapers with gold-leaf decorations, sumptuous tassels, galloon trimmings, and bullion fringe completed the first Red Room, where the Polk court gathered beneath the new gaslight during the years of the war with Mexico.

The state floor was and still is where most of the ceremony associated with the presidency takes place. Its furnishing and general effect are therefore always important, and this has been true since the start. In the half-century after the rebuilding of the house, it was carpeted wall to wall, covering the wood-plank flooring entirely. When there was a dance in the East Room—which might or might not be the custom depending on different presidents' ideas of propriety—the carpeted floor was covered with linen crash, which was waxed and sometimes chalked with a design that the merrymakers wore off with their dancing feet.

Paint covered the halls—entrance and transverse—but the rooms themselves were always wallpapered. After the completion of the reconstruction of the house, the architect of the Capitol, Charles Bulfinch, found "the walls generally of plain grounds, blue or green, with as much of gilding as to give to each apartment the air of a

Earliest known photograph of the White House, daguerreotype by John Plumbe, Jr., circa 1846

James and Sarah Polk on the south portico, 1849. The Polks, on a winter afternoon in his last year in office, are accompanied by Thomas Hart Benton (to Polk's right), Dolley Madison (to his left), James Buchanan, far left, and next to him his niece, Harriet Lane, who would be hostess at the White House on the eve of the Civil War. Mrs. Polk (center), considered a beauty, was called the "Spanish Donna."

North front of the White House, circa 1860, as Lincoln first saw it. The statue of Jefferson by Pierre David d'Angiers was set up before the White House in 1848 on orders from James K. Polk, who saw a parallel between himself and that earlier expansionist. The statue stands in the center of a lawn, which was cut and rolled and seasonally decorated with flower beds. Cut off from the driveway by a fence, this small garden was open to the public every day.

Opposite:
The East Room in the time of President Lincoln, from a stereopticon view, the only known photograph of this interior as Lincoln knew it. Rich floral carpeting, shimmering with the reds and blues of the new aniline dyes, complemented the wallpaper, with its heavy gilt highlights. The regal effect, so odd in a republic, was always given free reign in this room.

palace." Into this scene by day hundreds of tourists passed to inspect and react to the house they provided for the president and to judge how well he treated it.

On rare evenings artificial light illuminated crowds large or small—five thousand for a public reception, forty for a dinner—as they were received by the president. The rooms then served as background for the always somewhat tense presentation of the president. No detail was unimportant. Everything must succeed. For heroes the entrance could be grand. Jackson appeared beneath his golden arch of stars in the East Room; William Henry Harrison entered gracefully on the grand stair; Zachary Taylor, scruffy and dumpy, stomped uncomfortably into the East Room, for he loathed both ceremony and tight trousers.

Others not in the heroic military mode, still thinking it essential to be ceremonial, proceeded hesitantly. Jefferson, for all his republican simplicity, stood grandly in the exact center of the Blue Room, where callers approached to shake his hand. Neither George Washington nor John Adams had felt it appropriate for a president to shake hands. An appearance of some ceremonial sort seems to have worked, man after man, until Polk, who faced a dilemma. A hero he certainly

Overleaf:
The Republican Court in the Days of Lincoln, by Peter F. Rothermel, represents a state reception held in the East Room during the Civil War. Depicted is the end of the affair, when the president and his party paused beneath the great chandelier at the center of the room to meet honored guests before he bid the crowd good night. Rothermel imparts the flavor of the great receptions that characterized the room at least several times a year from its completion in 1829 until the last of the public receptions in 1932. According to the artist, "The scene is laid at the second inauguration," but it strongly suggests Lincoln's triumphal reception for General U.S. Grant, held in 1864. That event celebrated Grant's elevation to general-in-chief of the army, a turning point of the war and one remembered in highly emotional terms for years to come.

105

did not look to be, yet his administration took place during wartime, when heroism is held at a certain premium. Polk was small like Madison and lacked any special presence. Several of his predecessors had been criticized for seeming too showy, and he was wary of the same trap. The Polk solution, reached by his resolute wife, was that the president walk into the room to music after the crowd had assembled, with his wife on his arm. She directed the marine band to play "Hail to the Chief" to accompany them. The song was from the musical play *Lady of the Lake*, heard at the White House before. For Sarah Polk the march was a childhood favorite she had transcribed, words and music, in her copybook.

The manner of presenting the president to his guests was not the only ceremonial problem to be addressed, but the others fell under social forms that were less personal. Dinner guests and their partners marched, two by two, to music to the table, where they were arranged according to seating charts. If diplomats were present, they were carefully seated by the secretary of state, according to rank. Questions of rank at the White House extended to the order in which carriages formed on the driveway to receive departing guests, and even today tempers flare over perceived affronts to official status among the chauffeurs in the lines of black limousines at state functions.

Lincoln's seating charts survive, showing about forty at a long, rectangular table, with the president and Mrs. Lincoln facing each other halfway down the table and the president's secretaries at each end. The president was always served first. No one was to rise from the table before the president, and guests were not free to depart from the house before the president retired. After dinner the ladies retired to a bedroom or upstairs sitting room equipped either with close stools containing chamber pots or with a nearby water closet. For the men chamber pots were put out in the dining room, English style.

In the receiving line, usually just inside the Blue Room door, the president was introduced first, then his wife or hostess. Men always preceded women through the line of guests, which, on days of large public receptions, might extend out the north door and several blocks down the street—snow, rain, or shine. Beginning in the 1850s temporary wooden steps were put up to the north windows of the East Room to encourage early departures. The steps were kept busy by a combination of heat, human bodies pushing against each other, sweat, smells from the lights, soot from the furnace, noise, and sickly sweet odors from flowers, together with no food whatsoever and at most only the prospect of a sip of ice water (a concession to frequent fainting).

Private and official dinners were, of course, more manageable. From the receiving line the guests moved about the parlors and East Room under the magic of the great glass chandeliers, before the mighty mirrors, over the floral sprawls of Brussels carpeting—watching others, conversing, and promenading until the Marine Band announced the march to dinner. In the 1820s the time at table was about four hours, beginning at four o'clock in the afternoon; by the mid-1860s the time had shrunk to about an hour and a half.

After Lincoln's tenure the White House became his, in the public mind, as it had once been George Washington's. The bittersweet association of Lincoln and his family with the house, reinforced by the American experience in the Civil War, is expressed fancifully in this simple vignette. Father and son are reading inside the White House, with its north front in view through the open window.

Another function of state ceremony required of the White House was the state funeral. Such ceremonies were not accorded presidents who died out of office. But when a president died in office, the successor was faced with a problem not wholly unlike that of how to present himself at a reception. It was an extraordinary situation that required a carefully crafted form. Augustness and emotion demanded response.

President Lincoln and General Winfield Scott, head of the armies, review General Irvin McDowell's regiment, marching on Pennsylvania Avenue in late June or early July 1861, before the disastrous battle of First Manassas. The sketch, by war correspondent Alfred Waud, is of what was probably the first reviewing stand ever built in front of the White House.

General William Henry Harrison of Ohio, hero of Tippecanoe, died in his bed at the White House on April 4, 1841, thirty days after his inauguration as president. He was 68 years of age. The widow, awaiting the spring thaw, had not yet crossed the mountains from Ohio. Daniel Webster, secretary of state and thus the chief ceremonial officer, took charge and appointed two Washington merchants, Alexander Hunter and Darius Clagett, to organize and prepare the first funeral ever held for an American president.

The White House was draped in black and white crepe. Harrison's body was wrapped naked in a winding sheet and probably embalmed by the insertion of salt. The body was ultimately contained within four coffins; the last two, an inner one of lead and an outer one of wood painted with inscriptions and his name, were not put into use until after the funeral. The grieving public was admitted to view the remains, which were placed atop a table in the entrance hall outside the glass screen. Funeral services were held later in the East Room beneath the black-draped chandeliers, the body in the center of the room on a table covered with a deep black pall trimmed with silver fringe. Atop the coffin was a centerpiece of wax flowers arranged around crossed swords and a copy of the Constitution.

At the conclusion of Harrison's funeral the coffin was taken to a large float, or funeral car, which had been brought up beneath the north portico. The float was an elaborate canopy mounted on a wagon bed, all festooned in cambric and cotton in black and white. Drawn by black-draped horses, the car was accompanied by white-dressed black grooms and black-dressed white pallbearers to the receiving vault, where the body was kept under guard until the cold weather was over and Harrison could be returned to Ohio on the train.

Lincoln's funeral and all presidential funerals

to follow were based in their essentials on this first one, including the most recent, John F. Kennedy's, in 1963. The two merchants had established the tone. Time and attitudes would simplify the details, but certainly not during the forty years discussed in this chapter. Lincoln's family, like Harrison's, was not available to direct matters. Mary Lincoln's thin emotional edifice collapsed after the assassination, distancing her in an abyss of grief. The sons were too young. Political sensitivities wrought of a long war and its bloody conclusion led Lincoln's political colleagues to turn his funeral and his return home to Illinois into a mass public ceremony for their benefit. Nothing would have seemed more inappropriate to Lincoln himself.

The event began at the White House. Lincoln's closed coffin sat unattended in the middle of the East Room as carpenters borrowed from the Treasury expansion next door built bleachers to

ually refreshed with the heavy use of cosmetics. The minister called for revenge. Later the funeral procession, with a black-draped car much like Harrison's, rolled slowly along Pennsylvania Avenue in the boiling heat to the railroad station for its fourteen-city tour.

The White House up until this time had been Washington's house, his vision, built by him, but never his home. Now it was Lincoln's, whatever it had been since Washington took leave of its construction. Lincoln inherited an accumulation of what others had done to the building, but did very little to the house itself. His mark was to be indelible in another way. The White House that received Lincoln in 1861 was different from the house Washington had envisioned. A palace it was not. Its stone exterior might have evoked the old manor houses of England, but the interior was all-American. Wooden floors sagged in their long span; at great receptions during the Civil

After the completion of Lincoln's bier in the East Room artists from the magazines and newspapers were allowed to enter and make their sketches, for they were not to be given entry to the funeral. This is Alfred Waud's sketch with the coffin as he saw it but the people added according to a description of the upcoming service probably given by Major Benjamin B. French, commissioner of public buildings. The room was ringed with wooden platforms on which six hundred spectators would stand crowded shoulder to shoulder in the stifling heat. General Grant is shown as he was to be, stationed at the head of the coffin, while Mrs. Lincoln, in mourning, stands at the feet. (She did not actually attend the funeral.) The catafalque made for Lincoln's funeral and still used at presidential funerals is housed in the Capitol.

hold 2,000 invited mourners. When the room was finished masses of spring flowers were brought in, and in the hot days ahead filled the sultry air with their perfumes. At the funeral the victorious hero, General Ulysses S. Grant, sat on display beside the coffin. A black tent lined in white satin sheltered the open coffin, from which Lincoln's face appeared ghastly and pale, contin-

War years, logs were used to shore up the East Room from the basement lest the floors fall through from the moving, shifting weight of so many people. The house was still too large for its uses, although it was dwarfed by the new Treasury next door and, had its mass not been powerful, would have seemed foolishly obscure on the site it had once commanded.

110

Some visitors compared it to a hotel. Charles Dickens, for example, found it like a tatty English club and its grounds too new-looking. The house had not yet grown, as Washington had expected, but it did not yet need to. It was abundantly large. Washington might have raised his eyes at the homey character of its rooms. He might have expected something more palatial a good four score years into the republic. But by then almost everything American would have surprised Washington. The world of 1861 was one he would barely have recognized.

Great ports and factory towns in the East would have astonished him. Miles of tracks, columns of steam, the clacking hustle of the railroad cars were nothing he could possibly have anticipated, although his vaulting hopes for the country could have embraced it all. The age of invention had been only in its dawning when he died in 1799. Steamboats did not appear until almost a decade after his passing. By 1850 gas lighted the nights, at least until ten, in the city named for him. By 1860 the nation was larger in size but smaller for the rails and steamboats and telegraph that knitted it closer than it had ever been.

The year that saw the Civil War end, 1865, beheld an America that had by the sheer energy of survival created a high level of industrial power and a level of human mobility that few people were able to comprehend. Who is to say that this visionary man, though startled to be sure, would have been dismayed? Washington might have gloried in it, he who dreamed of new cities and a conquered wilderness and who lighted his Argand lamps so soon after they were invented.

There is no question, however, about the horror that would have gripped him knowing the labor Lincoln had faced to prevent the dissolution of the Union. The White House, so little different on the outside since Jackson's day, was the stage upon which a new drama was played. The sooty kitchens and crowded pantries; rattling windows and vast rooms; tall, solemn hallways; acres of tall meadow grass that rose and fell in the wind; the East, Blue, Red, and Green rooms—all these were known to Lincoln in the years in which he came, for all time, to symbolize the presidency's trials.

Executive complex in the 1860s, showing the White House, center, with the new Treasury Building on the east and in the foreground on the west the War and Navy departments

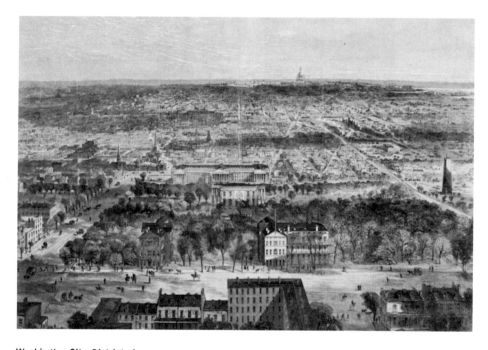

Washington City, District of Columbia, wood engraving by Theodore R. Davis, from *Harper's Weekly,* 1869

4

THE VICTORIAN WHITE HOUSE

Andrew Johnson, president from 1865 to 1869. Johnson modernized the office, expanding it to occupy the entire east end of the second floor, and installed the first telegraph inside the White House. In his time the executive branch faced its most deadly battle in an impeachment, which he survived.

N o decade in the presidency began with such storms and ended so calmly as did the 1860s. The mingling of victory and sorrow that accompanied the end of the Civil War folded into a congressional challenge to presidential power in the impeachment of Andrew Johnson. The scenes of this event were dramatic indeed. Johnson remained at the White House, not wanting to dignify the deliberations with his presence. The messenger who raced the final news from the Capitol barely beat the new White House telegraph in informing the president that one Senate vote had kept him in office, saving the presidency from suppression by the legislative branch. By a peaceful exercise of the election process, Ulysses S. Grant succeeded Andrew Johnson in 1869, bringing with him a feeling of public goodwill toward the presidency of a sort that had not been known since the election of William Henry Harrison, the last president who could claim nearly universal approbation.

It was clear that those who followed the unpopular Johnson would not dare try to exercise the great power Lincoln had amassed. Nor would there be so much as a rustling of effort until the 1880s, when Grover Cleveland showed himself to be a strong president. He, however, was defeated after one term. Cleveland served his second term four years later, after the intervening one-term administration of Benjamin Harrison. The power of the presidency from the late 1860s to the late 1890s ebbed under the somewhat corporate title of chief executive.

The novelist Thomas Wolfe looked back on these nineteenth-century executives as the bearded presidents, even though Johnson, Cleveland, and McKinley did not have beards. Others think of it as the Gilded Age, so named by Mark Twain and essayist Charles Dudley Warner. Although the Gilded Age slowed somewhat in the national panic of 1873, the idea prevailed in a certain tone at the White House until outbreak of the Spanish-American War in 1898. If the White House were to supply a physical image for these prismatic years, it would be the greenhouse. This house of glass was to grow and be cherished against the background of a continuing campaign to abandon, to demolish and replace, or at least to expand the White House.

Andrew Johnson inherited from Lincoln a house that had suffered abuse. Unable to move there for a month, while Mrs. Lincoln remained, Johnson had no power to stop the destruction by souvenir hunters. Silver was rifled from the sideboards; tassels were cut from the curtains. A curious public thronged the place. The doormen, lax in the absence of a president, were occupied recounting their recollections of recent events, while Johnson commuted from his hotel to an office in the Treasury.

Once he was in residence, Johnson undertook repairs, but he made no permanent changes. The gas system and the plumbing were extended. Office functions took over the entire east end of the second floor, which was equipped with new office furniture and a telegraph. Extensive cleaning, polishing, refurnishing, and painting took place under the direction of the president's daughter, Martha Patterson. She had taste and a knowledge of style, and by the spring of 1866 the White House fairly shone with her improvements.

As if in time for the age it was to symbolize, the greenhouse on the west wing was born again, in a more permanent form, as the conservatory. Originally it had been little more than a rectangular configuration of wooden window sash. Built by Lincoln's immediate predecessor, James Buchanan, the greenhouse replaced the old garden on the southeast, which had been lost when the Treasury Building was expanded southward in the late 1850s. The old garden, located at the spot designated many years before by Jefferson, had been especially cherished by the presidents,

Interior of the first greenhouse on the west terrace, 1861, with pots and tables brought from the orangery. Through the first seventy-five years of White House history American Indian tribes sent delegations to meet the presidents, at federal expense. The delegation members were received at the White House with ceremony and spent some time inspecting the rooms. The presidents and visitors exchanged gifts. During the Civil War, as President Abraham Lincoln hurried western territories into statehood, the Indians called in increasing numbers. None of the men and women here is identified by name except the central figure, who is Lincoln's secretary, George Nicolay.

The south grounds, circa 1867,
showing the first greenhouse,
built on the west terrace in 1857
and burned ten years later

beginning with James Monroe, who probably planted it. John Quincy Adams, an ardent gardener like his father, extended the garden concept with gravel paths and arbors. He is said to have planted an elm tree that still stands in the south grounds. Andrew Jackson built an orange house, or hothouse, in the shell of Latrobe's old Treasury fireproof, with tall windows looking to the south. Probably under the garden-minded Millard Fillmore it became a greenhouse in fact with the addition of skylights.

We know little else about the old garden. It was the sanctum of the presidents from Monroe to Buchanan, and Buchanan demanded a substitute when told it must go. Bills and receipts in the National Archives identify hundreds of plants, especially roses, spring and summer flowers, and the camellias and citrus trees that grew in the orange house. Plants and seeds were purchased mostly from Long Island and Philadelphia nurseries. There were large numbers of potted plants, all moved outside in summer and carried inside in winter. These were transferred to the new

greenhouse on the west terrace with the first sign of cold weather in 1859.

The president's greenhouse was an ordinary glass house, nothing elaborate. A narrow glass passage linked it to the western end of the transverse hall on the state floor. Old photographs allow estimates of scale. The greenhouse itself was some thirty-five by sixty feet, crowned by a hip roof made, like the walls, of window sash set into minimal wood framing. Twelve overhead panes of translucent colored glass symbolized the four seasons. Wooden steps lined the walls inside and formed a bank down the center; lined up on the steps were heavy terra-cotta pots with thick, round rims. A hydrant was provided to fill the watering cans.

The greenhouse was less a private retreat for the president than the old garden had been. Visitors to the house often went there, if the president and family members were elsewhere. Photographers took great delight in the natural illumination of the interior. The earliest known photograph taken inside the greenhouse was made during the Civil War; it shows Lincoln's secretary George Nicolay, a group of ladies, and a visiting Indian delegation from the West. The path between the plant steps is narrow, and the glass ceiling seems low around the edges.

Early in the morning of January 18, 1867, fire broke out in the greenhouse. The president stood on the stair landing and watched the conflagration below, the swirling flames accompanied by the sounds of smashing glass. Teams of men pulled to safety as many of the plants as they could, but more were lost than were saved, particularly large old fruit trees in tubs. A major casualty was a sago palm that had belonged to George Washington, a legacy that came to the White House either through the efforts of Andrew Jackson, who liked Washington memorabilia, or as part of the Custis and Lee possessions confiscated from Arlington.

The commissioner of public buildings, Major Benjamin B. French, set out to obtain plans for a new fireproof greenhouse. Acting on the advice of Alfred B. Mullett, supervising architect of the Treasury, he made contact with Lorde & Burnham of Tarrytown, New York, where an elaborate set of drawings was prepared for a sumptuous glass house of iron frame, with Gothic arches. But the plans appeared at an awkward time. French was dismissed as commissioner in March and replaced by General Nathaniel Michler of the Army Corps of Engineers. The inventive Michler spread the drawings before him and, with an eye on cost, began marking them up What he finally devised had a minimal cast-iron frame, with wooden sash somewhat as the greenhouse had before. The new conservatory was almost twice the size of the one that had burned. Michler himself selected many of the

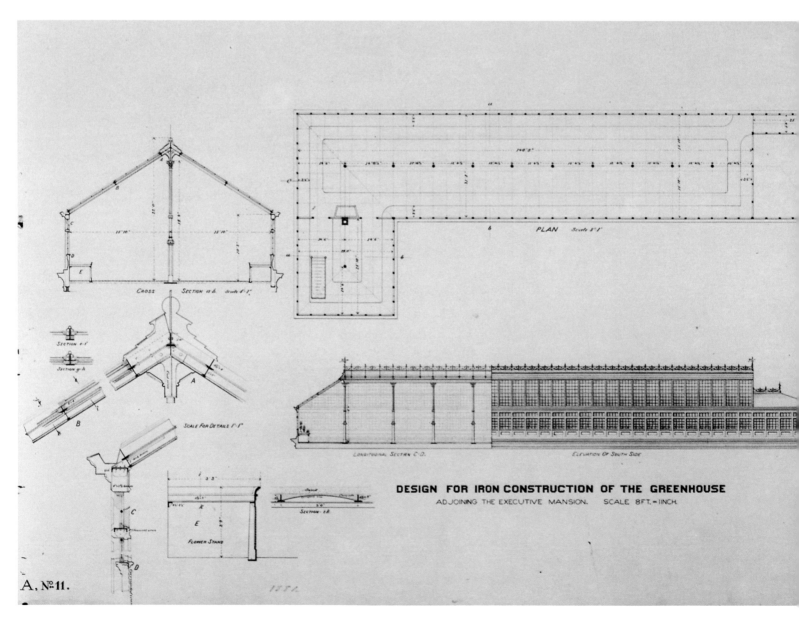

DESIGN FOR IRON CONSTRUCTION OF THE GREENHOUSE
ADJOINING THE EXECUTIVE MANSION.   SCALE 8FT. = 1INCH.

plants: "11 Azalia Indica. . .1 Magnolia Fuscata. . . Poinsettia. . .4 Acacias," and so on.

Overall, Michler found the business of the executive mansion in a confused state. Benjamin French, a Lincoln appointee, was a holdover into Johnson's presidency; his principal purpose was to please his benefactors. A large amount of work had been going on at the White House since 1865, and the costs were running high. For example, the recommendation of the supervising architect of the Treasury, Alfred B. Mullett, that the dilapidated east wing be demolished had been readily accepted and carried out in 1866. When it was gone the east side of the house looked gaunt and naked, so Mullett designed a one-story colonnaded porch to run along the basement level on that side. Its roof provided an unsheltered porch opening off the East Room. This porch greatly improved the aspect from the east, giving a formal entrance to the grounds, but in terms of cost it was an addition to the work planned at the outset. The entire effort showed poor management.

Johnson's almost continual infirmity from late 1865 until well into 1867 prompted those around him to seek a more healthful residence. Ever since John and Abigail Adams had lived there, the White House had been considered an unhealthy place. The manner in which it had been set into the hillside rendered its basement wall wet and mildewed, despite the annual lime washing of the exterior walls. Brick pavers on the basement floor had long since been covered with wood floors, yet moisture crept in and the ground level rooms were dank. Across the grounds to the south, beyond a stone wall built by Jefferson, lay a marshy area long believed to give off deadly vapors. Polk's early demise, a few

Opposite:
A simple orangery built by Andrew Jackson in 1833 led eventually to elaborate conservatories, which stood on the west terrace of the White House from 1857 until 1902, when they were demolished. After a fire in 1867 various projects were presented for building new conservatories with framing of modern and "fireproof" cast iron. This project, by Lorde & Burnham of Tarrytown, New York, was rejected because of its high cost, but it remained somewhat the model for the structure that was actually built, only partially of iron.

The East Room as redecorated by President Andrew Johnson, 1866–67. The room is seen in summer slipcovers, a custom followed until the era of air conditioning.

months after his retirement, and the death in office of Zachary Taylor had been blamed on the bad air.

Johnson feared the perils of the swamp. In the distant past, before Polk, presidents had spent their summers elsewhere. By the late 1850s, when the press of business made leaving town more and more difficult, Buchanan had taken over the cottage at the Soldiers' Home, several miles northeast of the Capitol, which Lincoln and then the Johnsons also used. It was small even for a retreat and a temporary solution at best. Martha Patterson considered renting a house on higher, drier ground and inspected about five before Johnson decided against moving.

He did not disapprove, however, of the idea of building a new president's house. Lincoln's assassination gave him and his successors pause to consider the dangers of living in so public a place. Security had been a concern at the White House for many years. James Monroe, responding to assassinations in Europe, placed sharpshooters on the walkway behind the stone parapet atop the walls. John Tyler had established the Metropolitan Police largely for executive protection, and a decade later Franklin Pierce was the first to employ a personal bodyguard, the faithful shadow Thomas O'Neil, who had been an orderly sergeant under him in the war with Mexico. Andrew Johnson had not been in office long when a minor shootout took place in the entrance hall of the White House. A would-be assassin had come to call on the president during regular morning office hours. One of the major advantages of a suburban mansion, with its greater privacy, would be its facilities for the better protection of the president.

In mid-July 1866 the Senate directed its committee on public buildings and grounds to look into acquiring a large tract of land for a public park and a new presidential mansion. The House of Representatives was to act in January on a similar objective, but meanwhile the Senate committee had asked Edwin M. Stanton, secretary of war, to detail a military engineer to the project. General Michler was given the assignment. He toured Central Park in New York in the summer, then through the fall inspected land and estates in the environs of Washington.

Michler's report, submitted January 29, 1867, read in part: "The Senate resolution would seem to imply that one and the same tract of land should be designated for a site for grounds for a presidential mansion as well as for a public park; but as it is not definitely so stated, it has been judged best by me to separate the subjects. . . . As it is designed to build a home for the President to which he can retire from the active cares and business of his high office, and where he can secure that ease, comfort, and seclusion so necessary to a statesman, it would seem best to locate it away from the constant turmoil of city life, at such a distance where his privacy cannot easily be intruded upon, and still sufficiently accessible for all practical purposes." Several sites were considered on orders from B. Gratz Brown of Kentucky, chairman of the Senate committee, and these included the present Rock Creek Park;

Opposite top:
The White House from the southwest, circa 1870. These conservatories, rebuilt in 1867–68, were continually expanded and remodeled. The brick structure to the left is of unknown origin but is probably the entrance to stables built as an ell to the west wing when it was reconstructed in 1815–18.

Martha Johnson Patterson conducted an overhaul of the White House, returning it from the shambles left by the Civil War years. She served often as hostess for her father, Andrew Johnson, and generally managed his household.

Opposite bottom:
East facade as remodeled in 1867–68 on the suggestion of Alfred B. Mullett, Supervising Architect of the Treasury

the Berry estate, known as Metropolis View; and Meridian Hill, an old estate then in ruin, its trees destroyed and its mansion a burned-out shell. To these Michler added Harewood, the unfinished country estate of W. W. Corcoran, where the grounds had been laid out following plans by the late Andrew Jackson Downing but the "princely mansion" never built. And he warmly recommended the Moncure Robinson estate, located several miles northeast of the Capitol adjacent to

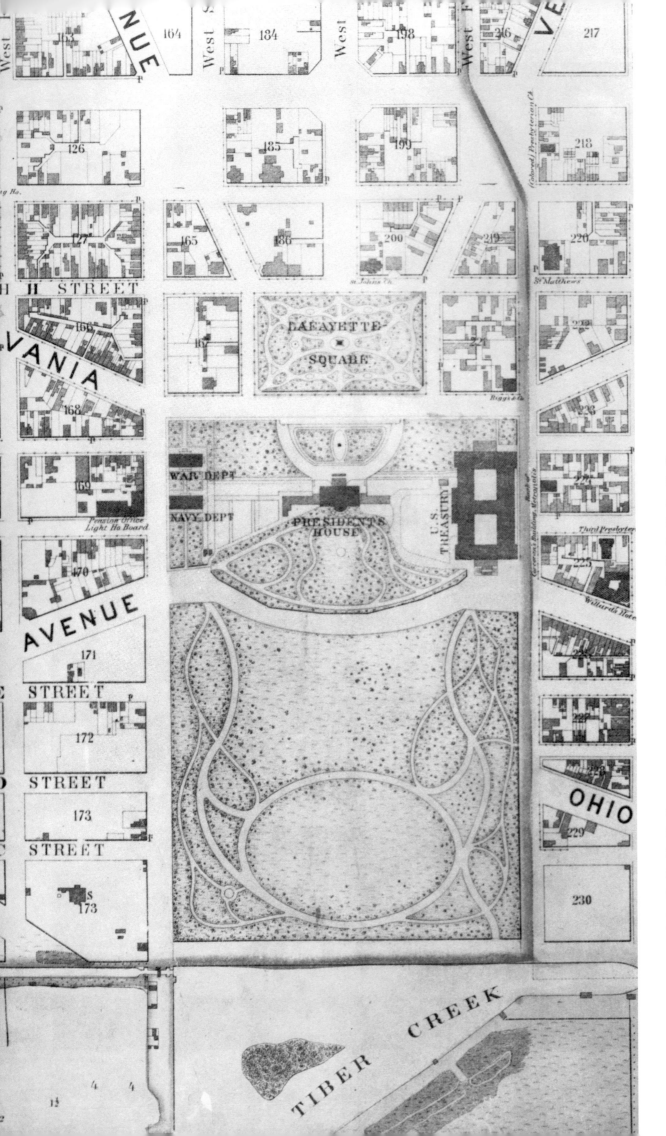

Unrealized project for the President's Park, reflected in a city plan, 1873. A modification of the plan opposite, this was actually adopted briefly by President Ulysses S. Grant and influenced some of the planting.

Opposite:
Unrealized project for the President's Park, 1873, showing public and private grounds, planted forests, carriage drives, and elaborate effects with water. With the exception of Lafayette Park on the north, it includes all the land originally designated for the White House in L'Enfant's plan.

the grounds of the Soldiers' Home.

Of "Mr. Robinson's beautiful locality" General Michler could hardly say enough in praise. "An extensive panorama of the surrounding country lies before the beholder; from every point of the compass the eye can dwell upon magnificent landscapes extending far into Maryland and Virginia, and combining all that is beautiful and picturesque." That the president should be provided with such vistas seems to have been well established. In such views George Washington had taken delight when he sited the White House. Today the president's prospects from his south windows are carefully groomed for distant splendor. The lofty sweeps of mountain and valley preserve this concept at Camp David.

The Michler report was imbedded in particular circumstances and, unquestionably, in politics as well. Moving the president to a distant location apart from the White House and its adjacent complex of federal employees cannot have been unappealing to Congress. Michler's repeated notations of the proximity of the proposed sites to the White House may have been delicacy on his part, for he never alludes to the future of the original house. By implication, perhaps, one can assume that the building was to be retained as a presidential office building and for official entertaining. But this is not recorded.

A drawing for a new house was prepared under Michler's direction. We know nothing of this plan, except that it was current among the Army Corps of Engineers for some years. Michler replaced Major French as commissioner of public buildings only six weeks after submitting his report. This marked a political change, placing the administration of the White House itself under the Army engineers and giving the Michler report a status just below that of official policy.

For reasons unknown, though doubtless related to the emotional moment of the impeachment and to the certainty that Andrew Johnson would not be elected to a full term, the Michler report was not acted upon, either for a new White House or for the other recommendation, a "national park" in the romantic terrain one day to become Rock Creek Park. Yet the spirit born in Michler's concept would not only live but would grow in the ambitions of the corps throughout

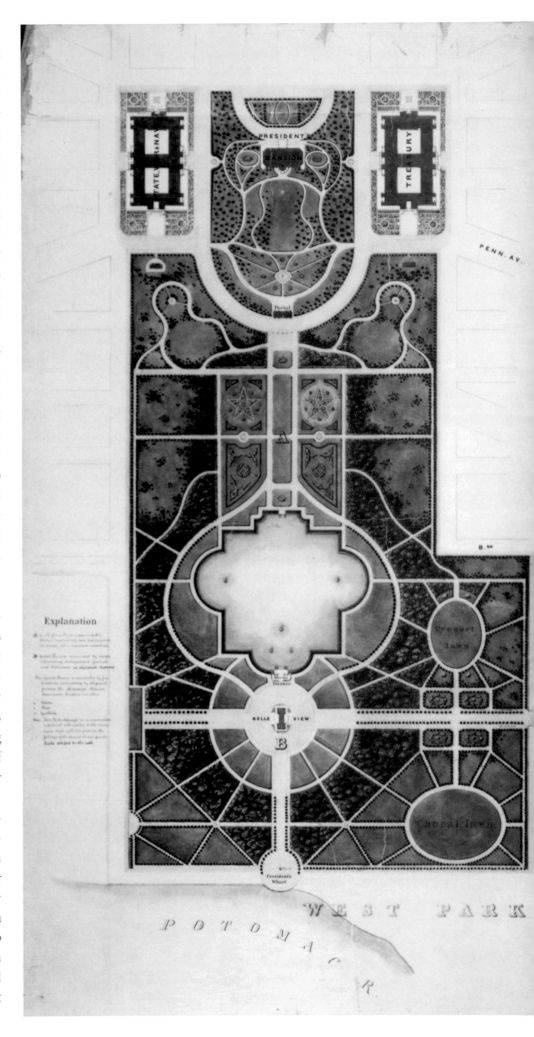

121

the balance of the nineteenth century. From the perspective of the present, when historic preservation enjoys wide support, the corps becomes the enemy of the physical White House, plotting its replacement with each administration. But such matters must be judged in the context of the times. To Michler and his era, the shackles of the past had been cast away by the war. Except for glorious reminders of that great contest, relics of the historic past were merely curious antebellum symbols of the vanished dark. Progress lay in the new-built and in technology. It must also be observed that the engineers were lavishing attention upon the home of their commander-in-chief. President-pleasing is an eager interest shared by all the agencies that have ever superintended the Executive Mansion.

General Grant, inaugurated March 4, 1869, wanted no part of a new White House, and while the issue came up again during his administration it never seems to have interested him. He made full use of Lincoln's house in his quest to symbolize peace and plenty as the nation's chief executive. Some presidents go into office to solve financial woes, some to fight wars, and still others to make peace. Grant's mission was to make the country feel good about itself, to fill the role of matchless hero representing the good life that postwar prosperity was to bring to all. With his wife, Julia, the new president worked to make the house more livable. They ordered Latrobe's double grand stair torn out and replaced in the same location with a single stair that rose along the north wall, landed, and continued on the south, allowing for new floor space in the upstairs hall beside the great fan window looking west. This was the origin of today's west sitting hall.

In the glass passage between the house and the conservatory Grant installed a billiard room. Billiard tables had appeared before – sometimes arousing moral controversy – but in the basement. More than any other room in the house the billiard room shows the president's bold self-assurance. Though no photographs of it survive, and it existed for only about eight years, the carpentry bills reveal a fashionable room in the English vernacular revival or reform style, framed in heavy exposed timberwork and paneled in beaded boards. Rows of tall windows

admitted light from the north and south. The heavy billiard table, gaslit overhead, stood on a floor of brilliant encaustic tiles laid in a geometric design. French doors gave into the billiard room on the west, at the end of the transverse hall. After dinner Grant challenged the heroes of the Union Army to serious bouts at billiards, and he spent many hours alone, polishing his game.

Another alteration by Grant, that of the East Room, no longer exists as he made it, but it was significant to the late nineteenth-century White House. In advance of the marriage of his daughter, Nellie, in 1874 he ordered the room refurbished. With the exception of gaslighting, introduced in 1848, the East Room was much as it

Ulysses S. Grant, president from 1869 to 1877. The idol of the nation, Grant made the White House the image of the American good life. He set up his billiard table in the greenhouse and drove his sulky at top speed on Pennsylvania Avenue. Grant declined the engineers' offer to build a new house for the president.

Opposite:
The East Room, prepared for Nellie Grant's wedding, June 21, 1874. A major redecoration of the interior had been carried out in 1873-74, with the original architectural scheme extended in heavy beams and columns and the continuation of the anthemion cornice introduced by Hoban in 1815-18. New mantels of wood were crowned by immense mirrors that reflected the new gas chandeliers purchased from Cornelius & Son, Philadelphia.

Julia Grant probably loved the White House more than any other president's wife. She decorated its rooms, arranged its flowers, cheerfully greeted the thousands who came to receptions, and wept on the day she had to depart the "dear old house."

had been since Andrew Jackson completed it in 1829. Wallpaper, Brussels carpeting, the three great chandeliers, and Hoban's Grecian decorations still characterized the most elaborate of the interiors.

What Grant did was to elaborate upon the original design. Under the direction of his old friend and comrade General Orville Babcock, who had been made commissioner of public buildings, the East Room was completed by the spring of 1874. Babcock turned to Alfred Mullett, who appears to have given the design work to the Austrian Richard von Ezdorf. Hoban's anthemia were carried across the room in two new beams, supported by Corinthian columns, further defining the three divisions of the room previously articulated only by the chandeliers

and tables beneath them. The resulting square ceiling areas were heavily tinted in rose and azure to suggest the sky as it might have been through the open roof of an atrium. Four rich new fireplace mantels were surmounted by great mirrors in frames to match. An infusion of new woodwork—columns, beams, mantels—was painted white, with a liberal trimming of bronze powder gilding, varnished to high shine. Climaxing the glittery decor were three new gas chandeliers with nickel-plated frames covered with showers of glass; these fixtures were larger than Jackson's and the delight and wonder of all who came to visit.

"New Grecian," the style was pronounced, a play on the smart *Néo-Grec* mode brought from France. If the *Néo-Grec* was subtle and intellec-

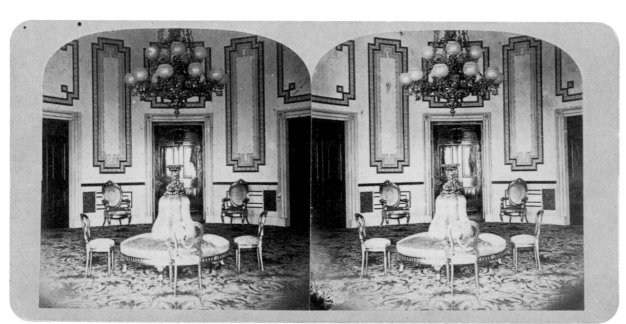

White House interiors in the time of President Grant. Stereographic slides such as these were produced for sale to tourists at hotels and newsstands and showed the rooms of the White House they saw on the daily tours. These date from about 1871. (Top) The Blue Room and (bottom) the Red Room

124

tual in its use of historical themes from classical antiquity, New Grecian assuredly was not. Nothing could have been bolder. In technical fact the East Room was probably neo-Federal in its friendly amplification of the decorations of 1818. Since the 1920s the Grant East Room has been characterized as "Steamboat Gothic," and, although only a memory, it holds its own as one of the premier American interiors of the Gilded Age. Its redecoration twenty-eight years later, in 1902, was not so universally celebrated.

The billiard room had an even shorter life. Rutherford B. Hayes, elected on the heels of the scandals that clouded Grant's last years in office—and the Hayes election itself a contested

The Lincoln bedroom furniture known to history was originally set up in this manner in the Prince of Wales Room, where the future Edward VII had slept on simpler furniture on his visit in 1860. The satin and lace bed draperies were purple, gold, and white. Mrs. Lincoln selected the furniture in Philadelphia in 1861.

one – set aside his whiskey and glass and pledged himself to be a model of propriety for all Americans. Whether the billiard room was banished as an expression of this attitude or whether the space was otherwise needed is not really certain. However, its demise appears connected to the problems that arose from not pouring wine at White House dinners.

Washington was a hard-drinking town compared to many other places. Hard liquors had been banished at the White House since Polk, but wine had been considered a part of hospitality, especially when diplomats were present. Now that Hayes had cast wine out of the presidential dining room as well, he determined to keep his guests too busy to think about drinking. After dinner, about the time the palate signaled for brandy, President and Mrs. Hayes rose from their places at table – no guest being allowed to rise before the president – and were followed by their company to a reception room or court, made of the old billiard room by removing the billiard furniture and lining the walls with chairs. From there the couple led the column of guests

Rutherford B. Hayes, president from 1877 to 1881. The richest president of the nineteenth century, Hayes was a lover of antiques and old houses. He did very little to the White House, wishing not to change it but to enhance it.

in a spirited promenade along the narrow conservatory paths. This exercise took about half an hour and ended at the foot of the grand stair, where Rutherford and Lucy Hayes bade their company goodnight. The evening was over.

President Hayes did very little to change the

Opposite:
Elevation of the conservatory, looking east and showing the small connecting space in which President Grant built his billiard room. This drawing, made in 1880, shows the area adapted to President Rutherford B. Hayes's new uses, with provisions for French doors to be added into the original west windows of the State Dining Room (see page 170).

Sketch of the White House, early 1880s, by Octavius L. Pruden, a member of the office staff

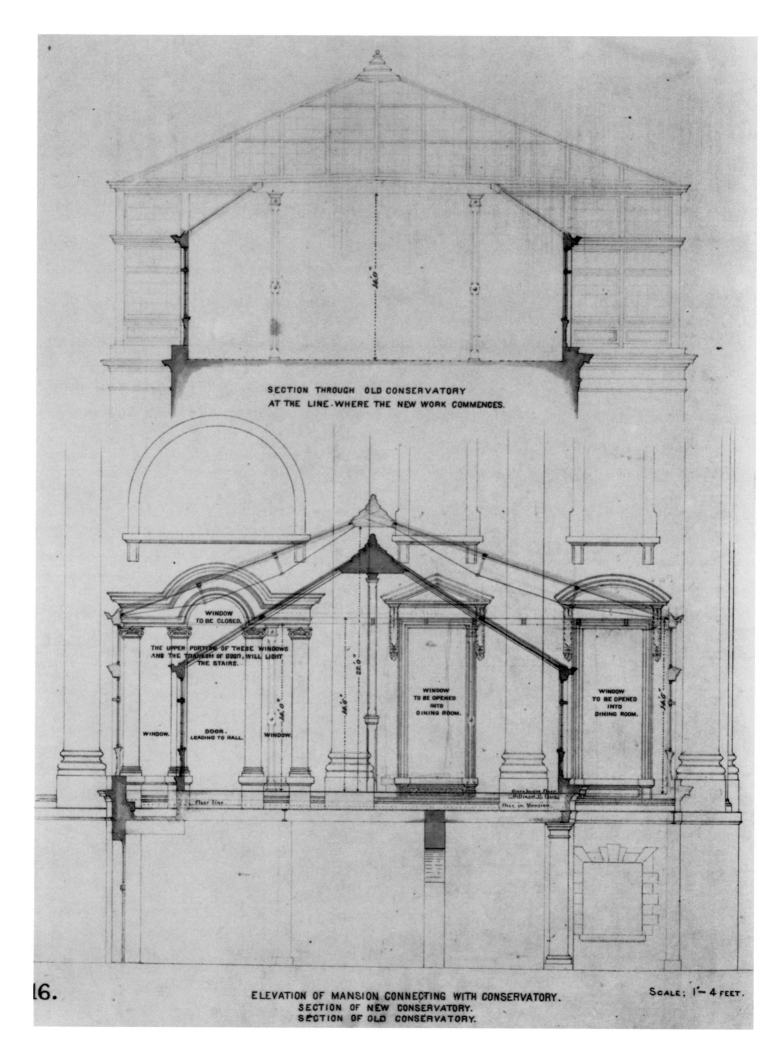

SECTION THROUGH OLD CONSERVATORY
AT THE LINE WHERE THE NEW WORK COMMENCES.

WINDOW
TO BE CLOSED.

THE UPPER PORTION OF THESE WINDOWS
AND THE TRANSOM OF DOOR, WILL LIGHT
THE STAIRS.

WINDOW.

DOOR.
LEADING TO HALL.

WINDOW.

WINDOW
TO BE OPENED
INTO
DINING ROOM.

WINDOW
TO BE OPENED
INTO
DINING ROOM.

16.

ELEVATION OF MANSION CONNECTING WITH CONSERVATORY.
SECTION OF NEW CONSERVATORY.
SECTION OF OLD CONSERVATORY.

SCALE; 1'— 4 FEET.

Right and overleaf:

By the late nineteenth century the conservatories had grown to great size and were among the notable ones in the United States. These views give an idea of the delightful retreat they provided for the president.

Opposite:

Mrs. Lucy Webb Hayes and her children, Fanny and Scott, with their playmate Carrie Davis in the greenhouse, 1879

White House. On May 10, 1879, he ordered a telephone installed, but there were few people he could call. Of all the executive family only Secretary of the Treasury John Sherman had a phone. The first typewriter came in under Hayes and found acceptance more quickly than did the telephone. Hayes dismissed the engineers' plans for a new house. He and the first lady—for Lucy Hayes was the first to be called that with any frequency—loved history and were ardent antiquarians. She often said, "I would not wish to exchange this [house] for any other. . . . I think it

beautiful. . . . I love this house for the associations that no other could have."

Hayes believed that in furnishing the house history should have its place. He consulted Librarian of Congress A. R. Spofford, who he assumed knew about such things. Spofford suggested hanging a collection of portraits of presidents and first ladies. As a result, the portrait by E. F. Andrews of Martha Washington hangs in the East Room today, companion to the earlier portrait of Washington by Gilbert Stuart. Spofford had wanted actual portraits or copies of

portraits that the subjects had sat for. Having new pictures painted, on a monumental scale, was an idea generated in the White House political circle. Although only three portraits were installed, of which the painting of Martha Washington was the most memorable, the idea began a tradition of large presidential portraits that lasted for many years.

Lucy Hayes was photographed on several occasions in the conservatory. Beyond her in the pictures the long plant tables brim with greenery. Under her patronage and that of her predecessor, Julia Grant, the conservatory multiplied into conservatories that filled the entire L-shaped roof of the west wing. Hayes brought Henry Pfister from Cincinnati to manage the conservatory and its growing staff of gardeners and "bouquet-makers." In 1879 and 1880 the billiard room space was torn away and the conservatory butted full width against the west wall. Space for french doors was made by cutting down the windows of the State Dining Room. At the same time the conservatory roof was extended to the south for the rose house, an enclosed garden in the same location as today's unenclosed Rose Garden.

The conservatory, steam-heated, had abundant running water. Its tenants included large numbers of tubbed palms, which were interspersed through the state rooms during receptions. Camellias were plentiful, as were small-blossomed japonicas in pink and red and white. Tubbed hydrangeas were massed along some paths, and many varieties of ferns filled the plant shelves. Julia Grant introduced orchids, her favorites, in a special orchid room. She institutionalized, if she did not begin, the custom of sending bouquets to visitors of importance in the capital in lieu of the traditional and always tedious first ladies' custom of making social calls in person. Sometimes as many as twenty bouquets might go out in a day, accompanied by engraved White House cards.

Orange, lemon, and lime trees, along with pineapples, grew in the palm house. Overhead pipes showered this area. But the White House favorite was roses. They bloomed in the rose house year-round. One resident recalled that the second floor west hall, when the windows were open, was moist and fragrant with their scent.

Late nineteenth-century presidents and their families took special pleasure in the conservatory. The private world under glass was a retreat from busy schedules, but it also provided practical comforts. By 1880 the long range of doors connecting the conservatory to the house brought in humidity during the long, dry winters, when the rarified air from the central heating system made the rooms of the house almost unbearable. Skin cracked and flaked, furniture came unglued and wood split, fabrics dry-rotted, and plaster weakened. The introduction of moist air through the conservatories added to the enjoyment of flowers and greenery when snow was on the roof.

The engineers kept their plans for the new house close at hand, alluding to them in their letters and sometimes in their reports. During his time with Grant, even General Babcock wrote, "With the growth of the country the Executive Mansion has become, with each succeeding year, more and more of a public office. . . . The large number of persons having business with the President renders the Executive Mansion unfit for occupancy as a private dwelling and entirely deprives the family of the President of ordinary privacy." This was written in 1873, in response to a request from the House Committee on Public Buildings and Grounds. Nothing came of it.

President James A. Garfield, military hero and history buff, shared an interest in architecture with his wife, Letitia. They were willing to redecorate the rooms but not to replace the White House. Like his friend Hayes, Garfield wanted things to be appropriate for so historic a place, but he was not such an antiquarian. He approved extensive redecorating. Mrs. Garfield met with Herter Brothers of New York and considered proposals. These were predictably modern, showing the trademark Aesthetic styles for which Herter was known. At the close of the social season in May she decided, having been ill, to have her summer holiday at the shore, then attend to the house.

On July 2, 1881, Garfield was shot while at the train station preparing to join his wife at the beach in New Jersey. He lingered in agony at the White House through the scorching months of

Exterior views of the conservatories, (above) from the southwest and (below) from the west, in the late nineteenth century. By this time they had reached their ultimate extent.

133

Chester A. Arthur, president from 1881 to 1885. Arthur missed the lights of Manhattan and found no charm in the White House he inherited from Garfield. To improve his interiors he called in Louis Comfort Tiffany.

Opposite:

White House teas are of unknown origin, but by the close of the Hayes administration in 1881 they were a part of White House life. (Opposite) Mrs. Hayes's "pink tea" in the State Dining Room. The decorations, the food, and the house party were all in pink.

In mourning for President Garfield, September 1881. Mourning customs were practiced at the White House as early as John Adams's tenure, when one of his sons died. There was no state mourning until 1841, for William Henry Harrison. Traditions established then are continued in part even today when a president dies. In this photograph the full extent of mourning decoration is still seen. In the twentieth century it would be simplified.

July and August. Every effort and invention was applied to make him comfortable. One device, a cooling system, opened the technical window on today's air-conditioning. In September Garfield seemed improved, so much so that his optimistic wife summoned the local decorating jobber W. D. Moses, who had worked many times before for the White House, and from his swatches and samples picked her favorites.

The fragile though massive form of Garfield was moved to New Jersey to the seaside by a legion of devoted attendants, rolling his hospital car over tracks laid to the cottage door. In Washington Moses's men began stripping wallpaper and sanding woodwork. Garfield died on September 19, the eighteenth anniversary of his triumph at the Battle of Chickamauga. His body was returned to the Capitol, not to the White House, which was in disarray. The widow returned with the coffin to Ohio. One day she would realize the dream she and her husband held and move to California. Years later, in Pasadena, she commissioned Charles S. and Henry N. Greene to build the bungalow in which she was to live out her days.

The successor, Chester A. Arthur, seemed as unlikely for the job as any other vice president does in the tragic moment of loss. History remembers only a few things about him and one is that he had taste. His reaction to the White House could not have been more negative. Historic or not, it was an unacceptable residence. He lodged with a friend until the situation could be remedied. To the delight of the Army engineers, he sought funds for a new house—perhaps the one they had in mind. They were less than enthusiastic when he decided that he wanted the same in-city location and that the old White House must go. Unsuccessful, Arthur proposed a residential wing on the south. The Senate appro-

(Top) The State Dining Room before it was redecorated by Louis C. Tiffany for President Arthur and (below) after it was redecorated. The walls were painted in many shades and textures of yellow and highlighted in silver. Reflectors of hammered silver backed the gas wall brackets. Stylish, low-back oak chairs replaced the fancy "French" side chairs President Polk had purchased in 1848.

priated $300,000, but the bill did not weather the House of Representatives. At last, getting nowhere, the president determined to refurbish the house as it was. For this he had $30,000, an amount he would greatly exceed.

He called to the work Louis C. Tiffany, a new lion of the world of fashionable interiors in New York. Son of Arthur's close friend the jeweler Charles Louis Tiffany, young Tiffany had just made his reputation with the decoration of the Armory and the Union League Club. His achievement of national fame would come with his work on the White House, some time before the appearance of his colored-glass lamp shades. The mention of Chester A. Arthur calls up the name Tiffany, and Tiffany's inevitably leads to mention of Arthur. No similar situation exists in the history of the house.

Arthur was required to honor the Moses contract, so Tiffany had limited space in which to exercise his creativity. The president cleared the stage: "Twenty-four wagon loads of old furniture and junk from the White House were sent off Tuesday to the warerooms of Duncanson Brothers to be sold," reported the *Washington Post* on April 15, 1882, the day after the auction. "Only curiosity and desire to examine the house-keeping of a President could have drawn to Ninth and D streets fully 5,000 people and caused a realization from the auction of such goods of about $3,000." Among the items sold were "hair mattresses, maps, chandeliers, four marble mantels, bureaus, bedsteads, two high chairs for children. . .marble top tables, leather-covered sofas, ottomans and dining room chairs, a lot of white matting, a plaster map of Santo Domingo, a lot of moth paper, a lot of water coolers . . . cuspidors, lace curtains, lead piping, old iron stoves. . . ."

By far the greatest cost of Tiffany's redecoration was in artistic painting. Practically every surface was covered. Some of this artistry was in decorative patterns, but most was complicated glazing, color laid over color, each one translucent and in sequences carefully calculated to achieve the proper iridescence; tinted shellac and varnish further deepened the effect. Tiffany worked in the East, Blue, and Red rooms; the State Dining Room; and the transverse corridor, all on the

Tiffany added his touch to the East Room in the delicate ceiling wallpaper that resembled Pompeiian mosaics and kept to the classical theme.

state floor. Very little furniture was purchased, but repair and reupholstery were carried out on the existing furniture for practically every room. The gilded rococo revival suite in the Blue Room, for example, purchased by James Buchanan in 1860 when he sold the Monroe suite, was re-covered in blue silk canvas. The suite included chairs, sofas, footstools, and the circular divan, the sole piece remaining in the house today. Only the Green Room and the family dining room on the main floor escaped Tiffany's brush. These fell under the Moses contract, and judging from photographs and written documentation they must have seemed dull by comparison.

Overleaf:
The Red Room, soon after its completion by Tiffany in the fall of 1882. Its particular glory was the dramatic, decorative paint on the walls, which made the room seem iridescent, an effect lost in this photo. The great distance between the architecture of the house and modern taste can be seen in the rather too-diminutive scale of the furniture in relation to the lofty room.

The family dining room, enveloped in pattern, contained in 1882 old White House furnishings reused. The dark woodwork was mahogany-grained with paint to match the mahogany doors. The sideboard, on the right, was carved by Henry Frye of Cincinnati and brought to the White House in 1880.

The president's study, the second floor oval room, was the family library. Seen here in the early 1880s, it has been refreshed but not entirely redecorated from Hayes's time, when the desk—a gift from Queen Victoria and made from the timbers of the HMS *Resolute*—was installed.

Opposite:
The Blue Room, by Tiffany. The effect of this space is entirely lost in this black-and-white image. The principal color was robin's egg blue, used both in its full intensity and whitened to pale hues. The design consisted of strong horizontal banding and an enclosure of silver embossed pattern.

~ DESIGN for TILE PAVEMENT ~
~ for ~
VESTIBULE
~ EXECUTIVE MANSION ~
WASHINGTON D.C.
Scale, Inch = One foot — Plan 938

Opposite:

Detail, project for the entrance hall floor, 1880. This last improvement of the Grant administration was probably completed under President Hayes. The encaustic tile floor was laid as designed but removed in 1902.

(Above) The entrance hall, 1882, and (below) the transverse hall, transformed by Tiffany with his trademark colored glass, shown ca. 1889.

Aesthetic effects played in whimsy, allusion, and with drama on the inherent character of interiors nearly seventy years old. The shape of the oval Blue Room suggested an egg, so Tiffany painted it an innocent robin's egg blue, starting at the base with the full force of the color and adding white as the color rose on the walls, until at the cornice it was light, and spangled it with silver-leaf snowflakes that gave the illusion of colonial doilies. The East Room ceiling was stripped of its atrium effect and stenciled and painted to suggest Roman mosaics. Yellow glazes enriched the walls of the State Dining Room, while in the Red Room Pompeiian red walls were crowned with stars and bars in copper and silver. The nuances of these colors in the hazy pools of gaslight must have given animation to the large, sharply defined spaces and pushed the walls away into a realm of half-being.

Tiffany's most famous touch was the insertion of colored glass in the draft screen dividing the entrance hall from the transverse hall. Van Buren had placed a screen made of window sash there

in 1837 to help increase the efficiency of his gravity heating system. This was replaced for Franklin Pierce in 1853 by Thomas U. Walter, who designed a screen of cast iron and ground glass. It was this screen that Tiffany altered by substituting colored glass in deep tones of red, white, and blue where ground glass had been. The colored-glass part of the screen stood about ten feet tall, and above it, filling the arches that sprang from the walls to the two King of Prussia blue marble columns, was clear glass to allow the passage of daylight into the transverse hall.

Seen from the entrance hall, the new glass made little difference. Its surface was faceted and textured in various ways, so it was interesting, but the light behind it was dim, even when the gas was lighted, and it was largely absorbed in darkness. On the inside, however, the blaze was memorable. A flood of light passed through from the entrance hall, projecting the full polychromatic richness of the glass screen on walls painted a simple cream color. High up on the ceiling the light from beyond the clear glass was captured in

Opposite:

The Green Room, as redecorated for Mrs. Garfield by W. B. Moses & Co. of Washington. Started before President Garfield's death, the work was completed for a dubious President Arthur, who considered the taste passé.

Elevation of a private residence for the president proposed by George Inslee, circa 1881, for President Arthur. This was only one of several unsuccessful attempts made by the president to improve the White House in a more substantial way than redecorating. The other schemes have not survived.

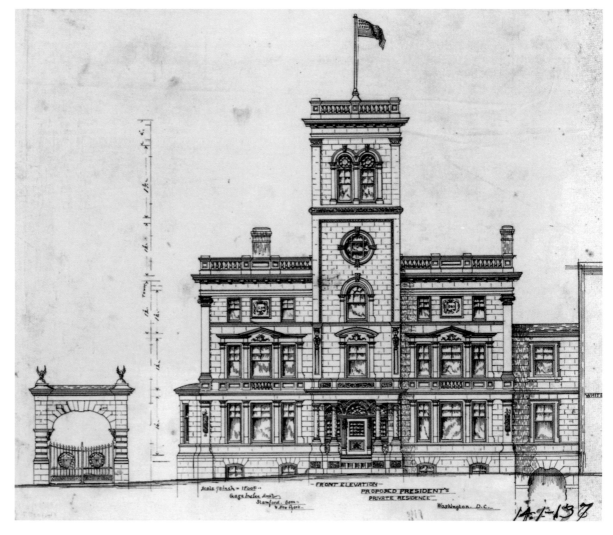

145

a silver spiderweb that formed a canopy over the brilliant colors projected on the walls.

Tiffany had created a striking ceremonial way from the grand stair to the East Room. Here the president first appeared to "Hail to the Chief," and along this long cross hall he led his dinner guests from the East Room to the State Dining Room. It made good theater for the more pompous affectations of the democratic palace. The wonderful screen was to stand only twenty years, almost to the day. In 1902, after it was removed as part of Charles McKim's restoration, a hotel owner bought it at auction. Presumably it was lost some years later when his hotel, near Annapolis, Maryland, burned. To recapture a bit of the flavor of the colored-glass screen today, one may cross Lafayette Park to St. John's Church. There on the south side is a glass mosaic window Tiffany made at the same time he made

the screen, in memory of Chester A. Arthur's wife, Nell, who died early, sending her husband a widower to the White House.

About a year after Arthur's term had ended and Grover Cleveland's had begun, Army Corps of Engineers officers had convinced the busy new president, a Democrat, to continue efforts toward achieving a new White House—not an entirely new one, but one renewed by additions. The promoters of this scheme had learned from their earliest efforts on behalf of Arthur that sentiment was a strong defender of the existing executive mansion. To this power they had necessarily surrendered. "The American people are attached to the old 'White House,'" wrote the officer in charge of public buildings, as he rose to flowery platitudes in the vernacular of such proposals:

"The character it has acquired from historic associations of the men of early days, having

Dolly Johnson, cook, in the family or everyday kitchen about 1888-90. Smaller of two, this kitchen was in the northwest corner of the White House basement, while the great kitchen, used for parties, was beneath the entrance hall. The plan (page 100) shows an 1856 proposed subdivision of the original space. In fact it was divided in two, leaving the above smaller kitchen on the corner.

Mrs. McKinley's bedroom, 1898, northwest corner, second floor. Her dressing room is through the door to the rear. This had been the Prince of Wales Room (see page 125) and is today the upstairs dining room.

been occupied by all our presidents, Washington alone excepted, makes it venerable, and lends additional charms to its classic proportions. Our citizens have long been wont to visit the place, and there to take by the hand such Chief Magistrates as Jefferson, Adams, Jackson, Lincoln, and Grant. They will not consent to surrender their prescriptive privilege to visit the President here for the drowsy chance of finding him not at home after a ride of miles away out of town. He must be accessible to members of Congress, to the people, and to those who go on foot; and we have never had a President who even desired a royal residence, or one so far removed as to be unapproachable save with a coach and four. Our institutions are all thoroughly republican in theory, and it will be agreed they should remain so in practice."

Nonetheless, the structure was now "found to

be insufficient," the officer reported. Action was demanded, he continued, because "the present mansion is old and dilapidated; its floors are sunken, its basement is coated with mold and infested with vermin, which it is impossible to exterminate. Whatever of the modern conveniences have been introduced, partake of the nature of patchwork, and are, at the best, greatly inadequate for the health and comfort of its occupants."

The condition of the house did leave much to be desired. Hoban had rebuilt it using more timber framing than he had in the original structure. Stretching over the long spans of the rooms, the floors could be quite lively. This was more a problem upstairs than below, for the East Room's floors could be given extra support from beneath. Work on the exterior walls in the late 1980s revealed that plugs were frequently placed

**Northwest corner
dressing room upstairs,
about 1890**

in the stone, most in haste, while the house was being painted. Sometimes concrete instead of stone was used to patch and, having a greater density than the stone, caused damage with temperature changes. At least once, with similar results, molten lead was poured into a crack at the place where the east side of the stone entablature of the south portico joins the stone walls of the house. About once a year the house was washed down by the fire department, with red engines in attendance and hoses trained on the walls. A paint touch-up usually followed this effort. Often, to save money, one or two faces of the house might be painted instead of all four. By various devices it was kept clean and white, as shown in early photographs.

Grover Cleveland did little to push the engineers' project, though he supported the idea in a distant sort of way. He was busy being a new sort of president. He was a Democrat, challenging Congress, cleaning house in the bureaucracy, and reviewing the nation's financial management. His secretary, Dan Lamont, was the first presidential secretary to have the management of press relations as his main function. The bachelor Cleveland was one of those hated and admired presidents, with no one lukewarm. His announcement in May 1886 that he would be married at the White House in June made him for a while the most fascinating man in the western world. The groom was 49, the bride 21. At the ceremony scarlet begonias symbolized fire, and a floral ship named *Hymen* was the dining room centerpiece.

The engineers must have been pleased to learn that the president was homemaking and might now notice that the house needed help. He disappointed them. Before his marriage he pur-

148

President's office, second floor, circa 1890, with stenographer Alice Sanger

chased a residence on twenty-three acres near the present Washington National Cathedral. This he remodeled into a comfortable, rambling house in the Queen Anne mode, crowning it with a red roof. Here he and Frances Folson and more than twenty pets kept house, full time from May to early December and part time during the social season. The president was driven to work daily in his carriage, with a small military escort, all moving at a steady pace, not stopping until the procession reached the north portico.

Cleveland was defeated in 1888. Benjamin Harrison, his successor, brought to the house the largest accompaniment of relatives who had lived there since Andrew Johnson. In 1889 the Army engineers made a proposal to transfer the greenhouses to the east side and put an executive office building on the west. The First Lady, Caroline Harrison, considered the possibility.

Encouraged, the engineers unrolled their old plan for her, and she began to develop ideas of her own, for she and the president had been looking for a big project with which to celebrate the centennial of the presidency. The engineers had found a comrade. The small, rosy first lady, a woman of many activities, was of an artistic bent. She deplored the cramped living quarters, where the only private bathroom was the president's. It was no longer possible for the family to use the state floor. Tourists thronged the East Room and parlors on weekdays all the more since Cleveland's marriage. Teas and receptions rescued the presidential purse from more costly dinners, but they were held weekly during the season and kept the state floor in disarray.

During the summer of 1889 Mrs. Harrison met in the Red Room with a select group, the main participant being James G. Blaine, secretary of

ELEVATION OF THE OFFICIAL WING

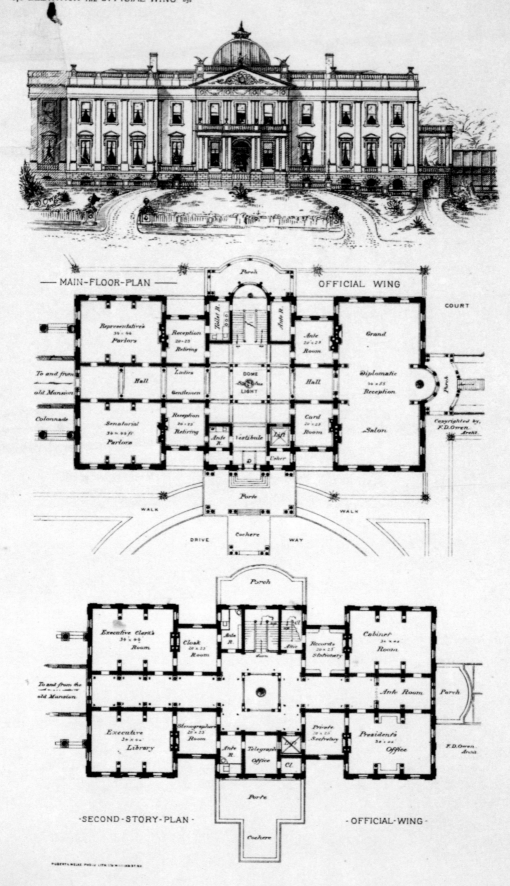

— MAIN-FLOOR-PLAN — OFFICIAL WING

-SECOND-STORY-PLAN- -OFFICIAL-WING-

Opposite:

Elevation and floor plans

for a new west wing, part of the

expansion proposed during

President Benjamin Harrison's

administration, 1889

North and south views of

proposed additions to the

White House, 1889

state. She wanted this session to result in a proposal for an improved White House. Blaine would speak to the need for a more expansive setting for entertaining. The other participants would do as they were told, of course, notably the public buildings commissioner, Colonel John M Wilson. Her friend Frederick D. Owen, an engineer, would help with the plan and had already made a sketch that illustrated her ideas. The feature of the meeting was her long discourse on the great discomforts of life at the White House. Her delight over being the first lady was widely advertised in the press, so her misery cannot have been disastrous. Secretary Blaine remarked that her effort to gain better quarters would be at peril if her plan included altering the historic house, for Congress would refuse to fund it, as had happened before.

Mrs. Harrison had explained what she wanted to Owen, at his drafting table, and a set of drawings was produced by the autumn. A new commissioner, Colonel Oswald Ernst, reported in September, and Mrs. Harrison reviewed the drawings with him and a group of reporters. The response was so positive that the first lady determined to try her project's political wings. Owen was employed by the public buildings office and worked to detail the schematics he had executed the previous summer. Meanwhile Mrs. Harrison gained an ally in Senator Leland Stanford of California, who promised to manage the funding bill through committees to the Senate floor. An oversight on the part of the president—failure to make a political appointment in the Maine district of Speaker of the House Thomas B. Reed—resulted in a roadblock. The bill never got to the

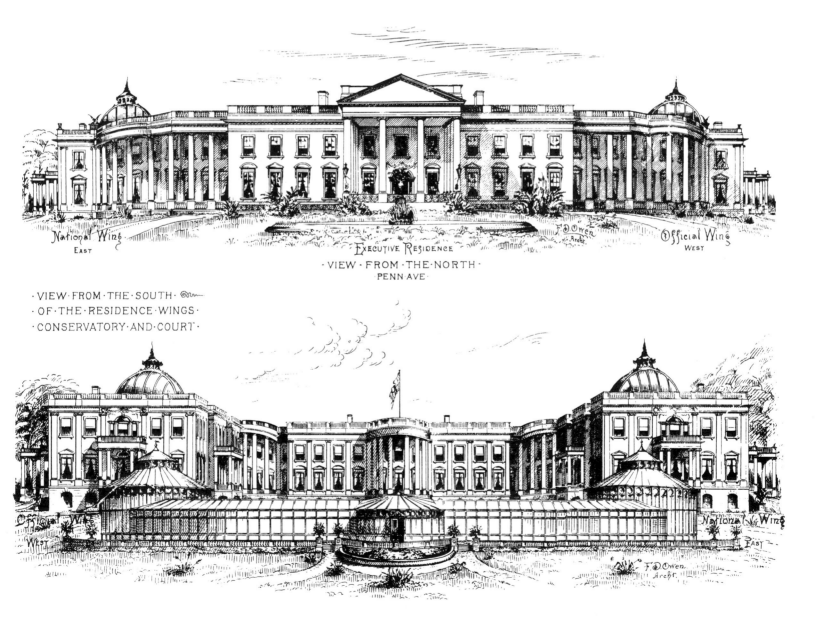

National Wing
EAST

EXECUTIVE RESIDENCE
·VIEW·FROM·THE·NORTH·
PENN·AVE·

Official Wing
WEST

·VIEW·FROM·THE·SOUTH·
·OF·THE·RESIDENCE·WINGS·
·CONSERVATORY·AND·COURT·

Official Wing
WEST

National Wing
EAST

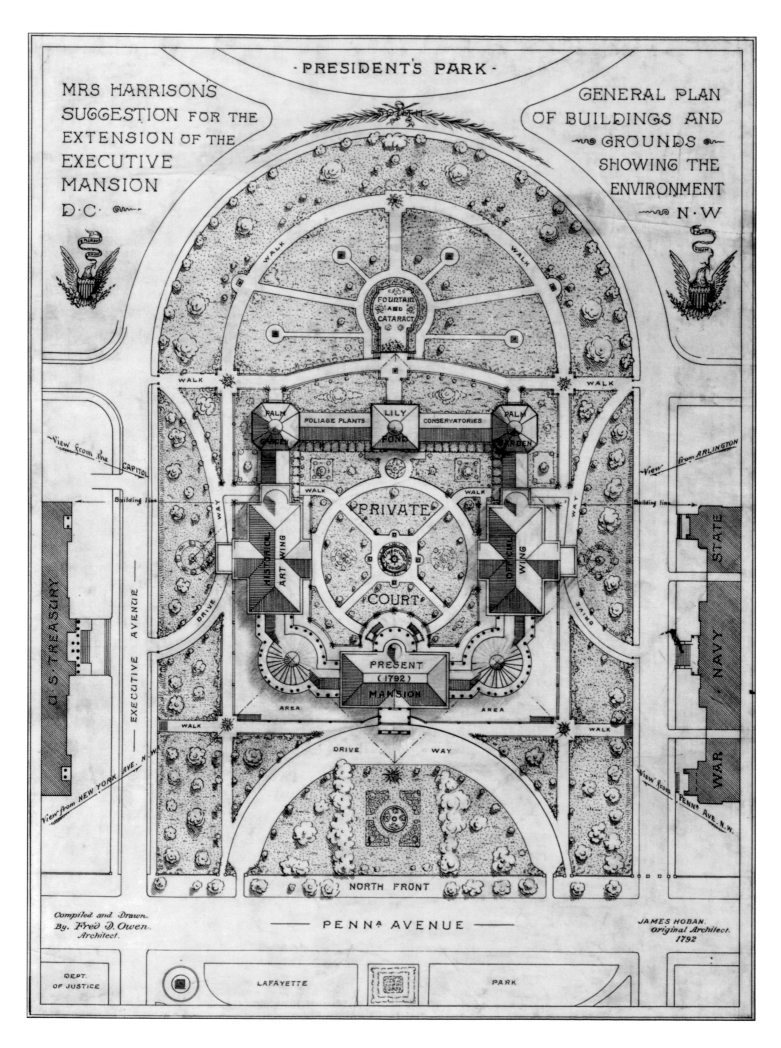

PRESIDENT'S PARK

MRS HARRISON'S SUGGESTION FOR THE EXTENSION OF THE EXECUTIVE MANSION D·C·

GENERAL PLAN OF BUILDINGS AND GROUNDS SHOWING THE ENVIRONMENT N·W

FOUNTAIN AND CATARACT

PALM GARDEN · FOLIAGE PLANTS · LILY POND · CONSERVATORIES · PALM GARDEN

View from the CAPITOL

View from ARLINGTON

Building line

Building line

U·S·TREASURY

EXECUTIVE AVENUE

HISTORICAL ART WING

PRIVATE COURT

OFFICIAL WING

DRIVE WAY

STATE

NAVY

View from NEW YORK AVE. N.W.

PRESENT (1792) MANSION

AREA

AREA

WAR

View from PENN! AVE. N.W.

DRIVE WAY

NORTH FRONT

Compiled and Drawn. By. Fred D. Owen. Architect.

PENN! AVENUE

JAMES HOBAN. Original Architect. 1792

DEPT. OF JUSTICE

LAFAYETTE

PARK

Benjamin Harrison, president from 1889 to 1893. During Harrison's administration the Constitution and the presidency reached the age of 100. He supported his wife's idea that a good way to commemorate was to expand the White House.

Opposite:
Plan of grounds and wings, proposed White House expansion, 1889

Caroline Harrison, an artistic woman, was a shrewd manager and found the White House inadequate as a residence. Her efforts to expand the house might have succeeded eventually, except that her death cut short the campaign.

floor of the House of Representatives.

The scheme came close to realization, however. It was therefore not tabled but kept in view, a future goal for the corps. The plan called for a perfectly logical expansion of the old rectangular house. Conservatories and west wing were to go, as was the porch on the east. A new quadrangle arrangement was proposed to the south, with the original house remaining as its northern center-piece. The interior of the White House was to be rebuilt to be fireproof, and the steps to the south portico were to be removed, making that porch a columned balcony. Two structures somewhat larger than the White House were to face each other across the south lawn. They were to be linked to the house from the east and west ends by two-story connectors, domed and colon-naded, with cylindrical sections placed halfway in each.

South of the new buildings, on the sharply descending grade, the quadrangle was to be closed at the end by a long range of conservato-ries containing palm gardens, foliage rooms, and in the center a lily pond, all under glass. People using the main and second floors of the White House and two annexes could easily see over the conservatories to the Maryland and Virginia vis-tas so long admired from the president's win-dows. The new building on the east was styled the Historical Art Wing, while that on the west was the Official Wing, with the president's of-fices. The wings were to be built around sweep-ing cross halls, framed by columns; at their crossings were to be tall saloons, colonnaded, with large glass domes, square-sided in a quasi-Second Empire mode.

All the prominent architectural details of the wings came from those of the White House. In theory the work was thus perfectly sound, but as architecture it was tedious, carousel-like in the extreme, and palatial in an almost comical way. The plan, on the other hand, as tailored to the needs of the house, would work well today. It supplied not only large rooms but also large numbers of rooms. There were spaces for dining and for receptions and offices so ample that the president's paltry five rooms and a hall in the east end of the second floor seemed a joke. The living quarters were sunny and roomy, with more bathrooms. On the ground level were ser-vice rooms more modern and numerous than the house had ever known.

Cleveland returned to office in 1893 and ac-quired another house separate from the White House. He and Frances Cleveland probably lived less of their time in the White House proper than any other full-term president except Harry S. Truman, who abandoned the house during the renovations of 1948-52. Mrs. Cleveland, who liked the Harrison proposals, had the engineers set them up on easels for tourists to see. It was a good time for thinking of palaces. The diplomatic

· PROPOSED ·
· EXECVTIVE MANSION ·

Paul J. Pelz
Architect
March 1893.

community gained its first ambassador to the United States, from Britain, in 1893; it was thus elevated to a level of official protocol not reached before. In the next decade Massachusetts Avenue and other streets would be decorated by elegant mansions, where public receptions would be held during the season. Young and beautiful, Mrs. Cleveland was at the head of society and may have wished for such a setting of her own.

She was also a fair politician, aware of how little time four years allows a president. Her second child was born in the White House, but Frances Cleveland seems to have been happier in the surrogate house. The engineers sketched modified schemes for an expansion. Perhaps she gave them some ideas. Even the panic of 1893 seems to have closed the subject for only a few months. It made the engineers consider realizing their grand plan in phases, beginning with a new office for the president.

In 1894 the officer in charge of public buildings wrote, "Surely the people of this great nation can afford to provide for its Chief Magistrate, outside of his home, a place where the immense business incident to his exalted position may receive attention." The Capitol had been enlarged, he reasoned, forty years before. Congress was moving the Library of Congress from the Capitol into a

"magnificent library building." One year later the officer described in his report how fine the executive office could be, built of granite. "This structure could be connected [to the White House] by a wide corridor with a large conservatory, fitted up as a winter garden with tropical plants, fountains, and statues of eminent Americans."

It seemed obvious that the White House would have to be changed. Washington was changing all around it. By the late 1890s the city had many houses grander than that of the president. Yet the White House was the White House. Invitations there were coveted by even the most jaded partygoers, and the public's curiosity about what went on there was boundless. The presidential occupants never felt a strong motivation to rebuild, much less an inclination to endure the misery of an expansion that might take years. Since Mrs. Harrison there had been no one truly inspired to become the project's patron.

When in 1897 William McKinley moved in, the corps tried again. This time under the direction of Colonel Theodore A. Bingham, the public buildings office geared up for a real campaign. Fred Owen became a full-time employee, and he and Bingham spread the drawings before them, Bingham with his blue pencil. As this was taking place, in 1898, the United States went to war

Rendering of a proposed new White House on Meridian Hill, Paul J. Pelz, 1898. This dreamlike palace scheme, perhaps recalling L'Enfant's and equally ill-fated, had no official support but represented the continuing effort on the part of a number of professional architects to break into the closed circle of federal building in Washington. For the time the Army Corps of Engineers held tight control, yielding not an inch.

Opposite:
The White House from the east, looking toward the north portico, at the end of the nineteenth century

with Spain. Congress loosened the purse strings and provided $50 million to the president to fight the war. McKinley carried the presidency swiftly to a level of power exceeding even Lincoln's. Nothing like it had been known since George Washington. The segment of political history that had begun with Grant was largely over in that seminal year of 1898.

Not long after the war was over Bingham pushed himself to revise the earlier plans. He did his homework thoroughly and never went into a contest unprepared. Where his predecessors had drowned in the rhetoric of sycophancy, he would succeed, he believed, by presenting an overwhelmingly complete and perfect package no sensible person could turn down. Research carried him into the documents of the early days of the White House. The papers of the builders of Washington were in his office, the minutes of the commissioners, the bills of the workmen, the letters. The map usually believed to be L'Enfant's original hung on his wall. He read the papers of Latrobe and learned to know Hoban and the visions of George Washington. Every decision he made he wanted footed in historical justification or good reason. He contacted officials at Leinster House in Dublin, the home for many years of the Royal Dublin Society, and they sent plans showing how they had expanded Hoban's model in recent years. Curiously, Bingham seems never to have realized that Hoban revised the Leinster House idea by removing the lower ground floor. Yet in practically every other respect his research was excellent.

By the turn of the century many historical influences had reshaped the Harrison plan of 1889. Even though other schemes for a better president's house presented themselves, Colonel Bingham had no reason to doubt that he would determine the course of executive housing. He was pleased with his and Owen's work and ordered a model built. The year 1900 was a major anniversary, with November marking a century since John Adams had moved into the White House, the first of the unbroken succession of presidents that continues today. What more appropriate time to introduce a bigger, more beautiful White House to serve the reborn presidency?

City of Washington, Bird's-Eye
View from the Potomac—
Looking North by Charles Parsons,
Currier & Ives lithograph, 1892

Opposite:
South portico
from the east,
circa 1895

5

BEAUX-ARTS RETHINKING

As the twentieth century opened, certain forces were at work that would transform Washington into the monumental city it is today. The Army Corps of Engineers were not alone in wanting change, but they were bureaucrats trapped in the forms in which they functioned. They had let their vision slip so that it was no longer relevant to the mainstream. Outside forces in architecture, meanwhile, had come into play. Heady from the triumph of the World's Columbian Exposition they had staged in Chicago in 1893, some powerful architects in private practice were showing an interest in the capital city as a place to establish permanently the ideals that had enjoyed only temporary splendor at the fair. Such a valhalla would also present endless possibilities for work. Their principal obstacles were the Treasury's Office of the Supervising Architect and the even more formidable Army engineers.

The engineers had heretofore enjoyed undisputed power over public building in Washington. In a clash with civilian architects over construction of the Library of Congress, the corps officers had at last gotten rid of the architect and finished the job on their own. The corps saw engineering as the preeminent discipline and

architecture as only a facet of it. Decades before, the engineers had adopted the French viewpoint that a professional was one employed and salaried to carry out a great public work—as the architect of a palace or a church—and that those who provided such services as a business were merely contractors, be they architects or engineers. All private practitioners were thus regarded by the corps as nonprofessional and second class. "Professionals" by their definition nearly always worked for the government.

In small ways this attitude is still reflected in government service; for example, government architects are not required to be licensed. In Colonel Theodore Bingham's day private architects were barred as a rule from federal projects. Fred Owen, the engineer who had made Mrs. Harrison's plans, is a case in point, for he had to be admitted into the corps as a civil employee before he could continue his White House work through the 1890s. Private architects fought back as best they could. They gained a victory in 1893 with the Tarsney Act, which, in theory at least, transferred government building projects from the exclusive control of the Office of the Supervising Architect of the Treasury to a contract system in which the work was bid upon. In fact it was a feeble victory. By the time the bill became law it was so weakened officials could effectively ignore it.

Neither the architects nor their Washington-based professional society, the American Institute of Architects, could be a match politically for the engineering establishment in the government. The engineers were held in high esteem at the Capitol. Their letters show that they moved freely among senators and representatives. The private architects had learned at the 1893 fair, however, that they had the ability to inspire. One of their most powerful admirers was Senator James McMillan, father of Detroit's magnificent parks system and chairman of the Senate committee concerned with the District of Columbia. From this relationship sprang the McMillan Commission, which was to plan for Washington an urban renaissance in public building based on the L'Enfant plan. Eventually the corps would be bypassed as designers.

Apparently oblivious to the changes that were coming, Bingham pursued his centennial plans for the White House. He sent to the Blue Room a white plaster model he had made of his great

Classic mode that had become somewhat archaic after the fair.

The idea of round elements, which had formed secondary motifs as part of the connectors in the Harrison plan, became the predominant feature of Bingham's and Owen's east and west wings. Girdled by heroic-scale Ionic columns, the domed wings were each about three-fifths the breadth of the house, so the resulting spread atop the lofty site was very wide. Because of their roundness, they seemed to frame the house, which on the south receded from their forward projection. The wings were highly decorated with the established White House stone ornaments—balustrades, window hoods, Ionic columns and pilasters—all against smooth ashlar walls above the rusticated basement level. Bingham, more completely immersed in the history of the site than anyone before, was aware that George Washington had wanted the house to grow with the country. This, he reasoned, was the sort of expansion Washington would have approved.

What little can be learned about the Bingham

Model of the proposed White House expansion scheme of 1900

project, and at President William McKinley's special centennial luncheon on December 12, 1900, he described the scheme his model represented. It still bore some resemblance to the Harrison plan, except that the quadrangle was opened up and replaced by large side wings added to the original house. Each wing was crowned with a shallow dome, and the composition had a certain resemblance to the new Library of Congress, an expression of the Free

plan comes from a surviving, but incomplete, set of drawings. The west wing was to contain state guest rooms and a banquet hall, with salons, baths, dressing rooms, and a hotel-type kitchen. The decorative treatment was rich, indeed fancy, with interior columns, parquet and mosaic floors, skylights, and opera house staircases. On the east an office complex was envisioned with spacious work areas, meeting rooms, and, to reflect McKinley's masterful control of the news,

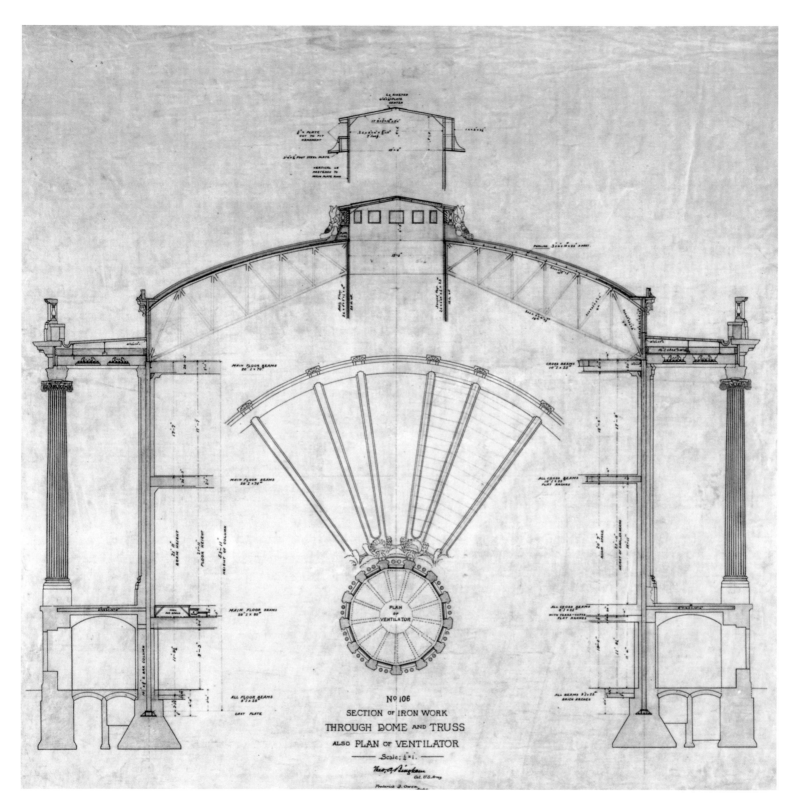

No 106
SECTION of IRON WORK
THROUGH DOME and TRUSS
ALSO PLAN of VENTILATOR
Scale: ¼=1.

PLAN
OF
VENTILATOR

Structural section of a pavilion and (overleaf) plan of the state floor with added wings, from the set of drawings made by Frederick D. Owen for the proposed 1900 expansion

quarters to house the press in comfort. McKinley had turned the second floor office corridor over to the press; before that reporters had usually waited on the north portico, some fifteen at a time, each with his bicycle-mounted messenger boy ready to fly to the public telegraph office.

When Bingham gave his centennial presentation it happened that the American Institute of Architects was in convention, and a group of the delegates accompanied Senator McMillan to the

president's luncheon. McMillan, who had approved in principle the idea of remodeling the White House, was angered to see that so complete a project had been brought forth without his approval as chairman of the Senate district committee. The senator was a believer in master plans and had no use for isolated programs such as Bingham's. Their difference of opinion touched off serious controversy at the luncheon. In the weeks and months to come Bingham faced

161

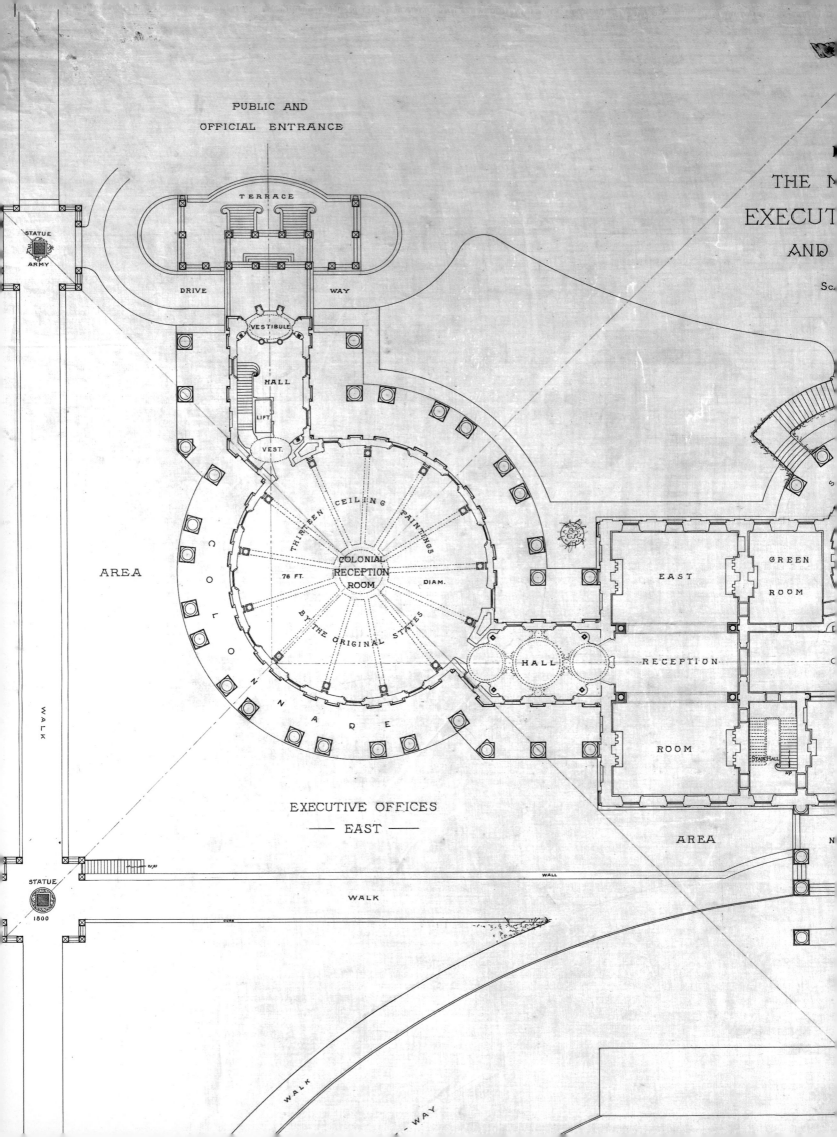

PUBLIC AND
OFFICIAL ENTRANCE

TERRACE

DRIVE   WAY

VESTIBULE

HALL

LIFT

VEST.

STATUE
ARMY

AREA

COLONNADE

THIRTEEN CEILING PAINTINGS

COLONIAL
RECEPTION
ROOM

76 FT.   DIAM.

BY THE ORIGINAL STATES

STATUE
1800

EXECUTIVE OFFICES
— EAST —

WALK

WALK

CURB

HALL

RECEPTION

ROOM

EAST

GREEN
ROOM

STAIR HALL
UP

AREA

WALL

THE M
EXECUT
AND

SCA

WAY

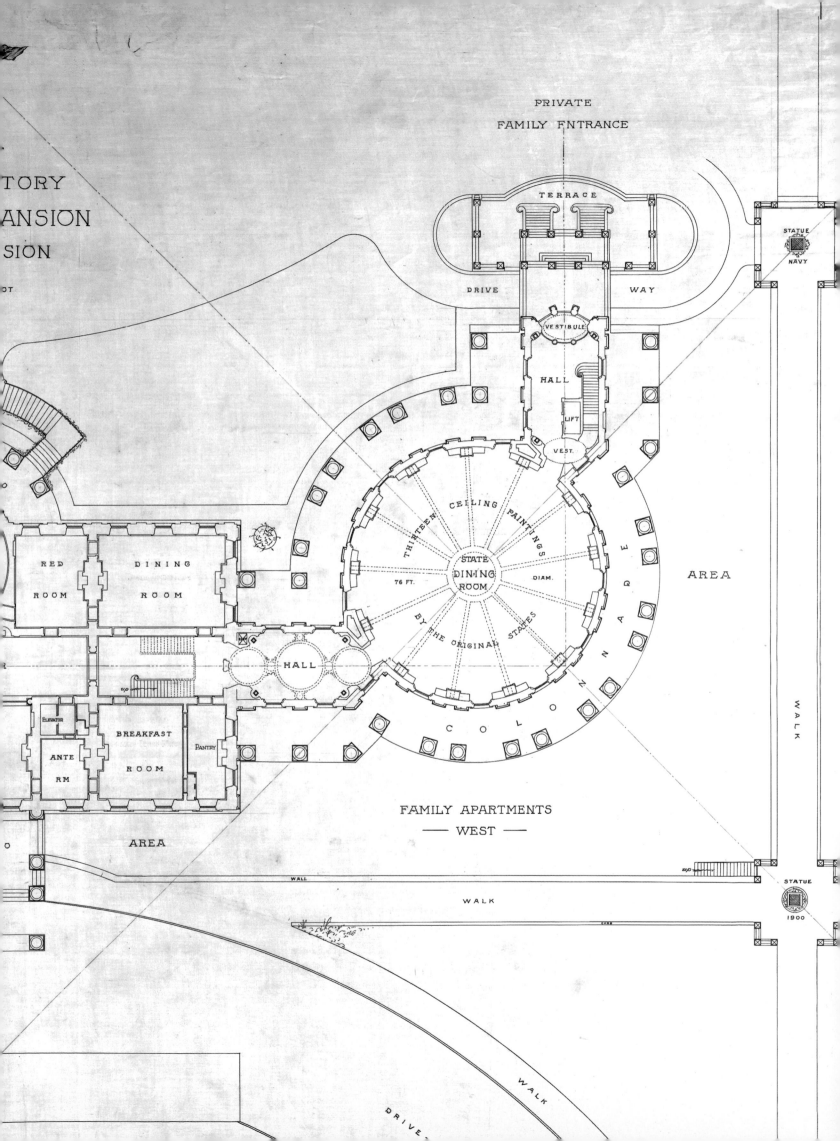

TORY

ANSION

SION

OT

PRIVATE
FAMILY ENTRANCE

TERRACE

DRIVE   WAY

STATUE

NAVY

VESTIBULE

HALL

LIFT

VEST.

RED
ROOM

DINING
ROOM

THIRTEEN CEILING PAINTINGS

STATE
DINING
ROOM

76 FT.   DIAM.

BY THE ORIGINAL STATES

AREA

C O L O N N A D E

HALL

ELEVATOR

ANTE
RM

BREAKFAST
ROOM

PANTRY

WALK

FAMILY APARTMENTS
— WEST —

AREA

WALL

WALK

STATUE

1900

CURB

WALK

DRIVE

Employees of the McMillan
Commission making a scale model
of a transformed Washington

THE
PRESIDENTIAL
PARTY
VIEWING THE
MODELS.

THE PRESIDENT
AND SEN. McMILLAN

SECRETARIES
LONG AND WILSON

President Roosevelt and the
Cabinet viewed the model and
drawings for the McMillan plan at
the Corcoran Gallery of Art.
The event is shown here as
depicted in the *Washington Post*,
January 16, 1902.

heated criticism. He often responded rudely, with damaging candor, feeling secure that he had the president's approval—weak though it may have been—as well as political connections on Capitol Hill. But wheels were turning elsewhere: On March 8, 1901, McMillan presented his dream of a master plan for Washington in the form of a bill before the Senate.

On September 6, 1901, McKinley was assassinated at the Pan-American Exposition in Buffalo, New York. Americans grieved over a president they had truly loved. The vice president, Theodore Roosevelt, came to Washington as president ten days later. In the months that passed he proceeded with caution, but it was clear early on that this man had a style of performance wholly different from McKinley's. Wearing the heavy mantle of renewed executive power bequeathed by McKinley, the youthful Roosevelt quickly filled the shoes of the presidency. He had a way of getting to the point of a thing by reducing it to its simplest element. In the office suite he surveyed a complex and often inefficient organization ridden with layers of tradition stacked atop temporary procedures. The stationery, with its unctuous legend, "Executive Mansion," seemed to symbolize it all. One of his earliest orders, given before McKinley's funeral flowers had wilted, was to change the name of the place officially to the White House. Things were to be different now.

Bingham's plan, for which he fought still, did not die all of a sudden; like most of the corps' projects that failed at that time it was overwhelmed by an emotional wave. In January 1902 the McMillan Commission opened an exhibition at the Corcoran Gallery of Art with drawings and models that proposed a renewed capital city, a resurrection of Washington's and L'Enfant's dream. Tree-lined streets, parks, and neoclassical buildings gave it the vigorous spirit L'Enfant and Washington had had in mind, only modernized, improved, and adapted to the needs of the twentieth century. The commission's advisers were distinguished figures in American design: architects Daniel P. Burnham of Chicago and Charles F. McKim of New York; the landscape architect Frederick Law Olmsted, Jr., son of the more famous designer of parks and estates; and the sculptor Augustus Saint Gaudens. They toured great cities in Europe to prepare themselves for the planning of the city.

Washington, model of the City Beautiful, as envisioned by the McMillan Commission

Theodore Roosevelt, president from 1901 to 1909. McKinley's mighty rejuvenated presidency found a dynamic salesman in his successor, who remade the White House to suit the new image. For the work he called in the leading architecture firm in the United States at the time, McKim, Mead & White.

Plan of the White House on its site at the time Roosevelt's renovation began. Structures on the right are conservatories.

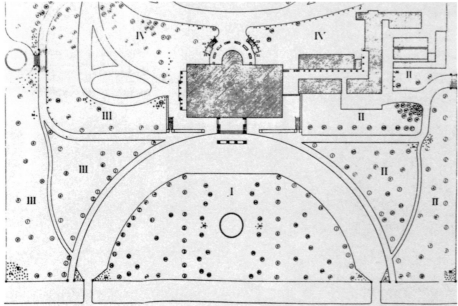

The Plan of 1901, as it came to be known, was fresh. It was crystal clear in concept and seemed appropriate to a democratic nation newly emerged as a world power. Roosevelt attended the exhibition at the Corcoran and was pleased with what he saw. He was to like it even better upon reflection. And, although nine years were to pass before the plan was adopted under the Taft administration, its presence set the tone for the future as early as 1902. The Corcoran show was still on view in the spring of that year, when Mrs. Roosevelt invited Charles McKim to meet

with her about some improvements at the White House.

As one who had never accepted the city of Washington as anything but secondary to New York, she turned naturally to one of New York's most respected architects to discuss her ideas. McKim was also a friend of Roosevelt's cousin Edith Wharton, who with Ogden Codman had written *The Decoration of Houses*, published in 1896. This volume had established her as an able promoter of the anti-Victorian sort of historical decoration one might call Beaux-Arts, relating it to the academic strain current in architecture. Mrs. Roosevelt was Victorian in her tastes and an ardent collector of antiques—evocative old teapots, mellow brass andirons, quaint old dressers, and the like. She and the president loved the White House for being "colonial." They believed the president of the United States should live there.

At the same time the Roosevelts had a large household of young children. The eight-room family quarters with two bathrooms were not satisfactory. Downstairs the rooms looked tatty and the floors sagged. The dining room seated a maximum of sixty in elbow-jabbing and breathless discomfort. The office space was overcrowded. There must be more room all around. Edith Roosevelt asked McKim for quick and easy solutions. After some consideration he said that a complete renovation was the only course that would both do justice to a great historic building and keep the president in the White House.

Through the intervention of Senator McMillan, who very much wanted the president to keep on living in the White House, money was soon appropriated. McKim received the news by telegram when he returned to New York from his visit with Mrs. Roosevelt. Several days later, when the president was in New York, McKim called to meet both Roosevelts, and they put him formally in charge. Now not only McKim but also the whole field of private architecture had the opportunity to shine. It could sell its neoclassical ideals to the world in a popular forum. By appointing McKim Theodore Roosevelt had recognized the profession of architecture, singling out for this major responsibility one of its most distinguished members.

The raw nerves on the scene in Washington, however, can be imagined. Bingham was both astonished and angry to hear about McKim's ascendancy, then hurt when informed that he was merely to manage the accounts on the government's side. In late April McKim made an appointment for Bingham to show the White House to him and to the contractor, O. W. Norcross, whose construction company, Norcross Brothers, had built the greatest buildings by McKim, Mead & White. The three walked through the Victorianized house attic to cellar. Tattered traces of Tiffany mingled with the efforts of a dozen lesser decorators. Ida McKinley's "colonial" Blue Room was stuffed and draped and carpeted; dim filament light bulbs in gilt metal bouquets peeked from the cornice, while the thundering gasolier of 1854, pearly now with necklaces of light bulbs, hovered like an inverted glass Christmas tree over the famous circular divan. Grease layered the two kitchens. The elevator stopped between floors and spit sparks before proceeding. Toilet flushes whispered in the walls of the State Dining Room. There was good reason for change. But Bingham had known that for years.

McKim was always emphatic with Bingham; he did not represent himself in the work, he said, but his firm. During the tour he observed without much tact that the job was his and the decisions would be his, but he would do few if any drawings, leaving this to the office in New York. Poor businessman that he was, he had no intention whatsoever of discussing money with anyone except perhaps the president. He wasted a minimum of words in explaining his position to Bingham and left little question that he alone would deal with the Roosevelts. Bingham so loathed this fine fellow for his victory and for his arrogance that he strained himself to make the architect look bad through the following months and on several occasions earned reprimands. His attitude would one day cost him his job, after McKim's White House had come to be.

The program for McKim was simple on the surface and in a sense wide open. He was to preserve the historic White House but make it work for the modern presidency. At the outset he took special note of the word "restore," and his

Edith Roosevelt and her husband let Charles McKim have his way in most particulars with the renovations of 1902. However, she loved Victorian furniture and, to the Beaux-Arts architect's utter dismay, rescued the Lincoln bed and other nineteenth-century furnishings from the auction hammer.

Edith Roosevelt's sketch of the crowded family quarters, at about the time she moved to the White House. "T" is Ted, which she called her husband.

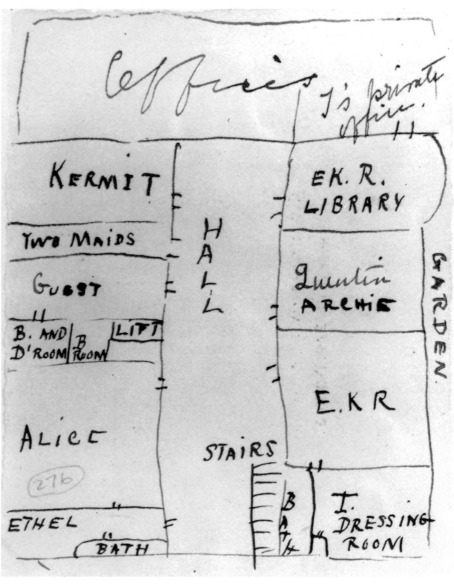

167

colleagues remembered that he used it often. Sketchpad in hand he visited the premises frequently, sometimes many times a day, through the spring and early summer, walking the grounds and imagining. On June 28, 1902, Congress appropriated $475,445 for the house and office. The president ordered that the house be finished in time to open the social season with a state dinner in early December. Five months were to be allowed for construction. The president had little idea of the extent of the work McKim had in mind, but his schedule was immovable.

As McKim developed his concept, he and the Roosevelts had only one controversy over the design. He was determined to tear down the conservatories; the Roosevelts liked the glazed paradise. The wonders inside, they felt, made an enjoyable diversion for guests when social functions became dull. Their feelings were strengthened by letters from the gardener, Henry Pfister, a Hayes appointee, who was urged by Colonel Bingham to speak his mind freely on the subject. McKim convinced his clients at last that the glass

houses were an encumbrance to the historical neoclassical purity of the house and had his way. They were demolished in the autumn of 1902, after forty-five years of service. Pfister watched many of his finest plants die with the first frost, for his substitute greenhouses on the Mall were not yet ready.

By the time the house was being stripped of its furniture in June, McKim's ideas were established and needed only the final details. "It is useless to expect to secure a harmonious structure," he wrote, "by doing over any one part of the house. If the work is to be done at all, the entire house should be treated as a single problem." He did just that. There is no question that the concept was McKim's alone. He rethought the White House in every particular, bearing in mind the two directives to restore the house and to make it function. Judgmental and often ruthless in evaluating the landmark's parts, he began to see a structure in his mind's eye that he as a modern architect could truly admire. The renewed house taking shape in his head was a far cry from what was there in terms of convenience, technology,

Clockwise from left:
The Blue Room and the corridor outside the State Dining Room, as they were at the time of the Roosevelt remodeling. For the better part of a hundred years the White House had been heavily used and reused, patched and redecorated, and hurriedly provided with new conveniences, and finally life there had outgrown the venerable building. The view of the Blue Room shows it as redecorated in a neo-Georgian style by McKinley, fashionable for 1902, but no setting for the revitalized presidency. The kitchen was built in the renovation of 1902, marking the appearance of twentieth century technical conveniences.

The removal of the conservatories, September 1902. (Below) Demolition has exposed the west exterior wall of the state floor, revealing the windows closed in by Hayes in 1880 to accommodate french doors.

and, yes, even grandeur. It soon became clear that one of the objectives of the work would have to yield somewhat. Since "function" was vital, McKim took a broader, more creative look at the word "restore."

To the Roosevelts restoration meant keeping the house about the same in appearance. McKim redefined the idea and instead decided that a better approach was to take the house back to what it had been originally–even to what it might have been had George Washington's designer been as able as Charles McKim. The idea of taking the house back freed McKim from any mandate to preserve what he could class as additions. As a concept this worked well. Under this banner he erased first the conservatories, then the heavy gas lanterns that had been mounted on the north columns at about the time the conservatories were built, the iron anthemion fencing along the driveway, and other external elements. If the same logic was followed on the interior he was given–or, if not, he certainly took–license to weed out the parts that conflicted with his vision. Given his knowledge of historical design he is sure to have realized that much of the interior detailing was changed when the house was reconstructed in 1815-18. He might also have categorized that work as added.

McKim moved the offices into a separate building. Because trouble brewed over putting the president out of the White House, as well as over adding a new building to the grounds, the structure was named the "temporary Executive Office" before working drawings were made. It was not, moreover, to house the president's actual office but that of his staff. With most of the office function gone McKim had the whole house to consider for a residence, two stories over a basement, or ground floor.

The family was fairly comfortable with the idea of living upstairs, except for the lack of space. Moving the office nearly doubled the space for family habitation. By relocating the grand stair McKim gave over the entire second floor transverse corridor to living quarters, divided as always by glass-transomed arches into three sections, with that on the east several steps up, to accommodate the extra-high ceiling of the East Room below. Bathrooms and closets could be fitted into the resulting twelve bedrooms. With so much space on the second floor, there was no need for a third floor in the cavernous attic. About one third of the attic was given to servants' rooms and storage, while the rest was unfinished. The middle one of the three corridor spaces, however, was given a large skylight. McKim wanted this to bring in sunlight during the day and, through rows of electric light bulbs concealed above ground glass, to provide an indirect light at night.

If the private quarters fell easily into place, the same was not true of the main or state floor. The requirements here were almost self-defeating. Great crowds had to come and go, yet it was an area that must sometimes seem intimate. Roosevelt had ordered a larger dining room. Men's and women's coatrooms and toilet facilities were necessary. There were also no places for men and women to retire to comb their hair or adjust their clothing after depositing their coats. Currently the men's room was in the conservatory, where President Chester Arthur had put it, abhorring as he did the custom of providing chamber pots

Charles Follen McKim at about the time he renovated the White House

for men in the dining room after dinner. A women's "retiring room" of undetermined origin had been built–possibly as early as 1848–in the hallway between the service stairs and the usher's office on the north. It was small, inadequate, and poorly placed.

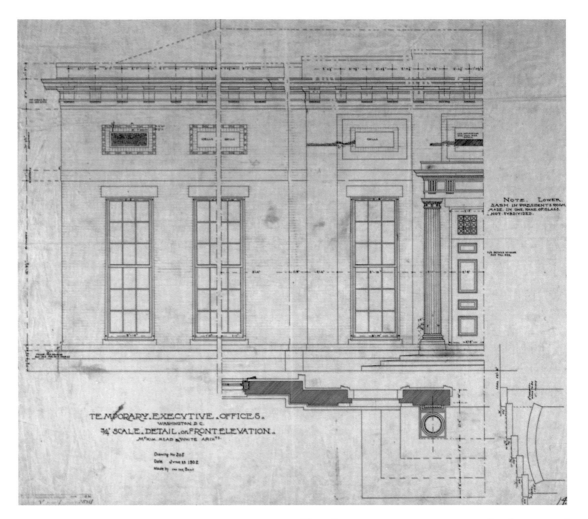

Elevation and plan of the temporary Executive Office, forerunner of today's west wing. This structure was actually a staff office, presided over by the president's private secretary and not intended as an official place for the president, who kept his association with the White House. The "president's room," carefully named at the top left of the plan, was for his use when he was in the building.

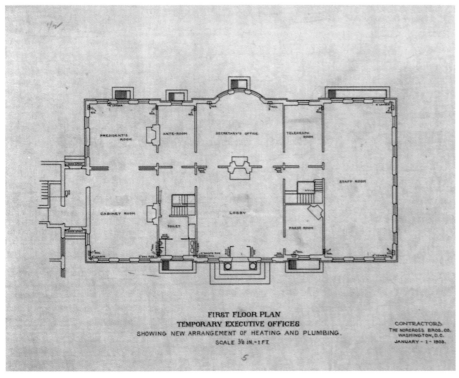

Opposite:

(Above) The conservatories and (below) the office building that replaced them in 1902

The obvious recourse was to make the ground floor serve the social needs of the state floor, but what was not clear was how to make it work. From the north or main front, the ground floor was a basement. Could guests be received as always at the front entrance, then sent downstairs, only to be required to climb up to the state floor again? McKim spent many an hour studying the exterior of the house. He had decided early to leave the west wing, after the conservatory was removed. In the glass-covered rose house he had admired the old west colonnade, its Tuscan columns largely obscured by rampant rose vines and jasmine, its rooms filled with storage and gardener's supplies. Old prints showed an east wing, and this he decided to reconstruct, to balance the other, giving the "cup" – the White House – its "saucer," as he liked to say. As it soon turned out the reconstructed east wing helped him solve his main floor problems. He created a new social entrance at the tip of the rebuilt wing to bring the president's guests in at ground level, then continue them into the basement ground floor of the house and up into

Plan of the McKim east wing of the
White House and (bottom) the
east entrance as completed in
1902. The long rows of cubicles in
the plan are "hat boxes" for the
use of guests, the idea being a
holdover from the nineteenth
century, when actual boxes were
set up in the entrance hall of the
White House to store hats at large
functions.

the entrance hall by stairs. Coatrooms, dressing rooms, rest rooms, and other conveniences would be built in what were then pantries, laundry rooms, and storage rooms.

The state floor itself was changed in one major way. To enlarge the dining room, the grand stair was moved and the dining room's north wall was cut away, extending the room about twenty feet. A new grand stair was built where the office stair had been, opening into the hall outside the East Room. The new stair from the ground floor would rise neatly beneath this, landing in the space between the East Room and the entrance hall. In his treatment of the five state interiors and the family dining room, McKim planned to take Hoban's Georgian cue and within that design vernacular reach for a more stately, ceremonial solution to suit the new presidency—and, indeed, the flamboyant president himself.

Demolition was probably well under way by July 1, 1902, the date McKim had final approval of his concept from the president and from Mrs.

Opposite:
Steel beams introduced to
support the floors, 1902. This
eastward view was taken in the
second floor hall where the
reception and waiting rooms for
the president's office had been
since the 1820s. The view
downward is of the East Room.

Overleaf:
Renovation in progress in the
East Room. Note Hoban's anthemia,
to be enclosed in the walls.

Roosevelt, who was spending the summer at Oyster Bay, New York. The president at first insisted on remaining in the house, but to the relief of everyone the plaster dust soon drove him across the street to his interim office in a neighboring row house. Because of the time constraint the demolition was not as extensive as it might have been. If only a portion of a wall was to go that portion was all that went, with any new surfaces put over what had been there before, be it wallpaper, decorative plaster, or paint. The old house was otherwise torn apart. All floors were removed from the three stories, so one could look from the dirt of the ground up to the ceiling of what had been Lincoln's office. Steel joists replaced those of wood, and Guastavino hollow tiles were cemented between, preparing a secure bed for wood and stone surface flooring to come.

A probe into the structure revealed that to enlarge the dining room as planned, forty-one feet of a brick bearing wall that extended a third of the way across the house would have to go. The engineers advised against taking out the wall because it was the only support from below for

in the remains of the brick interior wall on the east, was sandwiched into the rebuilt partition on the second floor. Tie rods dropped from it to secure the heavy floors over the dining room. This hidden truss would eventually fail.

Construction photographs, carefully dated, show a fast pace of work. July and August saw pulling down; after the middle of August rebuilding took place. Innumerable parts of the house were discarded at random—doors, windows, mantels, stairs and banisters, old cupboards, and the floors on which the early presidents had walked. Tiffany's hall screen went, and Hoban's King of Prussia blue marble columns were dumped into the Potomac. Whitewash-laden plaster was scraped off the basement walls. The groin vaulting of the corridor was stripped to the stone and brick, some of its arched parts copied in Guastavino tiles and plastered smooth. Utility pipes were buried in concrete chases beneath the corridor floor. The old furnace was removed from the oval room and a new one installed across the hall where the larger of the two kitchens had been.

Drawing of the truss designed by McKim, Mead & White to be installed on the west end of the second floor over the State Dining Room

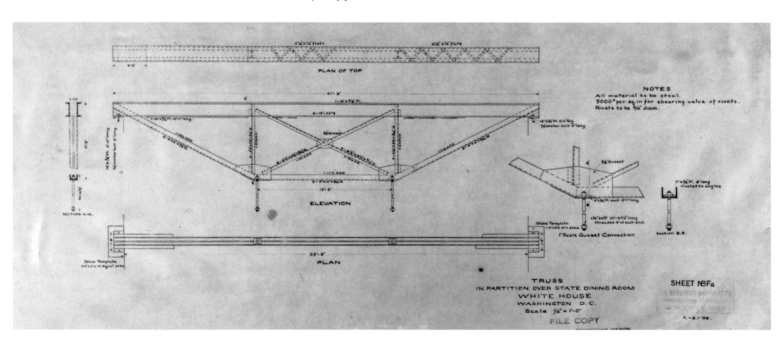

the long span of floors above the dining room. McKim insisted, however, that its removal was the only way to add the space he needed, so a dubious solution was found. The unwanted section of the bearing wall was torn out all the way from the state floor to the attic. A steel truss system, suspended from a pair of steel girders footed in the external stone wall on the west and

The architectural elements to be put in anew were made elsewhere and awaited installation in the fall. For every ornamental element McKim required a model in plaster, presented at his office in New York. To give some idea of how fast the project moved plasterers were already at work in late July. All steelwork was finished in early August. In that month excavations began

View during installation of the truss that was to cause serious structural problems a half-century later.

President Arthur's screen of colored glass has been removed in this view of the entrance hall in the early fall of 1902, and Hoban's columns of King of Prussia blue marble stand revealed as they were when the reconstructed White House was reopened in 1818. McKim would replace this light, arched screen with a column screen more monumental in scale.

179

Detail of the decorative plaster ceiling of the State Dining Room, 1902

Opposite:
Plasterers put finishing touches on the decorative ceiling of the redesigned family dining room on the state floor.

calmed the waters, aided by McKim's fairly easy access to Mrs. Roosevelt. The president was impatient with the controversies, so they rarely went to him. Edith Roosevelt can be considered the client.

Already in the summer of 1902 McKim had to confront the first lady's tastes in decorating. She and the president liked carved Victorian furniture, no matter how ugly McKim and Edith Wharton might think it. The White House held a treasure trove of pier mirrors, fancy tables and chairs, even statues. Though these things were hidden away in storage during construction, Mrs. Roosevelt had made mental notes about them. Her suggestions for using the furnishings horrified the architect. He wanted to sell all he could. When he sent the great gasoliers to auction he aroused not the ire of the Roosevelts but of members of Congress, who ordered them brought to the Capitol, where they can be seen today in various committee rooms. Still McKim fought his client, gently, to change her tendencies and allow the house to be furnished, he said, "for all the time." Many were the meetings, however, when he was received by the first lady amid fabric bolts, paint samples, and notes about how this or that might be.

Interior finishing began in October. Workmen from Herter Brothers and Leon Marcotte & Co. in New York installed paneling and silk on the walls. Both companies had made their reputations decades before furnishing houses built by H. H. Richardson, Richard Morris Hunt, and a younger McKim, Mead & White and their Victorian generation. Now, like architects, they specialized in modern historicism, rooms of the Louis XVI and Adam types, colonial American and Spanish Renaissance, and other affectations of the Beaux-Arts approach to design. Their work was superb, from the fine joinery to the surface application.

All the painted woodwork in the White House was sanded between paint layers, and the last coat was rubbed with pumice powder; the result was a porcelain-like surface. The oak parquet of the state rooms was lightly bleached and waxed, and the joliet stone floors of the entrance and transverse halls were scrubbed with sand and waxed. Upstairs the floors were of lightly var-

for the east wing, and not five feet below grade the shovels hit the footings of the original east wing built by Jefferson and Latrobe. These were exposed completely and in part incorporated into the new foundation. The walls of the temporary office rose faster. A photograph taken on August 7, 1902, shows the brick walls up, not yet stuccoed, and the roof two-thirds built.

Glenn Brown, secretary of the American Institute of Architects, was the architect on the job, and he pushed the work unceasingly toward the December deadline. His vigilant diplomacy kept McKim and Bingham apart—though Brown loathed Bingham—and also kept the president's representatives happy. Now and again a cost overrun threatened to halt the work, a panic nearly always sparked by Bingham. Brown

The new grand staircase, designed and relocated by McKim in 1902 to replace the 1869 grand stair. Heavy rolling gates of wrought iron could be drawn across the opening.

nished white maple. Pictorial East Room plaques were carved by a youthful Lee Lawrie, who would one day adorn the Nebraska state capitol for Bertram Goodhue. The cherubs and gardens on the White House plaques were not the subjects or forms that would make him famous, but they represent well one Beaux-Arts ideal in ornament.

McKim's rules of restoration were more sharply drawn at the conclusion of the work than they had been at the beginning, when he was careful not to bind himself too tightly to principles that might not work. He formally expressed three goals at the beginning: "to put the house in the condition originally planned but never fully carried out," "to make changes in such a manner that the house will never again have to be altered; that is to say, the work should represent the period to which the house belongs architecturally, and therefore be independent of changing fashion," and "to modernize the house in so far as the living rooms are concerned and provide all those conveniences which now are lacking." This was no more than proposal rhetoric, perhaps,

but McKim declined to edit it when the work was done.

Deadlines for the job were October 1 for the office and living quarters and December 1 for the rest, except for the new east social entrance, which was not scheduled to be complete before February. The office was ready exactly on time; the family's rooms a month and four days late. The Roosevelts prudently held back those invitations that would have launched the social season and finally issued them for a December 18 reception. The "east terrace," or east wing, was inaugurated for the New Year's Day reception of 1903. While there was a certain vacancy in the family's living area, for the budget had run out and Edith Roosevelt had cut costs in the private areas to complete the rest, the Roosevelts were delighted. The president pronounced as "yahoos" the few critics of the massive overhaul and looked the other way.

The White House was at once different and the same. Those who had watched the peeling away of the later additions during midsummer had reacted first with suspicion, then with dismay at

Plan of the state floor as remodeled by McKim, 1902. Note the relocated grand stair and the enlarged State Dining Room; these were the only significant alterations to the original plan. Red denotes walls that survived; blue shows walls McKim removed.

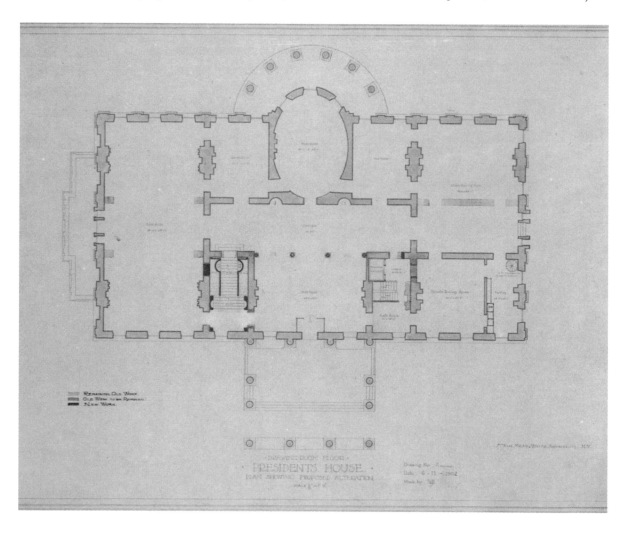

the loss of so much that was familiar, then with wonder over what emerged. McKim's process had been one of simplification. By the third week in August the return to an earlier sort of house was no longer an abstraction, but something one could see. The removal of the conservatories freed the rectangular central block and emphasized its stone embellishments as no one had seen them in nearly fifty years. Complaints were not voiced loudly. Much had been sacrificed, but much that had been lost earlier had been regained. American architectural taste, already responding to the colonial style, had before it a fine specimen freely called by that name. In the White House this new attitude had its first close association with historic restoration, however much or little purists in our era might think of McKims free interpretation of that word.

The exterior appearance of the McKim White House might be described as a fuller treatment of what had been completed when the north portico was finished in 1830, fuller in the sense that the grounds had been more effectively graded around the house to show the architecture. The effects of parapet walls and plantings had given

the house the effect of verticality, of rising from long horizontal lines. It seemed smaller, better proportioned, and almost understated in its serene whiteness, set on sprawling green lawns. A squarish entrance pavilion had been added to the east end of the east wing. This was a structure not unlike a neoclassical garden loggia with paired columns forming colonnades. The new temporary office building, on the west side, simpler and wholly different, stood appropriately apart from the west wing. Punctuated by rows of tall rectangular windows on the north and west, each crowned by panels with grilles, the modest public entrance faced Pennsylvania Avenue across the lawn, enriched by a shallow two-columned frontispiece.

The house in its simplicity was more effectively monumental than it had been. Yet this was not too pompous a monumentality for American democratic tastes. Many elements rendered it domestic in character, yet it was still formal, stately, and uniquely suited to its job. Most people, in recognizing it as colonial, felt that it was thus properly American. The use of painted stone made it seem sturdy and monolithic, with-

White House from the south, pencil sketch, Jules Guérin. Guérin, an advisor to many of the leading Beaux-Arts-era architects, lent his talent to McKim in depicting the renovated White House. This drawing illustrates McKim's "cup and saucer" analogy for the house and its restored image.

The newly renovated White House from Pennsylvania Avenue, circa 1909, with the fleeting image of Theodore Roosevelt

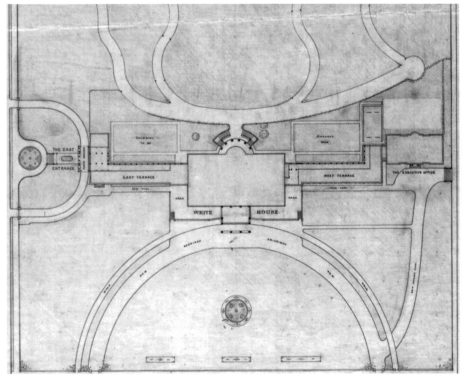

Detail of the White House
in a plan of the site after the
1902 renovation. (Compare to the
plan on page 166.)

out the richness of colored marbles and varied materials. To the more sophisticated eye it was Georgian and therefore Anglo-Saxon, like the blood of the founding fathers. (Feelings along this line ran deep in Theodore Roosevelt.) Over all, however, the great power of the revised White House was that it remained a familiar place.

Looking from the north the main difference between the house before and after was the aloofness of the central mansion from its wings and the new buildings on the ends. Before the removal of the Victorian conservatories, which had reached up into the second story level, the profile of the house simply stopped short on the east. Now the central mansion stood above everything else, its terraces sunk near grade, stretching low to the east and west, half-moon windows once again forming a balanced rhythm just above ground level. The south side seemed very different. Here the central facade with its rounded porch seemed to rest on a wide stone base formed by the wings and the exposed basement level. Flanking the south front, the wings

185

lormed U-shaped courts created on the left by the L-shaped 1818 stable wing and on the right by the east colonnade and entrance pavilion. Both courts were planted as small gardens.

Inside the mahogany and glass doors on the north the house was greatly changed, although the general layout was unaltered. For nearly seventy years the visitor entering on the north had not been able to see beyond the blue marble Ionic columns and glass screen—first of clear glass, then ground glass, and then, with Arthur, colored glass. Now the eye swept through a large white space, past a massive row of paired Doric columns, snowy white, and took in the transverse hall with its doors to the parlors. Hard stone floors, the stark cold neoclassicism of the architecture, and the shine of mirror and heavy bronze lanterns and torchères were more European than colonial American and far more splendid in tone than the old White House of wallpaper and jiggling plank floors had ever been.

In the three state parlors that opened from the transverse hall McKim attempted, in essence, to return the architecture to the Federal era—for which most of the original elements survived or could be guessed. In the great rooms at each end he merely used the existing White House as a

springboard for new design. The East Room, painted cream white, was to be the scene of brilliant receptions, while the State Dining Room, paneled in oak, stained and waxed, was for large seated dinners and seemed to enfold crowds within its mellowness. Both rooms were wood paneled and highly detailed, with carved Corinthian pilasters, medallions, garlands, and plaques; in the East Room, over the hall door, cherubs presented a draped plaque, which never received its cipher or coat of arms. For the East Room paneling McKim took for his model one of the rooms of the suite built for Louis XVI in the 1780s in the palace at Compiègne. Efforts to find McKim's historical source for the State Dining Room have yielded nothing specific beyond a general adherence to English tradition.

The three parlors—the Blue Room, flanked by the Green Room on the east and the Red Room on the west—were given their traditional colors, with white trim enamel on wainscoting and door and window facings and flat white on the decorated plaster cornices and ceilings. Traditionally the Blue Room had been the place where the president received ambassadors, and McKim made this the most formal room in the house. He covered the walls in dark blue corded silk with a Greek key border top and bottom. He hung silk

Entrance hall, 1902. McKim changed the character of this space with neoclassical detailing more suitable to a public building than a residence. The paired columns of plaster replaced the arcaded arrangement of single marble columns original to the house (see page 179). Fireplaces east and west were replaced by great built-in mirrors.

Opposite:
State Dining Room, 1902, with
rich oak paneling executed by
Herter Brothers of New York.
The silver-plated lighting fixtures
were by Edward Caldwell of New
York, and the furniture was made
by A. H. Davenport of Boston.
All of these elements survive in
the room today.

The rich white-enameled paneling
of the East Room was designed by
McKim and created by the
company of Attillio Piccirilli of
New York.

Overleaf:
East Room elevation, drawing by
McKim, Mead & White

Overleaf following:
The East Room after its
completion, 1902

of the same color, embroidered with stars, at the windows. Theodore Bingham's research had turned up the original bill for James Monroe's gilded French furniture, made in Paris in 1817 by Pierre Antoine Bellangé. Only a table remained in the White House, but furniture scholarship at the time readily supplied illustrations of the unmistakable style that had made Bellangé famous. It was assumed that the White House had the same style, so the furniture was copied on a larger scale by Leon Marcotte of New York, painted white, and placed around the Blue Room's oval walls.

In contrast to the icy formality and sparseness of the Blue Room were the Red and Green rooms. To these McKim had transferred from the State Dining Room two fine white marble mantels purchased by James Monroe in 1818 from British sources in Italy. He described them as "almost the only historic furnishings in the White House at the time when the restoration began." They remain in the two parlors today, resplendent with neoclassical figures supporting the shelf, their heads cushioned by curved marble pillows.

These and all the fireplaces in the house were wood burning. Only about half were left open. Roosevelt ordered several reopened, including the new one in the State Dining Room, even though dining room fireplaces are generally seldom used.

The wall covering in the Red Room was red velvet. The curtains matched, and the velvet contrasted with the white woodwork. Precisely the same effect was achieved with green in the Green Room. The two parlors were cozy, if dressy. Responding to the Roosevelts' affection for upholstery the Red Room was furnished in deeply tufted and fringed sofas and chairs that would have been at home in a parlor of 1885 or 1890. The Green Room would have merited Edith Wharton's approval, as it did McKim's. White-painted Adamesque chairs and sofas, produced by the A. H. Davenport Company, were covered in an Aubusson-like floral tapestry in soft rose and green. McKim had been shown an "old piece of Genoese velvet" at F. Schumacher & Co. in New York and used a reproduction of it on the walls and windows. The console table from

MᶜKIM, MEAD & WHITE ARCHITECTS
160 FIFTH AVENUE NEW YORK CITY

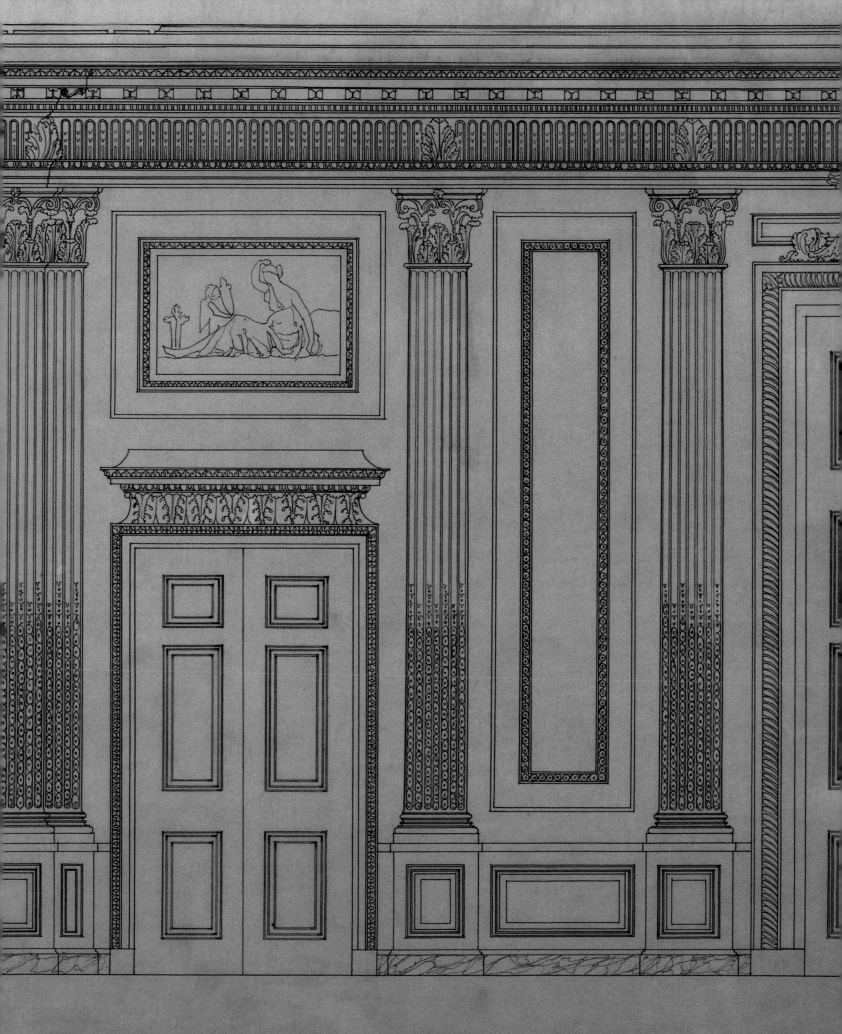

1/4 INCH SCALE DETAIL OF EAST ROOM
PRESIDENT'S · HOUSE
WASHINGTON · D · C ·

The Blue Room,
from the painting by
Charles Bittinger, 1903

The Green Room, 1902

The Red Room, 1902.
The crimson-colored furniture,
stuffed and buttoned, was not the
preference of McKim but that of
his presidential client.
Here, Edith Roosevelt displayed
her collection of dolls.

Monroe's Bellangé furniture was used here, as was one of Andrew Jackson's three round mahogany tables from the East Room.

The Red Room and the Green Room were both jeweled with light fixtures from the Edward F. Caldwell Company in New York; about these the architects could not say enough in praise. The work of some 2,000 craftsmen, Caldwell's production was enormous and of unequaled importance. It was one of the companies McKim insisted on using. Most of the fixtures bought there for the White House were chandeliers and wall brackets, all gold-plated bronze or, in the case of the State Dining Room, silver-plated bronze. These were cast from historic French or English fixtures, machined to perfection of definition, and at last given their surface treatment and decorated with glass. The surviving fixtures still at the White House probably comprise the finest single collection anywhere of works by Caldwell's company, which opened about 1900 and closed bankrupt early in the Great Depression of the 1930s.

The furniture was almost certainly selected with the help of McKim's friend and former employee Francis Bacon, who worked for the Davenport Company. Bacon, an architect, had taken an interest in interior design in the late 1890s as an adjunct to Beaux-Arts architecture. He was an artist and scholar of many parts, whose interests ranged from historic architecture and archaeology to the process of manufacturing quality woodwork products for houses, public buildings, and churches. Davenport had emerged late in the 1890s as the leading producer of fine furniture, which could be selected from stock, selected from a custom line, or specially designed. The Margaret Woodbury Strong Museum in Rochester houses the manuscript collections of the Davenport Company. Scores of scrapbooks of drawings and photographs chronicle years of distinguished furniture production. In the Depression years the company ultimately turned entirely to the manufacture of church fixtures in an attempt to rescue a declining luxury market.

At the White House Davenport enjoyed its high noon. Most of the furniture came from that single source, except for a small number of antiques; a scattering of mahogany cabinets, consoles, and tables by Retting and Sweet of Grand Rapids; and of course the East Room's grand piano from Steinway; Marcotte made the Blue Room's reproduction Empire suite and the French-style benches in the East Room. Davenport made the monumental eagle-supported marble-top tables in the State Dining Room and the two dining room tables – the Roosevelts could never agree on square or round so they had both. The dining room furniture is somewhat characteristic of the rest, heavy in its enlargement on historical models and made of very fine wood, with a rubbed shellac finish and rich brass fixtures.

In plan the second floor stretches, it seems, forever. Rooms of many sizes fall off the triple-divided transverse corridor that runs end to end, east to west. Here McKim faced the problem of introducing bathrooms and closets. He decided to save all the rooms rather than sacrifice a few and to add bathrooms by partitioning off the corners or ends of rooms. As is seen on the accompanying plan the result, though nearly a century old, is an arrangement predictable even today in adapting an old house to modern comforts.

Bathrooms, more numerous here than in most houses of the time, were added as necessities, not for idle luxury. Seven replaced the three that were on the second floor when the work began. Four bathrooms were partitioned off the ends of the four corner dressing rooms, which were sometimes also used as bedrooms. Elsewhere bathrooms were simply crowded in. The president's bathroom opened two ways, one off his and Mrs. Roosevelt's dressing room and the other directly off the west sitting hall, showing the still casual attitude toward privacy in these gleaming white-tile, nickel-plate, and porcelain conveniences. The bathrooms usually threw the rooms off balance, leaving the fireplaces pressed close against a new wall on one side and open as always on the other. Mrs. Roosevelt so disliked this asymmetry that she deleted closets from the plans for most of the rooms, preferring to resurrect the wardrobes rather than suffer the addition of

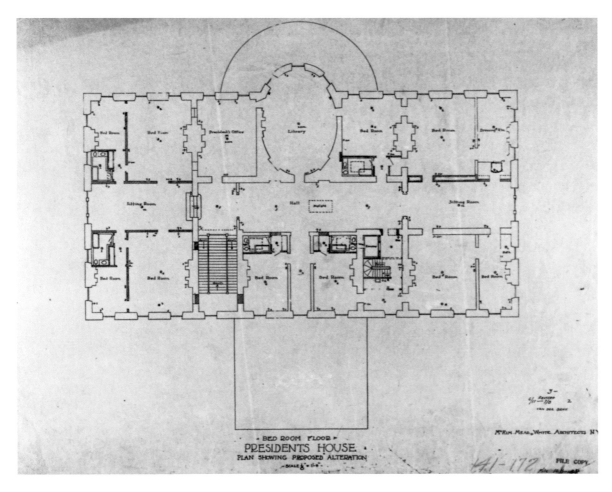

· BED ROOM FLOOR ·
PRESIDENTS HOUSE ·
PLAN SHOWING PROPOSED ALTERATION
· SCALE ⅛" = 1'-0" ·

Plan of the renovated second floor, showing the addition of bathrooms and the extension of the family quarters into the former office area on the east

(Top)The central corridor upstairs and (bottom) the president's study after the 1902 renovation. The study serves today as the president's office in the residence.

more partitions.

The family's library, or sitting room, remained the oval room upstairs, and the Roosevelts sometimes used it, but like most White House families to come they preferred the sitting area in the west hall, much more desirable after the relocation of the grand stair in 1902. Roosevelt's office was a square room just east of the oval room. This had been the Cabinet room since Andrew Johnson's time, and for Roosevelt it was in fact the office, not the study it would become in succeeding administrations. His space in the west wing was called the president's room, and he visited it and met in it informally, but his office remained in the White House. There he saw his most important callers, signed all important bills, and met with his secretary and stenographer. What might be called work sessions with his staff or group appointments were held in the temporary office building. This arrangement the president rigidly followed.

A general housecleaning sent most of the original family quarters furniture to auction. New furniture was introduced with great economy, nearly all from Davenport's line of Colonial Re-

vival bureaus, chairs, and tables. What remained of the White House inventory were the furnishings Edith Roosevelt would not allow sold. Notable among these were the Lincoln bed and other carved rococo revival pieces in rosewood that went with it. McKim had been so dismayed to see these used again that he made certain most of what else was left had no chance for rescue. The Lincoln bed was put in the president's bedroom, its gilded corona restored and draped; and generations to come would cherish it as the bed Lincoln slept in while president, although there is no record that he ever did. His wife had bought it, to his chagrin, in 1861; his son Willie died in it in 1862, and he was embalmed at its foot on an undertaker's slanted cooling board in 1865. Mrs. Roosevelt also brought back a marble-top parlor table carved with storks that is used in the Lincoln room today.

Except for the Lincoln bed, the other beds upstairs had heretofore been brass or painted iron relics of a craze for sanitation that had begun in the 1870s. Davenport replaced these with colonial-style beds. A donor produced a large high-post bed said to have been purchased from

Opposite:

Detail, *Reception at the White House,* **oil on canvas,**

William Baxter Closson, 1908

Original drawing for an eagle table for the State Dining Room, A. H. Davenport, Boston

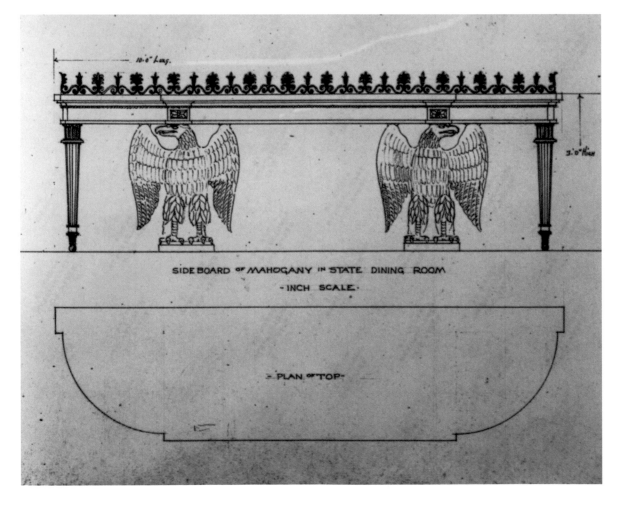

SIDEBOARD OF MAHOGANY IN STATE DINING ROOM

- INCH SCALE -

PLAN OF TOP

Andrew Jackson's heirs and to have belonged to Jackson. This was never documented, and while at first glance the bed, now in the Queen's bedroom, looks like a Davenport Colonial Revival confection, it seems on inspection that it might be an authentic 1830s bed. Roosevelt may have revived it through added carving and a replacement of some parts. In any case the bed was placed in the room that had been the president's office before the remodeling. In 1952 it was to be moved across the hall to the room it occupies today. The Lincoln bed replaced it in the former office, creating the Lincoln bedroom.

The interiors of the two wings were finished in plain neoclassical design, all cream color to white, with simple detailing that emphasized the spaces through light and shadow. Compared with the wings today these interiors were uncomplicated indeed. Visitors were enveloped upon entering the west wing by the confining

Line at a New Year's Day reception, circa 1905. The north door was still the entrance for this largest of the annual public receptions, which was held at the White House until 1932.

character of the entrance room. This chamber was just beyond a wall from the secretary's office and not more than fifteen feet from the president's room. Callers sat here on chairs and sofas, awaiting acceptance or rejection by the appointments secretary. A portion of the nonbusiness or citizen callers were received for a friendly handshake practically every day, during the late morning or early afternoon.

The east wing, on the other hand, was, in the warm months, simply an open porch facing east,

with the re-created Jefferson colonnade connecting it to the house. It seemed the barest, thinnest of appendages, bright with natural light and white and pristine in the fastidiousness of its Beaux-Arts neoclassical design. During the winter, window sash—like multipaned storm windows—fitted between the columns on the east and along the Jefferson colonnade, protecting the passage through which guests entered the White House. On the south, through the columns, was a garden with boxwood and grass. The north side was a long, narrow coatroom with racks and shelving. It was known as the "hat box" in memory of the happily obsolete custom of stacking boxes along the walls of the entrance hall of the house to receive hats, shawls, gloves, and scarves.

In the autumn the White House was reoccupied and a sweeping program of change applied to all its social, business, and domestic forms. Under the direction of Roosevelt's astute secretary, George B. Cortelyou, memorandum followed memorandum to various groups of staff, officials, and even the press. Printed rule books followed. Reading over these small books today, one can see the secretary meant business. In White House rules there was no gray area.

Cortelyou was a man born for the job. He joined Grover Cleveland's office staff as an assistant. He was secretary to the president under McKinley and the victor in a palace battle with the politically minded John Addison Porter, who had helped put the Ohioan in the White House. Cortelyou had held the wounded McKinley in his arms and been at his side when he died. Roosevelt, who appreciated careful management of details but was not interested in doing it himself, quickly recognized the qualities of Cortelyou and kept him on as secretary. This made Cortelyou the second most important man in Washington in terms of getting things done, even above the speaker of the House of Representatives and the vice president. His was a quiet power never symbolized in ceremony but well-known in the political community. His bow-ended office was on a line with the front door of the west wing, and architecturally it made a statement in the domain of the executive office.

The revisions in White House forms included

the reception of foreign diplomats, the march to dinner, the manner of organizing a state dinner, dress for office clerks, the effective disposal of waste office paper, and even the rules for riding horseback with the president. It is tempting to think that these new procedures and revisions of old traditions influenced McKim's decisions on the White House. McKim and Cortelyou did become friends, and Cortelyou came to McKim's defense against Colonel Bingham, whom the secretary thought insolent. But there is no reason to think that Cortelyou's programs were formulated before McKim's renovation and every reason to believe that they were not. Cortelyou had his say with McKim, for he was in a position to be helpful, but the basic genius of the White House transformation was McKim's.

The remodeling of the White House imposed a new life on its occupants. McKim had peeled his subject back to its essentials and molded it anew. A sharp, crisp image against the sky, a Georgian mansion of stone unique in its painted whiteness, the house seemed to be at last in architectural focus. Yet the main thing in 1902 was that it was the president's house, steeped in a century of tradition and now edited structurally to a new clarity of image and high level of efficient function that McKim believed would serve for a hundred years more. His restoration, for all its affronts to preservation, had preserved the White House as the home of the president. Casting aside the vast proposed expansions that had arisen from the engineers' narrow pragmatism, he had re-created the enduring symbol of the presidency.

The White House inevitably took on a more widespread and powerful meaning for the American people. Future alterations would be shaped largely by the McKim image. Patterns of use in the house had been established permanently, if perhaps with more flexibility than before. For all the awkward moments in the first events in this new house of stalled elevators and dimming lights, people marveled at the space gained, the convenience, and the elegance of the rooms that shimmered in the soft electric light. The president seemed somehow better sheltered than ever before.

If the house had become timeless, it yet remained subject to the everyday personal prerogative of the president. Roosevelt, for example, observed with increasing distaste the stone lions carved on the new stone mantel in the State Dining Room. He finally ordered them recarved into American buffaloes, just before the end of his administration. Presidents were certain to live here as they pleased, in spite of McKim's stringent standards of taste. Yet few adaptations of historic American buildings have been more successful than this. McKim grasped the real character of the old house and understood how far he could go in solving its problems without ruining either the building itself or, more significantly, the idea of the building. The White House he turned over to Theodore Roosevelt at Christmas in 1902 looked much like the White House we know today, even though hardly a brick or timber, plaster ornament or nail McKim put there survives.

Washington, the Beautiful Capital of the Nation, compiled and copyrighted by William Olsen, 1921

6

PRESIDENTS AND ARCHITECTS

T he architecture of the White House proper remained essentially unchanged for forty-five years after McKim's return to New York in December 1902. Theodore Roosevelt was so pleased with the restoration that he charged the American Institute of Architects with the "duty of preserving a 'perpetual eye of guardianship' over the White House to see that it is kept unchanged and unmarred from this time on." His successor, William Howard Taft, was even warmer in his feeling toward the institute, and as the McMillan plan got under way at last he approved L'Enfant's reburial on the hilltop near Arlington House, overlooking the city he had planned. A box of mere discolored earth was transported with military honors from the site near a Maryland farmhouse where he had been buried nearly a century before. Now raised from obscurity, L'Enfant was established as the spiritual link between a youthful, raw America and the seasoned grandeur of seventeenth- and eighteenth-century Europe. He became the justification and personification of the remaking of Washington along Old World lines.

Although the historic White House remained unaltered for many years, its wings, and particularly the west wing's "temporary" office ap-

William Howard Taft, president from 1909 to 1913. Taft cherished the historic White House but insisted upon expanded work spaces. Under him the west wing became permanent, and the first Oval Office was built.

pendage, underwent perpetual change. Taft shuddered at the thought of having to do business in the temporary building. On the day of his inauguration, March 4, 1909, Congress appropriated $40,000 with virtually no restrictions for the new president to enlarge and make permanent the executive office building completed less than seven years before.

Taft ordered a southward extension four-fifths the size of the existing structure. A rough sketch

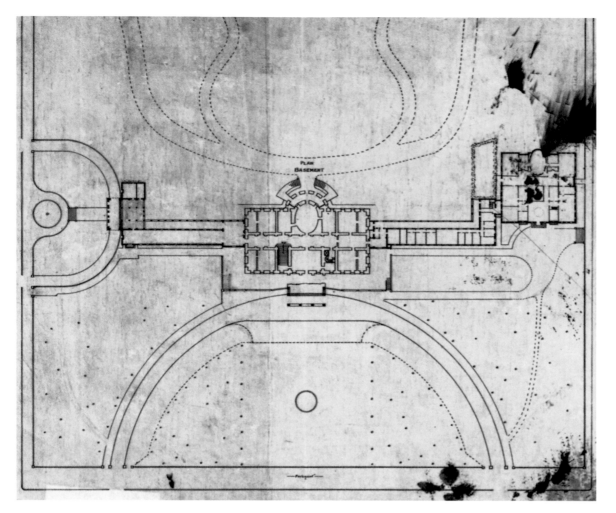

Ground floor plan of the White House and both wings, including the office building changes made for President Taft. Visible are the corridors of communication between the house and the offices, on the right, and the social entrance, on the left. The outdoor area marked just east of the executive office building was a drying yard for the adjacent laundry.

was provided to two Washington architects, who were to compete for the job at $250 each. Though an ailing McKim had advised against this approach, Taft believed the best results would come from competition. Entries were received on April 29, 1909, at the Public Buildings Commission headquarters in the Lemon Building, a four-story structure that would be demolished eighty years later to make way for the national headquarters of the American Institute of Architects, behind the Octagon on New York Avenue. Nathan C. Wyeth, architect of the Sullivanesque fourth floor addition to the Lemon Building, was the winner.

Work commenced at once. It is almost certain, though not firmly documented, that Wyeth followed the general plan presented to him from the president's office and presumably executed according to Taft's wishes. The project created what we know as the west wing. No longer was the office building to be a staff workplace; it was now to be the president's office. Every convenience was called for, not the least a central air-cooling system — fans blowing over ice bins in the

attic — which never really worked.

The simple overall plan called for a long transverse hall along the south side of the existing building, with new rooms built on the south. Of most interest in this now-vanished addition was the removal of the president's secretary from the main axis of the building and the placement in that premier position of a new office for the president.

Taking his cue from the Blue Room, Wyeth found an immediate identity for the president's office by making it oval. The Oval Office was therefore born in the expansion of 1909. It is all that remains of the interior of the enlarged office building, and while it has been relocated to its present site next to the Rose Garden — southeast of where it first was — it has otherwise remained about the same. Taft probably started work in the Oval Office in October 1909, and he used it every day, surrounded by a staff twice as large as Roosevelt's.

The architecture of the room was Colonial Revival, perhaps technically Federal Revival as well. Three tall south-looking windows stood to

Expansion of the executive office by the architect Nathan C. Wyeth for President Taft in 1909. Note, in the skeleton of the addition, the framework for the Oval Office, first built at this time. (Opposite) The plan shows the way in which the office building was enlarged to the south, with a new transverse corridor dividing the presidential quarters from the general staff and reception areas.

Postcard view of the Oval Office, circa 1909. The office is as originally completed, decorated with green burlap and ivory-painted woodwork.

The President's Office, White House, Washington, D. C.

61488Ⓖ

Edith Roosevelt's "colonial garden," designed by her and the White House gardener Henry Pfister, first planted in 1902. Filled with "old-fashioned" flowers in boxwood-lined beds, the garden existed for twelve years, until replaced in 1913 by the Rose Garden.

the rear of the president's desk, and he faced a fireplace across the long room. Broad, simple wood trim, plainer than that in the house, formed a vertical repeat in windows and doors, with the banding of wainscoting and bookcases. The floor was a parquet of Philippine mahogany and oak, like a checkerboard, with a border that showed around the edges of a broadloom rug. Seen in contrast to white woodwork, the olive drab color scheme dominated everything from the Tapestrolea, or burlap wallcovering, to the silk velvet curtains. The furniture was covered in caribou hide rubbed with red dye.

Although Taft was more than willing to overlook tradition and work in the new Oval Office instead of in the White House, the magnitude of some events gave him pause. He is believed never to have signed bills into law in this office, nor would he use the room to sign treaties or meet important guests where ceremony was involved.

Opposite top:
The Rose Garden, as planted in 1913 according to Ellen Axson Wilson's modifications of plans by George Burnap. A long, hedge-bordered "president's walk" was built to the executive office, along the Jefferson colonnade. Mrs. Wilson was a painter, and the trelliage, as well as being a background for the statue of Pan, was to serve as a place to hang her pictures during garden parties.

Opposite bottom:
George Burnap's 1913 sketch plan for the Rose Garden, including his notes

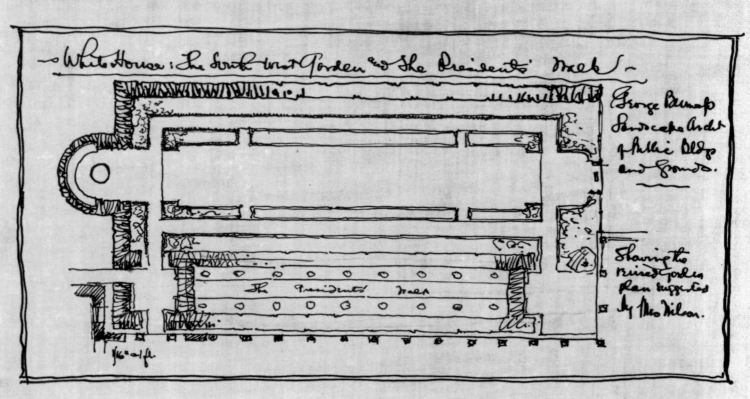

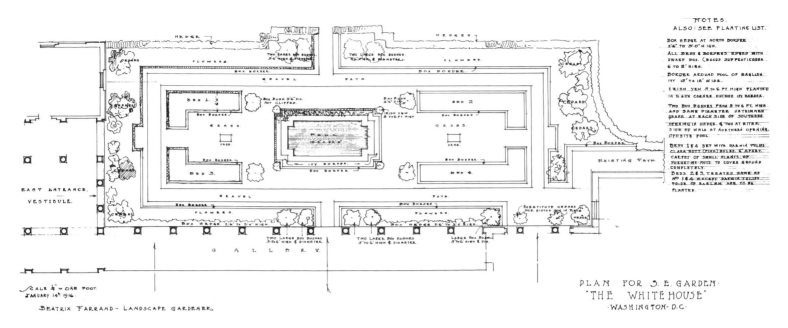

PLAN FOR S.E. GARDEN
"THE WHITE HOUSE"
WASHINGTON·D·C·

SCALE ⅛" = ONE FOOT.
JANUARY 14ᵗʰ 1916.

BEATRIX FARRAND - LANDSCAPE GARDENER.

For these occasions he always retreated to his study upstairs in the White House proper. No official ceremonies were to take place in the west wing until after World War I.

The east wing stood unchanged for nearly forty years, although some adjustments were made. The inconvenience of putting up and taking down the glass storm windows on the south was eventually remedied by their permanent installation. After some complaints about using the "back door," guests began to enjoy the east entrance. About five hundred at a time could stand in the colonnade and under the porte-cochère along the east driveway. A complex system of numbered cards and electric signal lights kept the carriages moving to deposit or load passengers. A vehicle was allowed to wait for three minutes and then dispatched to the end of the line.

Guests arrived for large receptions in various ways, some in their own equipages, others in fine rented coaches, while still others walked, galoshes over polished shoes, the women with dress trains over their arms, from the Pennsylvania Avenue streetcar stop. Almost any mode was acceptable in those days, when Washington had few pretenses to being a city. All but guests of honor, ambassadors, and members of the Cabinet registered at the east entrance desk, checked coats and hats, and moved on through the vaulted

Project for the east garden by Beatrix Farrand, 1913. Although it was under way, the east garden was not completed when Mrs. Wilson died in the summer of 1914.

basement corridor to climb the stairs to the state floor. Once there they were usually lined up to go through a Blue Room receiving line. As they waited, the president and the house party entered on the grand stair to a rousing "Hail to the Chief" and took their places in the Blue Room to shake hundreds of hands. Special guests were driven to the south portico, where they entered the basement through the diplomatic reception room. They were directed to the elevator to the family quarters, and from there they descended with the presidential party in the grand march down the stair.

Automobiles, which became increasingly evident under Taft, altered the procedures very little.

The long line at the east entrance included both cars and carriages. Flat tires, engine odors, and other new offenses were thereby added to the more familiar ones of horses. Car drivers were more cautious than coachmen, who sometimes got drunk in the boredom of waiting for their passengers and were taken to jail. President Taft bought an automobile, a great White Steamer, as soon as his administration got under way. With others who enjoyed the new invention he tried to make records on the Speedway, the paved road that rounded the north end of the Tidal Basin. Through the influence of his wife, Helen, this area would, in 1911, be planted with cherry trees, the gift of the mayor of Tokyo.

President Wilson and his second wife, Edith Bolling Wilson, whom he married in 1915. They were photographed by an early color process in the east garden, after its completion and some maturation of the plantings, probably in the late spring of 1916.

Opposite:

In the east garden, looking west, circa 1925. A view of this garden was the first "picture" presented to the White House guest, and though the garden is different today it remains the scene through the glazed colonnade of the east entrance. Following Beatrix Farrand's original scheme, the form was defined by grass and a skeleton of boxwood and the beds and borders were lavishly planted in flowers. The stone garden stools were designed by Farrand for Ellen Wilson.

The wings were enhanced in 1913 by the addition of gardens planted by Ellen Axson Wilson, Woodrow Wilson's first wife. These were different from what had been there before. On the east the court was landscaped with evergreens. Edith Roosevelt had ordered what she called a "colonial garden" planted on the west, a fancy-patterned parterre filled with roses and old-fashioned flowers she believed appropriate to the historic house. Mrs. Wilson invited Beatrix Farrand and George Burnap to make plans. The two celebrated landscape designers were acquaintances of hers, and she was an avid gardener.

In their entirety Farrand's plan for the east garden and Burnap's for the west proved too expensive, but they were carried out in part. The gardens were trim and green, with more of an architectural character than had existed before. On the east a lawn framed by undulating lines of boxwood had at its center a rectangular lily pond. The southwest garden, as the other was called, was more intricate in its design of paths and lines of shrubbery and trees. A "president's walk" paralleled the colonnade to the west wing. Pan played his pipes, a statue in white marble, at the end of a long boxwood vista. Behind him a wall of lattice formed a background, as well as an outdoor picture gallery wall, where Mrs. Wilson intended to hang her paintings to show at garden parties.

In 1923 the Army engineers found trouble in the roof structure of the White House. This discovery came not long after Calvin Coolidge entered office on the death of Warren G. Harding. A presentation was made to Coolidge that included an elaborate description of how poor the structural work had been in the renovations twenty-one years before. The truss that had allowed McKim to expand the State Dining Room was fast failing, the supports of the principal beam crumbling under the great weight. Old hand-hewn timbers to which tie rods were attached in the attic were found to be splintering. It would take half a million dollars to remedy the situation with a new roof structure of steel. "If it is as bad as you say," Coolidge asked, "why doesn't it fall down?"

The project got nowhere until 1925, when, after futile efforts at repair, it became obvious that the cracks in the second floor walls were not going away. Coolidge pressed for every other possible alternative to abandoning the house for a major overhaul. At last, in March 1927, he moved, to 15 Dupont Circle, the marble-and-tile palazzo McKim, Mead & White brought to completion for Mrs. Robert W. Patterson during McKim's White House work. It still stands today as the home of the Washington Club. The contents of the upper floors of the White House, including guest rooms the first Mrs. Wilson had

Construction under way for the new third floor, seen from the east wing in the summer of 1927

added in the attic, were stored in the state rooms, in the basements of the wings, and in the coatroom.

A temporary wooden roof was built on framework covering the house. By the first of April the old roof and all of Hoban's timber structure of 1817 were torn away. U. S. Grant III, the Army Corps of Engineers officer in charge of public buildings, had combined engineering drawings made in 1923 and 1925 with new ones of his own. For architectural advice he called in William Adams Delano of New York, a principal in the fashionable firm Adams & Delano, best known for Manhattan town houses and apartments and fine suburban homes in traditional styles. Delano was the architect on Grace Coolidge's advisory committee on the decoration of the White House rooms. This was an ad hoc group that had come into being in response to Mrs. Coolidge's wish to make the house look patriotically "colonial," like the historic rooms in the new American Wing of the Metropolitan Museum of Art in New York.

The president disliked the snobbish and troublesome advisory committee enough to ban it from the White House. But Billy Delano, as he was known, was an entirely agreeable man, and Grant, who never doubted for one minute that he was the social equal and political better of Delano and the committee, felt comfortable calling in that direction for help. There were not so many small problems to solve as one great one. Grant felt at home with the structural details, and the interior finish was a matter of repeating what was there; it was the roof that concerned him. Mrs. Coolidge had made the new attic the end-all solution to the problems of convenience inherent in living on the second floor. The program called for guest rooms, ironing rooms, cedar closets, servants' rooms and a sleeping porch, a small greenhouse, and a special room Mrs. Coolidge wanted, a "sun parlor." The shallow, slanting ceilings were to go, for the attic's rooms had never been comfortable to stand in.

Many drawings were made in determining the new shape of the roof. Colonel Grant and Billy Delano stood on Sixteenth Street and studied their problem, looking at the north facade dead-on. The south view presented no special problem, because the house stood on an elevation sufficient to shrink even a steep roof into visual insignificance. On the north, however, the roof loomed. The original stone balustrade would not do enough to screen the expanded scale.

Hoban's 1793 drawing, unearthed at the Mary-

land Historical Society, had been published in the historical writings of Fiske Kimball, the scholar who took an interest in the architecture of the White House and wrote on the subject around the time of World War I. Because it was the earliest known representation of the White

Opposite:
Aerial views of the White House, circa 1927. (Above) The roof before and (below) the heightened roofline after the rebuilding and enlargement of the old attic into a third floor

Calvin Coolidge, president from 1923 to 1929. Cramped quarters and a crumbling roof structure led to the demolition of the attic under Coolidge in 1927 and its replacement with a third floor of steel and concrete.

Grace Coolidge began what might be called the "antiques movement" at the White House when she decided to furnish some rooms with antiques to evoke American history. During the Coolidge administration the remodeled attic gained several guest rooms, which Mrs. Coolidge furnished in "colonial" style.

House, this north elevation was then believed to be the actual competition drawing, both because it looked like the house as built and because it had been found among some of the competition drawings. On this basis Kimball identified Hoban's source as Plate 53 from James Gibbs's *Book of Architecture*, published in London in 1728, being unaware of the earlier three-story project for the house that had been abandoned in the fall of 1793. The roofline shown in the Hoban elevation, representing the house as built, is quite lofty but pitched toward its long ridge in a way that makes it vanish except when seen from a distance.

The result of the Coolidge roof project was a new third floor with guest and service rooms. Little else can be said for the change. To accommodate the required new space the pitch of the roof was finally increased sharply, ending in a central platform some thirty feet square, which

reduced the roof's height somewhat. But try as they did to minimize the roof, Grant and Delano ended up putting a clumsy lid on the venerable stone edifice. There were other negatives, the worst of them entirely unseen – the structural engineering, the special expertise of Grant. The third floor was rebuilt as a skeleton of steel, with concrete-block infill, resting directly on both the masonry shell of the building and the bearing walls within. The second floor trusswork that had allowed McKim to enlarge the State Dining Room was supported in part by being suspended from the new structure overhead. This assignment of tremendous weight started a ruinous process that would climax in the reconstruction of the White House by President Harry S. Truman between 1948 and 1952.

Coolidge's administration, from 1923 to 1929, was the last of what might be termed the old-style presidencies. Taft's modernization of the

Rooms built in the attic of the north portico and intended for storage

office served Woodrow Wilson, Warren G. Harding, and Coolidge. A certain almost quaint personal quirkiness lent a special character to each of these presidential generations that today would likely be concealed in the vastly larger scale of the office operation. Wilson's staff performed its duties while Wilson typed his own letters, either in the Oval Office or in his study in the house. Harding, surrounded by people all the time, allowed a level of public access to himself heretofore unknown under any president. Coolidge would not talk business on the telephone, thinking it undignified for the presidency. His schedule was leisurely. The general office staff wore morning suits, changing to business suits to go outside the White House compound. Few women served in the west wing, although there had been women on the president's office payroll fairly continuously since Benjamin Harrison employed the first in 1889. In its tone the west wing

One of the new third floor bathrooms

Central hallway of the new third floor as completed in 1927 and before the furniture was moved in

The "Lincoln study," upstairs in the White House, so designated by President Herbert Hoover and reserved for his personal use. The room had been Lincoln's office and cabinet room and is today the Lincoln bedroom.

was quiet and soft-spoken. Breezes swept through its open windows into rooms where forty employees attended to their tasks, some having served there since the time of President Grant.

The tempo hastened markedly with the appearance of Herbert Hoover in 1929. He was not in office a month before he had increased his staff by half and put offices in the unused west wing attic and in the basement. Even so, the space was inadequate. U. S. Grant III began making plans for rearranging partitions according to the president's wishes. As quickly as he had abolished morning suits and introduced business suits for his employees, Hoover erased other work traditions. Clerks' rooms were subdivided into three executive offices with anterooms for the president's three secretaries. Private waiting rooms for senators and congressmen were abolished. Everyone now used the same lobby, which was extended into the private transverse hall Taft had added, making the waiting room T-shaped, with easy communication between the president and his staff. Guard stations were placed at the two entrances to the Oval Office.

Work on the west wing continued through the summer of 1929, with official business conducted there throughout. Hoover met many ap-

Opposite:

Clerks' room in the west wing, circa 1913. By Hoover's time this space had not changed, even though the staff had nearly doubled to some forty people.

pointments in a single morning and often used the sitting rooms at the White House for these. Five minutes was ample time for most meetings with staff members. Such sessions might follow in staccato sequence for several hours, the president opening all discussions. The last work of remodeling was on the unused basement. It was subdivided to make new offices, with windows cut into an areaway on the west side, abutting West Executive Avenue.

The year 1929 came to a grim end after the stock market crash in October. On Christmas Eve the executive office caught fire. Watching the blaze with his dinner guests on the roof of the west wing, the president shouted orders to rescue important papers. To preserve Hoover's heavy desk with its locked drawers, firemen soaked the rug on the floor and threw it over the desk. Film footage shows the great flurry that accompanied the fire fighting and the papers being dumped from the windows; hoses lay spaghetti-like over the ground. On Christmas morning the gutted wing was an ice palace created by freezing temperatures the night before. Colonel Grant studied the ruin and pronounced it not only stable, but reparable.

For a while the prevailing idea was to demolish the west wing and convert the flamboyant old

Opposite:
President Franklin D. Roosevelt's
swimming pool, designed by
Lorenzo S. Winslow with
Douglas H. Gillette as engineer,
and completed in 1933.

State, War, and Navy Building entirely to executive functions. This made sense, but the great granite pile projected the wrong image and, though nearby, was not a part of the White House. Hoover believed it important to remain where he was. The executive office was rebuilt within the existing walls, beneath a new roof. It was put back more or less as Hoover had remodeled it before, with all the work of a more permanent character than had been possible in the hasty remodeling several months earlier. Some discussion was held about expanding the office, but the country's sinking economy made it probable the president would have difficulty getting the necessary appropriation for more than a rebuilding. There were small improvements: an extra toilet room, a finer woodwork finish in the entrance, restrained Georgian embellishments of the woodwork in the rebuilt Oval Office. The main change was the installation of a central air-conditioning system by the Carrier Engineering Company. This system was effective. The need for more space, however, remained.

The Jefferson west wing—the "west terrace"—had been made by McKim into servants' quarters and a laundry. In the eternal quest for space, this range of rooms was too conveniently located to be so humbly used. Hoover was the first to invade it by putting several offices in the laundry space, the end nearest the executive building. That was in 1931. Two years later, at the beginning of the administration of Franklin D. Roosevelt, a national campaign was under way to raise money from schoolchildren to build a swimming pool for the new president. Roosevelt's suffering from polio was eased by exercise

Franklin D. Roosevelt, president
from 1933 to 1945. Amateur
architect and lover of old houses,
FDR was fascinated with
improving the White House.
Among his many projects was the
building of the east wing as it
stands today.

218

NEW CRYSTAL LIGHTING FIXTURES
WITH HIDDEN REFLECTORS
CURTAINS & VENETIAN BLINDS
BOOK CASES IN NICHES
NO CURTAINS ON WEST WALL BUT FOUR ARCHES
TO BE TREATED WITH FELT COVERED WITH FABRIC
The Cabinet Room

Eric Gugler's sketch for the Cabinet Room

in a pool, and the *New York Daily News* sponsored the fund-raising program as a human-interest promotion in his honor. The idea caught on quickly. Money poured in. The president asked Colonel Grant for designs and rejected several projects he considered excessive—one because it interfered with his vision to expand the executive office. The final decision, to put the pool in the west wing, removed the servants' quarters, the last domestic space along the colonnade.

The architect of the pool was Lorenzo S. Winslow, who served on Grant's staff as a civilian architect. Because the autocratic Grant was otherwise occupied, he had Winslow deal directly with the president, apparently unaware that Roosevelt took personal delight in building and remodeling. So pleased was Roosevelt with the pool design that he eventually made Winslow the White House architect. The relationship was to be closer than that of Washington and Hoban, if less personal than that of Jefferson and Latrobe, but it should be considered analogous to both. Winslow met with the president several times a week, early in the morning, often in the president's bedroom over breakfast. They sketched and planned. First it was the pool, next the office, then the east wing and a hundred small projects, such as the library they built on the ground floor and the chimney opened up in the diplomatic reception room to end the embarrassment of holding the fireside chats beside a fake fireplace.

For the final design of the pool Winslow worked closely with Major Douglas H. Gillette, who devised an elaborate system for steam heating the water for winter use and worked out details for indirect lighting. The pool and two dressing rooms occupied the portion of the west wing closest to the house. Winslow cut french doors beneath the existing lunettes facing out on the colonnade, gracing the long, narrow swimming pool room with an arcade on one side. The ceiling was arched to give it the impression of greater height; the rectangular pool took up the greater part of the floor. It was an elegant treatment of a small space, showing Winslow at his best.

As a young man Winslow had traveled extensively, studying architecture in Europe. For a while he was enrolled in the Ecole des Beaux-Arts in Paris, where, he later remembered, his watercolor instructor was Libby Custer, widow of George Armstrong Custer. His job with the Public Buildings Commission was enviable in Depression times, even if it was seldom challenging; it did, however, carry with it the tension of having to keep the president amused. The opportunity at the White House was to change Winslow's life. He would rebuild the White House fifteen years later, giving us the structure we know today.

Roosevelt was president for twelve years, and he practically always had a building project in mind, on paper, or under way. Bethesda Naval Hospital displays the linen napkin on which he sketched his idea for the hospital building that stands today, its tower inspired by Bertram Goodhue's Nebraska "skyscraper" capitol, which Roosevelt admired. During the winter of 1934 he summoned Winslow with a new scheme. There was no longer the need to go through Colonel Grant. Responsibility for federal buildings in the capital had been transferred from the Army Corps of Engineers to the National Park Service. Winslow found the president studying a set of sketches he had made for a new executive office, where the old one now stood. Within a short time Winslow produced a formal project, but for an addition, not for the new building that Roosevelt apparently wanted. The architect was clever enough, though, to encourage what he called "the active advice and interest of the President in all the various details." The president penciled the plan avidly and decided that an addition was indeed a good idea.

To carry out this expansion proved difficult. First, Congress opposed it at the committee level

because at this time the emergency public works law did not allow new construction. Roosevelt then called it a remodeling of what was there. Next, it became clear that the Fine Arts Commission would not approve it because the understanding had always been that the "temporary" office would be demolished one day and its functions moved to a remade State, War, and Navy Building, revised from Second Empire to a more Beaux-Arts neoclassical appearance. Roosevelt, absolutely furious, determined to have what he wanted.

Meanwhile, forces behind the scene in the person of the Fine Arts Commission chairman, Charles Moore (Senator McMillan's former secretary)—and, from another direction entirely, Mrs. Roosevelt—brought to the project Eric Gugler, a gifted Manhattan architect. He became the mediator, the solver of conflicts, though the president was the last to cool down on the subject. Gugler disliked the Roosevelt-Winslow scheme, but he agreed that a larger executive office was quite possible in that location. At last he gained the president's confidence. To keep peace with the Park Service, Gugler agreed to a title on the project no grander than consultant, although he was in fact the architect. Winslow saw to it that he received little cooperation from the Park Service, and the president offered no help, so Gugler called on the American Institute of Architects. The AIA provided him with work space in the parlors of its headquarters at the

Architect Eric Gugler at work on his drawings for the expansion of the west wing, 1934

221

Eric Gugler's sketches for (above) the relocated Oval Office and (right) the colonnade modified with a wheelchair ramp for FDR. No other modifications were needed to accommodate the president. The White House elevator went from the ground floor to the attic, and two men lifted the wheelchair up or down any short flights of stairs.

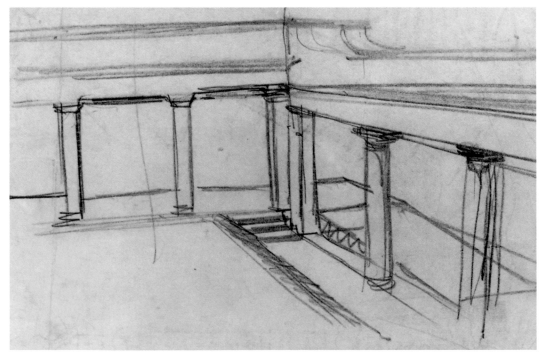

Octagon, two blocks from the building site.

Construction commenced about August 20, 1934. The president went to Hyde Park, and his staff was distributed through the state rooms. The project was finished in a typical White House heat, in little more than three months. N. P. Severin Company of Chicago was the contractor. This large firm had built the roof for Coolidge, and federal officials had been pleased with its work. Little seemed different about the finished building from the north, the only wall that survived in its entirety, but the remodeled west wing was a new building, completed only four years after Herbert Hoover rebuilt the old temporary office. It was decidedly a permanent structure, built of steel and masonry with an outer coating of smooth stucco.

Hoover had expanded the office staff from forty to about seventy. One hundred twenty employees returned to the west wing in November. Everyone now agreed with Roosevelt that the old executive office had barely functioned at all. Its size was doubled in the new. Gugler had done his layout in close concert with the president's staff, for his plan presented a maze of halls and rooms of all sizes tailored to the network of working relationships that characterized the office. For security reasons, west wing plans are not published here after the earliest one. The space has changed constantly, resulting in a crazy quilt sort of plan. An intruder would have to be blessed with a sharp sense of direction to find his way through the labyrinthine clusters of rooms and streaks of corridors.

Gugler called heavily on his skills to conceal the large volume of space he added. Considering the office building as a box, he built a second story that receded behind a parapet into the attic, for all practical purposes out of sight. He excavated a large basement that not only included the entire area beneath the exposed building but also extended the office space an equal amount underground, to the south. The subterranean section was pierced, doughnut-like, by a sunken court or light well, which Gugler planted lushly and centered with a fish pond. This bit of light, air, and greenery transformed the basement rooms from catacombs into tranquil, peacefully remote workplaces.

The original Oval Office, demolished in the course of the work, was built anew in its present location. Gugler seems to have changed the design somewhat, perhaps playing on Roosevelt's love for Georgian architecture. The simple wood trim of Taft's and Hoover's Oval Office was abandoned in favor of a playful rendition of the Georgian motif with a faintly Moderne flair, incorporating pediments over the doors and fluted seashell coves crowning built-in bookcases. Roosevelt selected the colors, gray-green walls and white woodwork. The contrast made the

decorative effects too noisy, perhaps, for on his own authority Gugler put drops of the green into the buckets of white enamel to muffle the blast.

The president did not put his pencils down for long. While the furnishings committee and Eleanor Roosevelt discussed work on the state floor, not always with success, Franklin Roosevelt directed Winslow in the building of a White House library on the north side of the basement corridor. It was a perfect image of rooms found in big houses in wealthy areas throughout the country, with books behind gilt wire mesh alongside marble-faced fireplaces. Under Roosevelt's direction Winslow also rebuilt the two basement kitchens streamline, as the term went, with the shine and compactness of a Pullman car, and Roosevelt, who loathed his wife's everyday White

The White House library as designed by Lorenzo Winslow, under the direction of President Roosevelt, in 1935, but shown later. The president's "Delft" tiles with views of Washington, D.C., surround the fireplace opening.

House fare for its boasted wholesomeness, ordered a small kitchen built upstairs for his own use.

He took an interest in the grounds, which had been revised in patches over the years but had been subjected to no cohesive plan since President Grant's in 1873. Roosevelt called in Frederick Law Olmsted, Jr., to review the drawings others had made, including Eric Gugler's effort to improve the link between the White House and

was the expansion of what we know today as the east wing. According to Lorenzo Winslow, this had been on his mind for some time. Advised that funding would be hard to get, Roosevelt kept his peace, but still envisioned an addition to the east of McKim's loggia entrance that would contain a museum. He took up his pencils again. Fearing calamity, the Park Service engaged Gugler in 1938 to do a project for an extension of the east wing. So ferocious was the criticism

the rebuilt west wing through the Rose Garden. Olmsted called for a major rethinking. His consultant was Morley Jeffers Williams of Harvard University, restorer of the Mount Vernon gardens. The Olmsted report, submitted to Roosevelt in October 1934, called for broader landscapes of groves and lawns rather than gardens with small flower beds. Olmsted proposed a southward vista, open and green, with trees planted thickly on the sides to frame it, both for beauty and security. The work of tree cutting began in the spring of 1935. Two years later Olmsted's ideas became reality, and they are the basis for the grounds today.

The last major project Roosevelt undertook

from the president and Winslow that the Park Service sent Gugler home. It was obvious that the president and his architect planned to do the job themselves.

On the afternoon of Sunday, December 7, 1941, only hours after the Japanese attack on the U.S. naval base at Pearl Harbor, Winslow was called to the White House, where Roosevelt received him upstairs. The president wanted plans started for temporary buildings on the south lawn to serve the war effort. "He gave me a detailed list of the people who would be housed in the quarters," Winslow recalled, and Roosevelt ordered that the architect's office be moved to the ground

**Above and opposite:
Views of the west wing as
completed in the fall of 1934,
after three months in
construction. Gugler has shifted
the location of the Oval Office to
the east, closer to the White
House, where it remains today.**

floor library immediately. In the midst of the move, at seven the next morning, Roosevelt called Winslow upstairs and told him that instead of erecting temporary buildings he had decided to proceed with the east wing. Temporaries would soon cover the east end of the Mall, in view of the White House, but no such structures ever marred the south lawn. Roosevelt was certain that at last he would have his museum.

Winslow brought out the east wing sketches he had been making for the president since at least 1938. They called for adding a two-story east front to the existing single-story wing and before it a new porte-cochère. With grassy, tree-planted

mounds thrown up on the sides, the new entrance would be unobtrusive. The loggia entrance built by McKim would largely go, but the idea would remain in a range of glass doors off the porte-cochère that would lead to a long, broad hallway and on through to the east garden. Some offices would be put upstairs and a police station below; still the president kept his main objective of a museum fully in mind. He presented Winslow with a list of memorabilia, objects already in the White House and ones he knew were in private hands and that he planned to press for as donations. Only Rutherford B. Hayes in the nineteenth century had matched

Overleaf:

The White House from Pennsylvania Avenue on the night of the attack on Pearl Harbor, December 7, 1941

Roosevelt's appetite for White House artifacts.

The final design Winslow likened to a "large theater entrance." Working drawings were prepared through the balance of December, and demolition of most of McKim's east entrance began at once. Meanwhile the Army insisted that an air raid shelter be included in the plan and that, of course, it be secret. Roosevelt balked, suspicious that military officials were trying to use the White House to promote themselves. They had suggested also that the place be painted in camouflage, which he rejected with not a little annoyance. He finally agreed to the bomb shelter, which would be the southward subbasement area of the new east wing entrance building. Temporary shelter was provided in the basement of the Treasury, with access from a garden mount northeast of the White House through a tunnel slanting uncomfortably to the Treasury "moat," or areaway, which one crossed in the open to the Treasury's cellars. The entrance to this tunnel, its rusty door, and its dank concrete walls survived, forgotten, well into the 1980s.

Basements and bomb shelter were gnawed out of the clay soil through the bitter winter of 1942. A national capital more populous than ever before passed by unaware that more was going on than a simple addition to the wing. There had been some public opposition to the expansion, but as news copy it was no match for the war. Behind a high board fence the steel and concrete had taken full form by the first anniversary of Pearl Harbor. All subterranean secrets were concealed by the unassuming white block of a building, which was crossed on the east by a long, single-story, columned porte-cochère sheltering a horseshoe driveway. To the rear the glazed east colonnade remained unchanged. The structure

Detail of a project for FDR's eastward addition to the east wing, office of Lorenzo Winslow, 1943

The addition to the
east wing, as it was
completed after World War II

229

was the simplest it could be, with more than a touch of the Moderne in its spare classicism.

Architecturally, the east entrance of 1941 and 1942 was a poor substitute for McKim's elegant loggia. It served a greater variety of purposes, but it did not, nor does it today, have that trim sort of elegance supplied by the first. For all the success of its work at screening, it is a heavy building, too heavy for the entranceway it is meant to be. Callers proceed from the columned shelter directly into the mass of the structure, meeting a broad dark hall that presents a tiresome, ill-conceived path of straight runs and steps that climb at last to an ell of the east colonnade. The colonnade, though it presents a green view along the side to the south, is yet another long passage that eventually ends in a third corridor beneath the house. This is very unlike the airiness of McKim's earlier structure, where one entered among columns and the garden's green and could feel at once a part of the house.

The vocabulary of the Moderne was more of a presence on the interior in panels, pared-down neoclassic effects, and rounded corners, but at most decoration here was limited. The project ran out of money. Drained by the high cost of its buried secret, the east wing was finished cheaply. Many walls intended for decorative wood paneling received not even plaster, but monk's cloth on lath to avoid the cost of finish plasterwork.

The availability of so much space at such a busy time changed Roosevelt's museum plans. Offices filled the east wing, upstairs and down. Winslow's drafting room was put on the south side of the second floor. Through open venetian blinds he could look out into the south grounds. The vice president and others were put in offices downstairs, furnished piecemeal for quick occupancy. What is today called the social office held

calligraphers, a photographer, and space for Edith Helm, the social secretary, whose main office was upstairs in the residence. The museum never came to be. Such artifacts as the president had secured—one of them, a medicine chest carried off by a British sailor the night the house was burned in 1814—were sent on to his library at Hyde Park, where they can be seen today. The president also converted the coatroom into a household movie theater for everyday use. It could be rearranged as a coatroom when necessary. A movie theater it remains.

Roosevelt made no further changes in the house. His health was declining rapidly, and the war demanded more strength than he had to give. His mind was drawn to things other than building—but not entirely. Those closest to him took an ongoing interest in his well-being through relaxation. The pool was not enough, and Hyde Park was too far away. Before the east wing was completed, in the summer of 1942, Admiral Ross McIntyre, the White House doctor, selected a 1930s Civilian Conservation Corps camp in the mountains of western Maryland as a presidential retreat.

Opposite:
Complete north and south elevations of the White House, 1946, by Lorenzo Winslow. These drawings show the extent of the structure east to west, without the screens of grass-covered earth mounds and plantings that emphasize the earliest center block and minimize the wings.

Norman Rockwell visited FDR's west wing waiting room in 1943 and produced this impression of callers with appointments to see the president for the *Saturday Evening Post*.

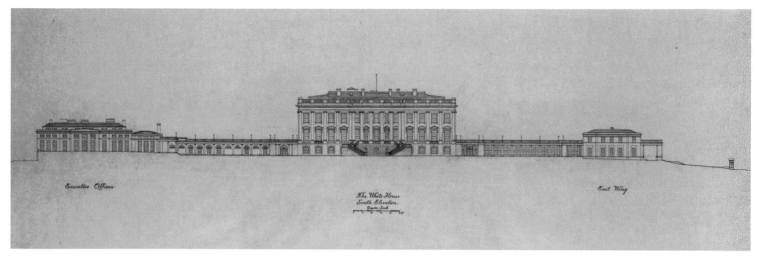

Executive Offices

The White House
South Elevation.
Graphic Scale

East Wing

East Wing

The White House
Pennsylvania Avenue Elevation.
Graphic Scale

Executive Offices

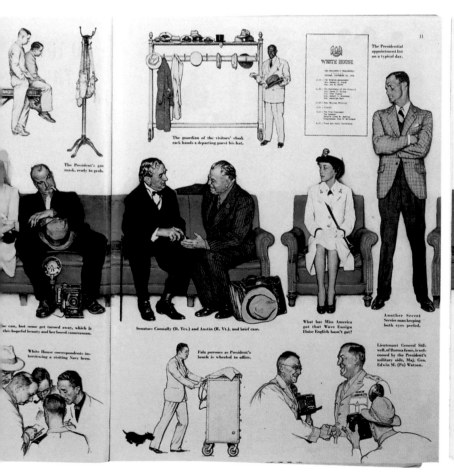

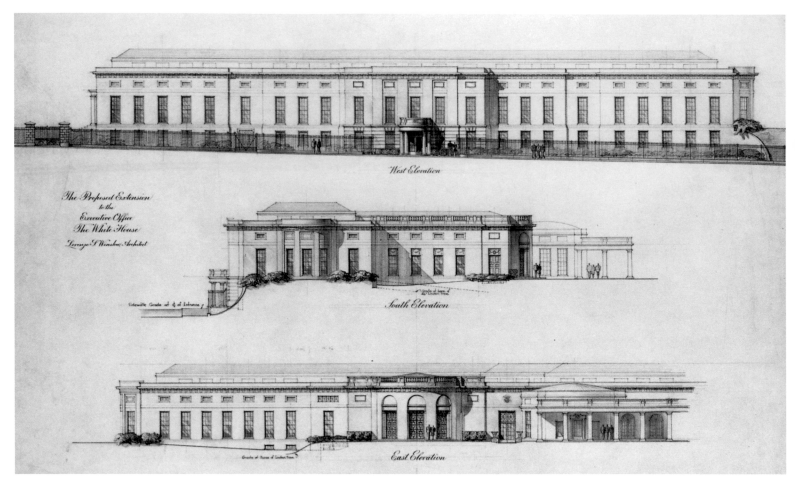

West Elevation

The Proposed Extension
to the
Executive Office
The White House
Lorenzo S. Winslow, Architect

South Elevation

East Elevation

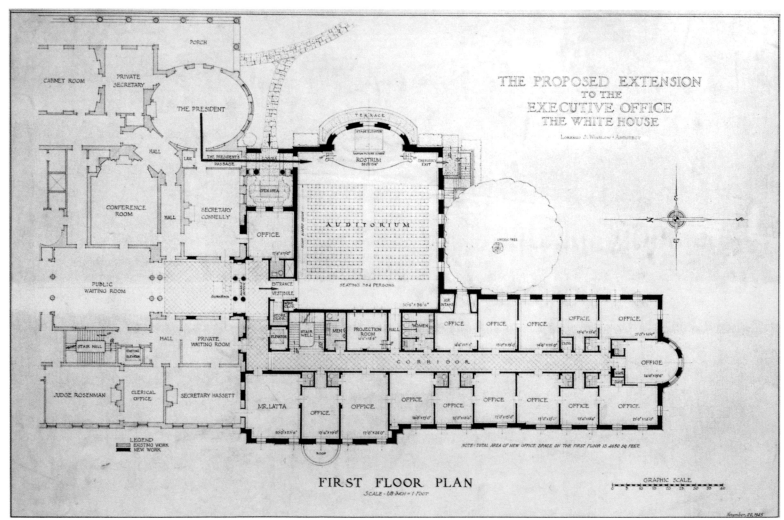

THE PROPOSED EXTENSION
TO THE
EXECUTIVE OFFICE
THE WHITE HOUSE
LORENZO S. WINSLOW · ARCHITECT

CABINET ROOM

PRIVATE SECRETARY

PORCH

THE PRESIDENT

HALL

CONFERENCE ROOM

HALL

SECRETARY CONNELLY

THE PRESIDENT'S PASSAGE

LOGGIA

OPEN AREA

OFFICE

TERRACE

ROSTRUM

EMERGENCY EXIT

AUDITORIUM

PUBLIC WAITING ROOM

ENTRANCE VESTIBULE

STAIR HALL

EXISTING ELEVATOR

HALL

PRIVATE WAITING ROOM

ELEVATOR

STAIR WELL

MEN

PROJECTION ROOM

HALL

WOMEN

SEATING 264 PERSONS

UNDER TREE

OFFICE

OFFICE

OFFICE

OFFICE

OFFICE

CORRIDOR

OFFICE

JUDGE ROSENMAN

CLERICAL OFFICE

SECRETARY HASSETT

MR. LATTA

OFFICE

OFFICE

OFFICE

OFFICE

OFFICE

OFFICE

OFFICE

OFFICE

OFFICE

LEGEND
EXISTING WORK
NEW WORK

NOTE: TOTAL AREA OF NEW OFFICE SPACE ON THE FIRST FLOOR IS 4650 SQ. FEET.

FIRST FLOOR PLAN
SCALE · 1/8 INCH = 1 FOOT

GRAPHIC SCALE

Opposite:

Soon after coming into office in 1945, President Truman determined to add to the west wing office building. The executive staff had risen in number from 140 before the war to 225 when Truman became president. Lorenzo Winslow's design for a southward addition included 15,000 square feet of new space, with offices, a cafeteria, and an auditorium for press conferences. The scheme fell before fierce political opposition in Congress.

Fascinated by this pseudo-pioneer village of logs, Roosevelt named it Shangri-la, his favorite name for a remote place, borrowed from James Hilton's novel *Lost Horizon*. He planned improvements in the rustic log mode, moved furniture there from the war-bound presidential launch *Potomac*, and took special pleasure in the place President Eisenhower was to rename Camp David, for his grandson.

The decade of World War II was not to close without a drastic change in the White House: the addition of a balcony to the south portico. This was made by Roosevelt's successor, Harry S. Truman, in 1947, two years after he took office. The motives for building the Truman balcony may not be as clear as they appear on the surface. The president was angry over losing his battle to quadruple the size of the west wing, and he was in no mood for further criticism of his architectural ideas. He could understand the politics of his loss on the west wing, but he resented the negative opinions art critics had expressed of the design.

Then he made it known in the summer of 1947 that he thought the second floor oval room above the Blue Room would be a better sitting room if it had a porch. Truman had various stated reasons for wanting to build one: He disliked the canvas awnings put up to shade the south portico in the summer, and he said he thought the design of the building would be improved by a porch like those of old mansions in the South. The Fine Arts Commission was aghast. A *porch* halfway up the beautiful south colonnade? But realizing the commission had been weakened by Roosevelt's continual opposition and its life was now precarious, the commissioners, rather than face Truman's anger, decided to suggest to the president that a leading architect in the traditional style be engaged to make proposals. The Fine Arts Commission assembled with the president on the south lawn and gave this view. David E. Finley, director of the National Gallery of Art and a commission member, remembered the session with Truman as uncomfortable.

The president interpreted the commission's re-

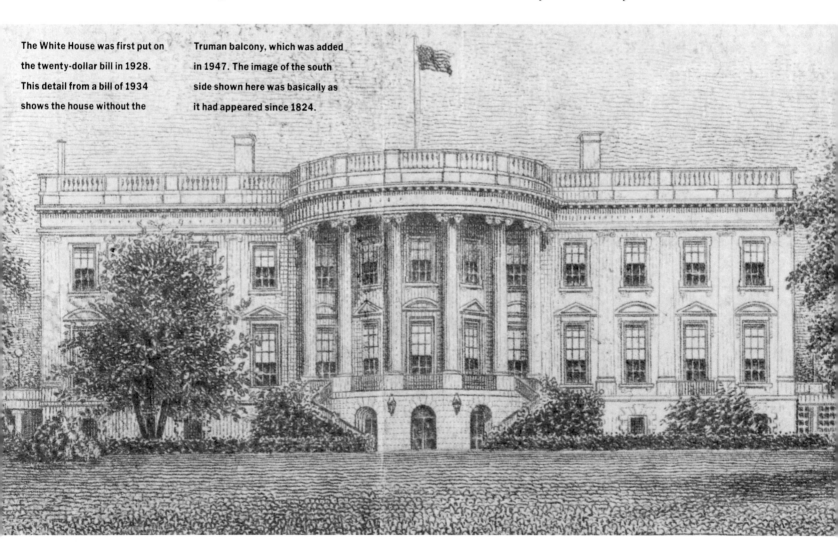

The White House was first put on the twenty-dollar bill in 1928. This detail from a bill of 1934 shows the house without the Truman balcony, which was added in 1947. The image of the south side shown here was basically as it had appeared since 1824.

sponse as approval, with the proviso that an architect of note should be consulted. William Adams Delano, the architect of the White House roof addition and a former member of the Fine Arts Commission, was recommended to Truman by the commission and invited to Washington. The commissioners had hoped, of course, that he would discourage the balcony. If he did he was characteristically mild in his opposition and soon approved the idea. On an enlarged photograph that still exists he inked in white a balcony of the sparest sort. The Fine Arts Commission declined to approve it.

A waiting period ensued. Pressure was exerted from the White House, but still the commission stood firm. To a letter from the chairman, Gilmore Clarke, Truman snapped back that he believed that permission had been given and that "you didn't enter into the matter at all with an open mind." He left no doubt that he would make the final decision. Delano assisted Winslow with final drawings in November 1947. The two devised a balcony in metal and concrete. This was ready for use in the spring of 1948.

The Truman balcony was and remains an unhappy architectural appendage. Perhaps some modification could have saved it; it might have been cantilevered from the bow wall and not reached all the way to the columns. As built it is an awkward encumbrance upon the semicircular colonnade. It causes problems on the state floor as well. No longer is the south portico the lofty tribunal it once was, opening from the state parlors. The balcony has done away with the verticality, the upward soaring of the open places between the columns from which a seemingly endless vista of earth, water, and sky was once enjoyed.

The balcony was the most significant change made in the exterior of the White House proper since Andrew Jackson built the north portico in 1829–31. Even more drastic change was to come, but it would be contained within the old walls. Four years after the balcony's completion the White House would undergo the most radical alteration since the British burned it. The work would be carried out with only the token acknowledgment of the Fine Arts Commission, under President Truman's personal prerogative.

Before and after: The south front of the White House (opposite above) circa 1947 and (opposite below) after the addition of the Truman balcony in 1948

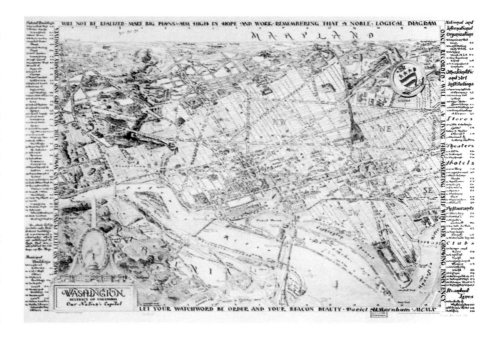

Washington, District of Columbia, Our Nation's Capital, **drawn by Oliver Whitwell Wilson, architect, New York, with the aid of Fairchild Air Views, 1948**

7

THE IDEA PRESERVED

Harry S. Truman, president from 1945 to 1953. Truman saw history in broad sweeps and appreciated symbols. To him the White House was bigger than its timber and bricks, and he took drastic steps to save the idea of the house that had sheltered all the presidents since Washington.

I mmediately after Pearl Harbor, in the rush to protect against expected bombings of the White House, a structural survey was made of the building to help determine how best to secure it. The resulting long-winded report was presented on December 14, one week after the Japanese attack on Pearl Harbor. In addition to proposing to camouflage the house, it offered many other suggestions rejected by Roosevelt, including painting the colonnade windows in the east wing black and, with mounds of sandbags, setting up machine-gun emplacements on the roofs of the east and west terraces.

After the war this report was a relic indeed, except in one particular: The house was vulnerable to air attack and to fire. This verdict could be translated into grim peacetime possibilities. A firebomb set off in the Blue Room, for example, could start a conflagration. And what of a kamikaze-style assault on the building? The 1927 roof structure of steel and concrete would deflect some of the worst, perhaps, but the extent of the damage would depend on the size of the plane and its speed. Those assigned to protect the White House, as well as the regular staff, took this to heart. From the architects and engineers to the chief usher, danger of this sort hovered so

fearfully near as to change the attitude about the permanence of the structure.

Introduce to this a president with a meddlesome fascination for making things that are out of kilter stand up straight. Harry Truman was as determined a builder as Roosevelt had been, but he wished to make things shipshape, not to redesign them. The White House, Truman liked to say, was a place where "some lived it up and others wore it down." There was no question that

237

the structure was not entirely stable. Some of the floors sagged. Cracking in the plaster was constant. Removal of the Roosevelts' thirteen truckloads of furnishings revealed many cracks in the walls. Patched and painted, the cracks soon returned; some of them not small hairline breaks but clefts of some size, stretching from ceiling to floor. Truman demanded to know what was wrong.

The commissioner of public buildings, W. E. Reynolds, had a team of engineers carry out a stress test on the second floor oval room. It was judged unsafe with more than fifteen people in it. Obviously this would not do. An appropriation of $50,000 was made on May 10, 1948, to do a structural survey of the house and devise a plan to stabilize and fireproof it. This work was undertaken in the summer. Meanwhile, as it progressed, a leg of the piano in Margaret Truman's room broke through two floorboards and knocked plaster down from the false-vault ceiling of the family dining room below. Fears many had shared now had their common symbol, and the origin of rebuilding the White House would be remembered as the moment the piano fell through the floor.

The structural analysis was directed at finding all possible danger. Sections of wall were stripped to the wood framing or to brick. Even

deeper cracks were exposed. Hoban's joists had been drilled for gas pipes, plumbing pipes, and electrical wires; in places repeated intrusions had cut structural elements in half. When the south wall of the west sitting hall was opened up, McKim's steel trusswork revealed all manner of damage. Its enormous weight had been reassigned in 1927 from a single crossbeam to the new steel framing of the third floor. The whole upper mass thrust down on the old walls with a force greater there than in any other part of the house.

There was even more of a story than the engineers could find with their survey. The president was disturbed by noises in the structure at night and by odd moments of movement, when the building seemed to shift slightly. Not until later would this movement be understood. The weak link was not the stone or the steel but the bricks that lined the stone walls. Vast spans of wood flooring, which McKim had stabilized with steel, threw their natural vibration into this deep inner walling of soft brick. Great stress came also from above. The immense weight of the 1927 third floor pressed down on the brick rather than the stone of the old walls. Had the walls been of solid stone, they might have supported the weight.

In laying blame it is well to trace the origin of the brick linings. The walls were commissioned at the outset to be entirely of stone. This decision was revised in 1793 to provide stone outer walls lined with a massive thickness of brick that would never be visible. While this was not unusual in British building, it caused George Washington some disappointment. The bricks were of soft clay and could not be exposed to the weather, but under the certain protection of the roof they were laid up twenty-two or more inches deep against the sandstone shell. First wooden timbers, then, in 1902, steel I beams had been mortised into the brick walls, which, over time, were less and less structurally competent to hold them.

The White House was not, as Truman suspected, falling down. But its waning structural security had been dramatized well enough to more than confirm the fears raised by the 1948 structural report. It was generally agreed that something drastic had to be done. Little time was

The second floor truss, installed by McKim in 1902 (see pages 178-79) to support the upper weight of the house is exposed in the interior demolition of 1949–50. This truss, which was by now suspended from the steel framing of the 1927 attic, was the source of much of the structural deterioration of the house.

In the entrance hall, demolition work in 1950 exposed Hoban's original plaster cornice, beneath McKim's cornice of 1902.

Famous near-disaster: the floor joists broken by Margaret Truman's piano in 1948, photographed by Abbie Rowe, photographer for the National Park Service and recorder of the gutting and rebuilding of the White House, 1948-52. Virtually all of the extant photographic coverage of the renovation was his distinguished work, carried out to exacting standards.

allowed for debate. When the engineers in charge assembled on January 14, 1949, they were greeted by Lorenzo Winslow with an entire program. Already the previous November the president and his family had moved across the street to Blair House, the historic town house purchased by the government during the war and taken over by Franklin Roosevelt for use as executive guest quarters.

Historic restoration of the sort we know today was never considered. One could argue that there was not much left of the original house anyway, that McKim had buried it beneath his Beaux-Arts veneer. Restoration skills in 1949 were, however, not as rare as the impulse to preserve and restore. This course could have been a possibility. Perhaps the president's personal involvement kept the National Park Service, the Smithsonian Institution, and other agencies quiet. The Commission of Fine Arts, fearing for its life, said little and gave rubber stamp approvals later on, after the fact. Because of the political implications of any protest and the threat of presidential wrath, the American Institute of Architects stayed away from so personal a Truman project; it was that organization that might best have led the attack. Truman assumed as much a free hand in this work as George Washington had had in building the house.

The plan was to gut the house to the stone walls, leaving only the 1927 third floor and roof structure. A house of steel and concrete was to be built within the walls to support the roof. The arrangement of rooms on the ground, main, and second floors was to be more or less the same, so that the new house would be recognizably the White House. At the meeting on January 14 the president's program was approved. The principal figures in the work would be Winslow; W. E. Reynolds; Major General Philip F. Fleming, who was federal works administrator; and Edward F. Neild, an architectural engineer and shrewd businessman Truman knew from Shreveport, Louisiana. (Some years earlier, while a county judge, Truman had engaged Neild to design the Moderne high-rise courthouse in Kansas City, Missouri.) But the final authority would be the president.

The proposal to Congress, over Reynolds's signature as public buildings commissioner, called for a house within the walls of the old, a new house with more floor space than the existing one and more secure. Congress, which had opposed demolishing the White House for more than eighty years, was assured that "no work is proposed in scope or detail that will alter the

The men in charge of the White House renovation of 1948-52. From left, Colonel Douglas H. Gillette, assistant executive director of the Commission for the Renovation of the Executive

architectural or cultural features or impair the integrity of the building in its role of a National Shrine. In all respects the historic and traditional symbolism of the Nation's most revered mansion must be preserved to the greatest degree consistent with the use of modern materials and equipment that will be incorporated into the project." That the builder of the balcony on the south portico was to be the ultimate authority might have given pause. The White House had always

Mansion and an engineer; Major General Glenn E. Edgerton, executive director of the commission, also an engineer; Lorenzo S. Winslow, architect of the White House; and Harbin S. Chandler, Jr., assistant to the architect and chief designer.

240

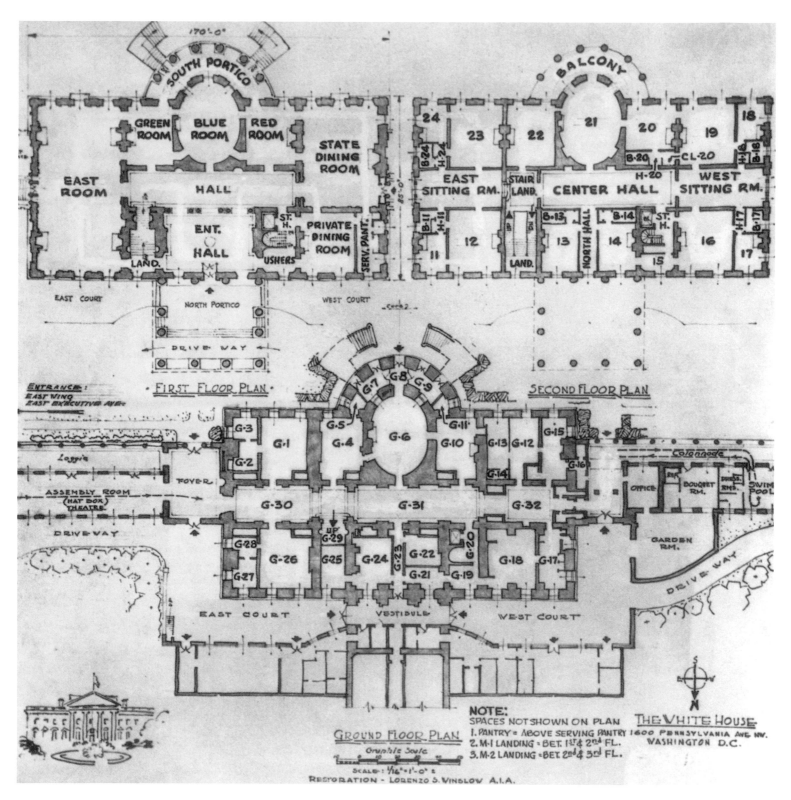

First Floor Plan · **Second Floor Plan**

SOUTH PORTICO 170'-0"

GREEN ROOM · BLUE ROOM · RED ROOM

STATE DINING ROOM

EAST ROOM

HALL

ENT. HALL

LAND.

PRIVATE DINING ROOM

USHERS

SERV. PANT.

ST. H.

EAST COURT · NORTH PORTICO · WEST COURT

DRIVE WAY

ENTRANCE: EAST WING EAST EXECUTIVE AVE.

BALCONY

24 · 23 · 22 · 21 · 20 · 19 · 18

EAST SITTING RM. · STAIR LAND. · CENTER HALL · WEST SITTING RM.

NORTH HALL

11 · 12 · 13 · 14 · 15 · 16 · 17

ST. H.

LAND.

GROUND FLOOR PLAN

Graphic Scale

SCALE: 1/16" = 1'-0" ±

RESTORATION - LORENZO S. WINSLOW A.I.A.

G-7 · G-8 · G-9

G-3 · G-5 · G-11 · G-15

G-1 · G-4 · G-6 · G-10 · G-13 · G-12

G-2 · G-16

G-14

Loggia

FOYER

ASSEMBLY ROOM (HAT BOX) THEATRE

DRIVE WAY

Colonnade

OFFICE · BOUQUET RM. · PRESS RM. · SWIM POOL

GARDEN RM.

DRIVE WAY

G-30 · G-31 · G-32

G-28 · G-29 UP

G-26 · G-25 · G-24 · G-23 · G-22 · G-20 · G-18 · G-17

G-27 · G-21 · G-19

EAST COURT · VESTIBULE · WEST COURT

NOTE:
SPACES NOT SHOWN ON PLAN
1. PANTRY = ABOVE SERVING PANTRY
2. M-1 LANDING = BET. 1st & 2nd FL.
3. M-2 LANDING = BET. 2nd & 3rd FL.

THE WHITE HOUSE
1600 PENNSYLVANIA AVE. NW.
WASHINGTON D.C.

been the president's. If anything whatsoever were approved for it, the president's power in the matter was understood by all. One did not question it, just as one did not question the authority of Congress over the Capitol. But still it was Congress that had the power to fund—or not to fund—the White House project.

Truman sent a budget to Congress in mid-February 1949. There was silence. In March he requested the appointment of a commission to supervise the work. He observed that he had originally planned to do this himself, but feared he would not have time. On April 14 the Commission for the Renovation of the Executive Mansion was established, without an appropriation. The president appointed to the commission popular men of both parties and called them to the White House on June 3. They secured the necessary appropriation—$5.4 million—on June 23.

To think that Truman would yield one grain of

Plan for restoring the White House, Lorenzo S. Winslow, circa 1947. The plan makes few alterations and suggests little removal of original materials, but includes the addition of rooms under the north lawn.

authority was to misunderstand the situation. Lorenzo Winslow was to function under his direct orders, much as he had with Roosevelt. William Adams Delano was to be the design consultant, by virtue of his nearly quarter century of White House projects. The commissioners cautiously placed architect Douglas W. Orr of Connecticut as the liaison between themselves and Winslow. Thus the order of rank was the president, Winslow, Orr, the commission. This organizational structure was followed until near the end, when the president tired of Winslow. By now Winslow had become rather highhanded, but Orr managed him very well. At the meeting where the protocol was laid down Winslow said that 60 percent of the renovation drawings were finished and approved. Orr responded calmly with a list of reports he wanted on various subjects, including analysis of historical materials. This was more Orr's statement of power than a genuine wish for information. Orr's

later relationship with Winslow was to confirm this tactic as his way of handling a peer who might, at some time, become too strong.

All the drawings were produced in Winslow's small east wing office. Delano came down by train from New York every other week. His influence seems to have been slight. Of new importance was Harbin S. Chandler, a government employee who did much of the design, according to Winslow's personal notes. Billy Delano had proved himself perhaps too agreeable and was much in demand for bestowing blessings on Winslow's and the president's ideas. He is on record as objecting only once in the entire design process. Winslow took all drawings directly to the president. From there they went to the renovation commission, where in all but one instance they were approved. Congressman Louis C. Rabaut of Michigan said that if the walls were to be kept the state rooms should also remain. If the interior was to go, why not the walls also? "We

·VIEW·LOOKING·SOUTHEAST·
·PROPOSED·ALTERATIONS·TO·MAIN·STAIRWAY·SCHEME·"C"·
Lorenzo S. Winslow·
·Architect·of·the·White·House·

Two projects for the new grand stair. The scheme shown opposite required the extension of the entrance hall into the transverse hall and the relocation to the east of the modified column screen. The project above retained the column screen and turned the stairs into the entrance hall; it would have been adopted, for it pleased President Truman, but William Adams Delano threatened to resign if it was built. For the Delano version, which was adopted, see page 265.

cling to the word 'preservation' in one sense," he wrote, "and entirely disregard it in another." In a way he seemed to be trying to turn the project toward a restoration, yet he was fully aware that the president meant to have it his own way. Rabaut gained no support and cast the one dissenting vote against Truman's plan.

The schematics folded smoothly into actual drawings through the summer and fall of 1949. There was a consensus to return the state floor to the way McKim had designed it. This plan went smoothly until the president decided he wanted the grand stair turned away from the transverse hall into the entrance hall. His reasoning made sense. McKim's long final flight required an awkward trip down from the upstairs, and the location of the stair made the grand march not only uncomfortable but also out of the vision of most of the guests waiting below.

Winslow presented several projects for the revised stair. The one the president approved

would have altered the character of the entrance hall so greatly that Delano rose in protest. At first he was sidestepped, but when he threatened to leave the job, both Winslow and the president took heed. The new stair had been devised to land in an open alcove on the east side of the entrance hall, forming a broad landing a few steps up from the hall floor; today we would call the landing a stage for photo opportunities. What offended Delano was not so much this redesign of the stair but that the plan entailed a stripping down of the hall. Winslow would have removed the column screen entirely and much of McKim's ornament along with it. This Delano would not have, and he did not move an inch from his position until columns and decorations were returned to the scheme; he ordered an archway cut on the stair's second landing, looking out into the transverse hall.

The gutting of the house began on December 7, 1949, eight years to the day after Pearl Harbor,

243

with the erection of a support system of steel. Securing the outside shell and removing the rest was an engineering challenge given to the firm Spencer, White & Prentis, leading specialists in the stabilization of old buildings. A plan was devised for support from within and without, beginning with new underpinnings for the walls. Hoban had dug his foundations no more than five or six feet to a clay stratum, on which he had laid a firm bed of stones, gravel, wood, and sand. Over time this had weakened through deterioration and shifting.

The new structure needed a more secure base, and this was found about twenty-five feet down in a twenty-foot-thick layer of gravel. Piers of steel-reinforced concrete were poured into forms that rose from the gravel stratum to the level of the base of the old walls. More or less evenly spaced, 126 of them were placed around the perimeter of the house. The old shell rested temporarily on these, riding steel footings, or plates. A new inner frame of steel was to be built just inside the rectangle of the old walls, dropping two stories below the ground floor (the lowest original level of the house) into areas to be excavated as a new basement and sub-basement. Once the digging was done, heavy concrete foundations were to be laid as permanent supports for the original stone walls.

Demolition of the interior actually began before December 1949. The commission had pledged itself more or less to removing and keeping for reuse such things as the door trim, ceiling ornaments, windows, and some pine timbers to be milled for paneling. Only Winslow really took this seriously, and he had each item carefully photographed and numbered. Abbie Rowe's day-by-day photographic coverage – of which a small sampling can be found in this book – built a visual record of remarkable extent. Hundreds of crates of paneling, mantelpieces, doors, and windows were sent to storage from October to December. In anticipation of change Winslow had made on-site drawings a year before. No one matched his knowledge of what went where or his sense of the importance of putting back as much of the original house as possible.

As soon as the Blue Room and the other oval rooms above and below it were stripped of their ornaments and trim, the center one of three shoring towers was built. The towers had two purposes, the first to support the 1927 third floor and roof structure, which were to remain, and the second to serve as a channel through which the debris of demolition could be hauled up and out. Some of the steel members of the towers were to stay as part of the permanent framing, concealed in the walls of the rebuilt transverse hall. In the commission's report February 14, 1950, is given as the date the first steel member was installed. It was put in place of the easternmost pilaster of the hall's column screen and marked the beginning of a tower that included the central part of the transverse hall and the north end of the Blue Room.

Winslow finished with his removal of artifacts on March 23, 1950, not at all to his satisfaction, for he had been hurried along. Thereafter, nothing was sacred about the house but the stone walls. All was carelessly reduced to debris – plaster, wood, bricks. As the parts were torn away, further steel was introduced; that which was to be temporary was painted one color and

Section of the White House by Spencer, White & Prentis, engineers, showing the new concrete underpinnings of the original stone walls and the steel frame within

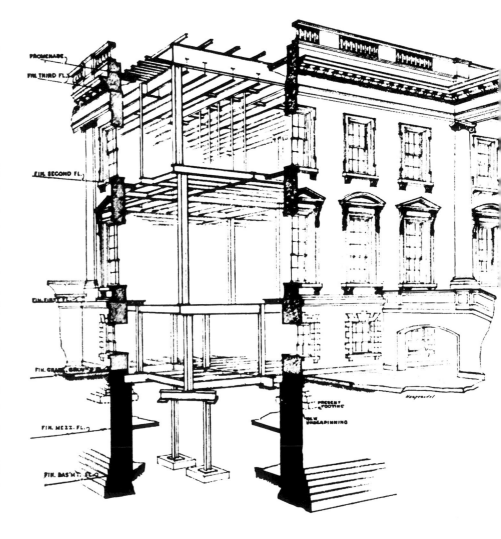

The dismantling process included the removal and packing of plaster architectural ornamentation, as well as the wooden parts that were considered worthy of rescue. (Above) A centerpiece from the East Room. (Below) At Christmas 1949 Joliet stone floors of the entrance hall have been taken up, and the plaster ornament awaits removal.

These views (top) of the East Room and (bottom) of Mrs. Truman's bedroom on the second floor, in 1950 show the final stages of the careful removal of decorative and other parts intended for reuse.

Opposite:
Removal of the sandstone stairs to the south portico, 1950. Built by James Hoban for James Monroe in 1824, by 1952 the stairs had been rebuilt with granite treads but retained the original handrail.

Overleaf:
One of two steel-frame "towers" built into the old structure to support the heavy third floor and roof while the house was dismantled. The towers acted as wells through which debris was removed; chutes from second floor windows on the south carried the debris to the ground.

The south front, from the southeast, during demolition, 1950. This view shows the general character of the construction site, within a high board fence that surrounded the grounds.

Opposite:
Interior of the gutted house, showing the soft brick lining of the sandstone walls and the cavities built to receive wooden timbers

Groin vaulting in the old basement corridor during its removal. Parts of these vaults had been torn away in 1902 and replaced with tile vaulting suggesting the groining, but large portions of it remained from the original eighteenth-century construction of the White House.

Installation of a new ceiling on the south portico. Removal of the ceiling of the original revealed the cornice of the bow, closed up in the added portico since 1824.

the permanent steel framing another. Through the tower shafts the refuse went, to chutes at windows down which it rolled into dump trucks. By special permit a motorcade worked morning and night for twenty-two days hauling the wreckage to Fort Myer and other locations as landfill.

When the stone shell at last stood empty, there remained a somber open interior crisscrossed by steel I beams of all sizes. The powdery red-orange bricks that lined the stone formed a tall, pocked, crumbling wall pierced by the open window sockets. The shell made an enthralling sight, much in demand among those who could get clearance to go and see it. President Truman delighted in showing the spectacle, and the more closely he looked the more another problem presented itself. He believed the demolition had gone far enough. There was to be no more. When the digging of the sub-basements came up and the president was told a doorway was to be cut wider to allow passage for a bulldozer and several dump trucks, he put his foot down and refused to allow it. All that was left intact of the

White House were those stone walls, and they were not to be touched. So the machinery was dismantled, taken inside, reassembled, and put to work. As the basement levels were excavated, the ground was dug away on the west beneath the bottom line of the stone walls to allow for a temporary driveway to reach the enclosure.

By Christmas 1950 the steel framing was in place, and the excavations were complete. From that point on the work was to build anew. The weight of the structure had been transferred to the steel frame. Between the old walls and the inner steel framing were six to ten inches of space, for the irregular surface of bricks for the most part made it impossible to press the two together. It had been deemed inadvisable to remove the bricks because they helped support the stone. On the outside, all along the stone walls, the mortar was raked out as completely as possible–the joints being very thin–and replaced by cement inserted at high pressure. By the end of 1950 the shell stood strong and solid. Such historic preservation as there was to be had been done.

Opposite:

Digging the new basement levels within the gutted shell of the White House. The bulldozer was dismantled and its parts were brought in and reassembled, to keep the machine from damaging the stone openings. As the grade level was dug out, passage was gained under the original walls.

Opposite:

South front, in February 1950, with the debris chute fitted to a window of the Monroe sitting room

The new entrance hall under construction. Delano's grand stair can be seen in its beginnings, against the east wall, as can the steel cores of the white marble columns to come.

Before the steelwork was completed, the Korean War began. Costs rose sharply. Winslow and the commissioners worried lest the project run out of money, and this fear was to play its part in the modification of many of their plans. They continued the work, hurrying the schedule almost obsessively. Truman had told them he wanted to live in the White House again. His second term—his first full term—was to end in January 1953. The commissioners faced wartime prices and labor conditions and a tough deadline less than two years away. They laid aside some of their priorities, but not hurriedly.

The subfloors were all concrete; the finished tile, wood, and masonry floors were to be laid over them. In most partitions hollow tiles filled the spaces between the steel members, and the whole surface was plastered on steel-mesh lath. Vibrations, it was believed, would never again be a problem in the floors and walls of the White House. In fact, the new frame introduced its own problems. Not twenty years later Lyndon B. Johnson was to find the second floor intolerable at times when the swaying lines of tourists on the main floor below created a humming sound in the steel innards of the building. Ducts, conduits, and pipes of many sizes were threaded through the walls. Often the partitions were rebuilt to match or approximate the external thickness of the original walls, leaving hollow space within that could be used for any purpose that seemed desirable. These spaces were especially useful in introducing the vast air-conditioning systems that cooled, heated, and ventilated the house. The convenience of the hollow spaces continues to be put to use today, when additional traceways or even new cabinets are needed.

Plastering was under way in late February. A special shop was set up to make the molded decorations. Whether Winslow or the president made the decisions about what to use and what not to use is not known, but one suspects that Truman was involved, for he approved everything before the commission saw it. Winslow did ask for the commission's vote on the plaster decorations. If the general idea of the house remained McKim's, the details were juggled extensively. When the cornices were pulled down

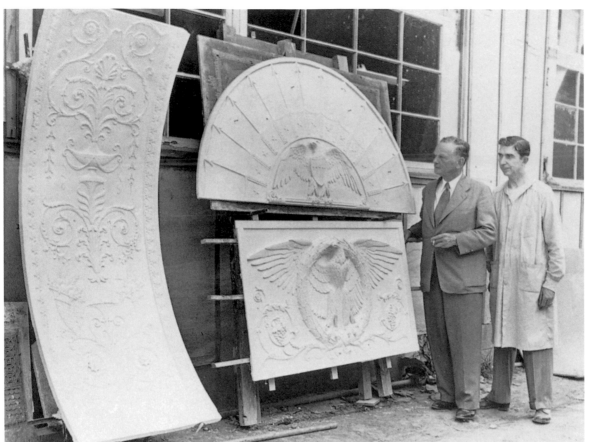

Sculptor F. Bruyninck displays his new plaster ceiling decorations for the East Room to Lorenzo Winslow, 1951.

Opposite:
New ceiling decorations for the East Room, freshly cast and prepared for installation, which began in 1951

in the state parlors, what had been there before— presumably Hoban's from 1818—was revealed. This, not McKim's cornice, was copied and re- placed. In the East Room McKim's "bold high- relief ornament" was given "a certain gentle sim- plification," according to the commissioners. Original parts were reviewed and many dis- carded. Those reused were in actuality recast for sharper definition, because the old parts were caked with paint, victims of maintenance that relied on repainting rather than on routine washing.

By June 1951 the effects of the war on the project were severe. Construction costs had made it clear the house could not be finished within the original appropriation. Two new ap- propriations would raise the figure by $361,000, but the work was only barely finished for a total of $5.76 million. To complicate matters, in the summer of 1951 the plasterers went on strike for two weeks. This, together with money woes and an almost constant need to cut corners, rendered impossible the president's deadline of January 15, 1952. When January came he set a new date of April 1, which would be met.

But not without certain sacrifices. Already by the fall of 1951 it was certain that Winslow's

archive of White House parts was not, by and large, to be reused in the finished interiors. Here the influence of an architect with a strong per- sonality would have changed the course of White House history. Winslow was not such a man. He was accustomed to doing as he was told. He complained, but his loudest objections seem to have been confined to his diary. The

Below:
Wood pilasters for the East Room at the woodworking shop of Knipp & Co., Baltimore, ready to put in place. These were simplified versions of McKim's pilasters of 1902 but replaced the originals, which were not saved.

Electrical panels located
in a new utilities room

Central panel of the Honeywell
Thermo control system for the
renovated White House, 1952

president, who might have intervened, had no grasp of the fine points of architecture and offered little influence in the direction of reusing the woodwork and other elements. As usual, the agreeable Delano kept his own counsel. Members of the commission, running scared, understandably – if barely forgivably – wanted the job done, at almost any cost. They allowed the introduction of machine-pressed woodwork for trim, in place of the original, and put no premium otherwise on the relics Winslow had set aside. By the winter of 1952 the old pieces, crates and all, were being thrown on the trucks and removed to landfill.

The commissioners seem never to have been comfortable with this turn of events. In their final report they would say, "One of the most difficult phases of the work was the careful removal of the materials in the White House. Almost all of these were of irreplaceable value: stone, woodwork, marble mantels, chandeliers, hardware and the many things, hidden and visible, which required preservation for reconstruction and for strong sentimental reasons." They claimed to have re-

(Above) Decorations and (below) hardwood parquet are restored to the State Dining Room, 1951-52. Most of the original oak paneling was restored to this room, making it the lone room actually restored from original finish parts. The paneling, which had been left natural-colored and waxed in 1902, was filled and painted pale green to cover the nicks and gouges suffered in its removal in 1949.

The house is brought together, 1951 and 1952. (Below) Decorators install silk on the walls of the Blue Room, and (above) a painter finishes the new barrel vault that spans the east ramp in the central corridor on the second floor.

Opposite:
A workman enters the north end of the East Room during its reconstruction. McKim's Beaux-Arts designs were modified somewhat, but the style of the paneling, influenced by eighteenth-century French designs, was to remain.

used more than in fact they did: "This rebuilding of sentiment into accurate restoration, by use of the actual materials formerly in place, is the result of the patience . . . of the battalion of workers . . . who eased valued shapes from their places and after many months, carefully eased them back into their former locations, so that they gave no indication of the far-reaching structural operations that had gone on during their absence, indeed gave no indication that they had ever been absent."

It was purely and simply a problem of money. The object of the renovation was to build a new house inside the old stone walls; on the principal story and on the second floor original architectural elements—plaster, paneling, flooring, doors, and windows—were to be preserved and reinstalled. But there were problems. As these pieces were removed they often splintered. Paint chipped off in such chunks that a total stripping of wooden parts was necessary, particularly with the earliest materials where decorative paint graining had been used to imitate varnished wood. McKim's elegant rubbed paint surfaces

had been repainted instead of cleaned, and they did not hold paint well because of their deep build-up of shellac. Digging for nails during removal left ugly pocks. And even when the material was removed, it was to return to locations that might differ in measurement from the original.

To have followed the reuse part of the concept would have meant setting up a large repair operation. It became evident early on that the old plaster would best be simply recast. After this decision was made, molds were cast in place and the originals sent out with the debris. This was much less trouble and saved money to help pay for the plaster workshop. The problem of the other relics came later, after the Korean War had started and prices had gone up. Although the president never said so, he would have been unlike any other in his seat of power if he had not been concerned that his enemies might make political hay out of his multimillion-dollar "palace." So he pressed hard for completion as early as possible in 1952.

Reasoning that practically every architectural

The new basement extended beyond the old walls of the White House. (Above) It is shown in construction by the north portico. (Opposite) The basement's long central corridor, bordered by thick concrete walls, before the installation of the floor.

The entrance hall, showing the
new stair landing, after the
completion of the renovations of
1952

Opposite:

The State Dining Room, (above)
before and (below) after the
Truman renovations. By 1952 it
was restored to its enlarged size
as established by McKim in 1902
and the oak paneling was painted
green.

memento they saw dated only from 1902 and
thus qualified less as historical than as simply
out of style, the commissioners did not hesitate
to issue a death warrant. All the time they knew
they would have done otherwise, under ideal
circumstances. Most of the window sash on the
first and second floors was repaired and rein-
stated in the frames, which had in most cases
stayed in place. The only room really put back
together again with old pieces was the oak-
paneled State Dining Room. When the panels
were lined up against the concrete walls and put
in proper order, their disrepair was extensive,
with splits in the wood and chips in the finish.
The cheapest solution? "The beautiful carved
wood of the Dining Room was given new life,"
wrote the commission in its report. "Formerly
showing a somber natural finish of the deep dark
tone associated with the shadowed great halls of
British manor houses, it was felt that the American idea was best expressed by the soft green
shades found in American Colonial decoration.
The room in these tones assumes a graceful
lightness and sunniness." It was painted.

The house externally showed no change. It was
the same White House. East and west wings
were unaltered, as were the porticoes. The largest
additions were below grade. A warren of underground rooms beneath the north portico and
driveway reached from the unroofed areaway
that fronted the basement on that side of the
house. Built of concrete blocks, with concrete
floors, these rooms sheltered air-conditioning
machinery and some domestic offices. Beneath
the house two new basement levels housed further domestic service rooms clustered along narrow concrete hallways. In total the house of
about sixty-five rooms had become one of 132,
including all major and minor rooms, with only
thirty-three of these on the ground, main, and
second floor levels. The substantial increase gave
space far beyond any the White House had ever
known, and it is still not crowded, though nearly
all the space is in constant use.

Inside the north door the alterations of the
renovation assumed a striking presence. The use
of cream-colored marble had transformed the
entrance hall from country house monumen-

tality to something chilly and institutional. Joliet stone flooring pavers had been replaced by grayish white marble, and the column screen, though designed somewhat after McKim's, was not plaster but marble. McKim's pilasters, rebuilt in marble, rose to a cornice that was the McKim design revived in plaster. Centered on the east wall, where McKim had placed a great mirror—with one opposite it—was the opening to the revised grand stair. It was a better solution than McKim's, featuring a single range of stairs rising in several comfortable lengths. The bottom landing, where the president appeared, was wide and elevated sufficiently so that even a hundred dinner guests filling the hall could see him with relative ease.

If the entrance hall looked at once familiar and different, the transverse corridor was much more as it had been, except for the coldness of the marble. During demolition it was found that McKim had reduced the size of the original stone niches on the south wall. These were returned to their earlier size in the renovation and embellished as places for plants. The marble floor was crossed by a red chenille carpet runner linking the East Room and the State Dining Room.

The East Room, streamlined somewhat, was still essentially what McKim had devised half a century before. Wherever alterations had been made they were touched by the Moderne hand of the era. Some of the old detailing was gone, its foreignness offensive to postwar American eyes. Notable among the elements omitted were the cherubs and shield surmounting the wide doorway to the transverse hall. (These were to turn up thirty-seven years later in a Georgetown garage, painted gold.) McKim's gray-and-white marble mantels were replaced with Knoxville red marble to please the commission chairman, Senator Kenneth D. McKellar of Tennessee. The sprawl of bare, waxed parquet, bleached light, the off-white walls, and the white ceiling blared with bright reflection. Edward Caldwell's mighty chandeliers were once again reduced in size, and it was by mere chance that they were used at all, for Truman tried hard to persuade Congress to release President Grant's 1874 gas fixtures so they might be returned to the White House. Had his effort succeeded, the room would have been an odd specimen indeed.

Opposite:
The East Room presented more or less the same dazzling white space that had characterized it since 1902. Changes here were subtle. Winslow had the great chandeliers reduced in size and discreetly fitted with hidden spotlights, as shown below.

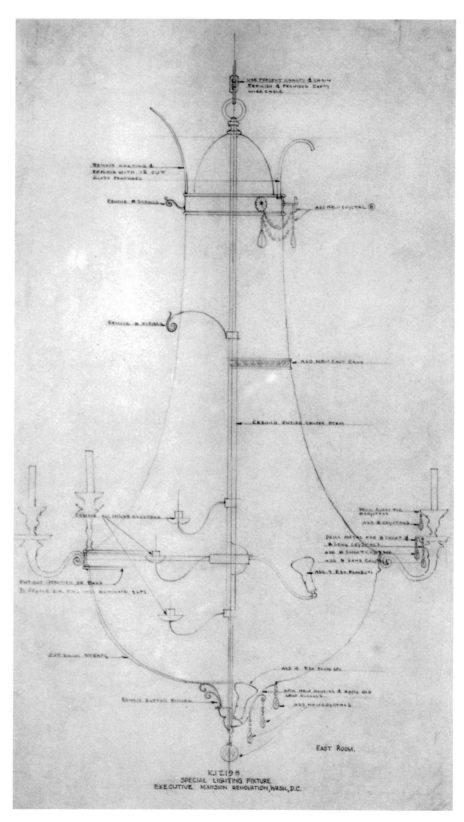

(Above) The Red Room and (opposite) the Green Room as completed in 1952. In their architecture the state parlors were fairly true to McKim, who had been fairly true to Hoban. No early materials survived, except the marble mantels. The colors remained the same, bearing only the nuances of their time, as had always been the case.

In most respects the three parlors were about the same. The ceiling of the Blue Room had always been lower than that of the Red and Green rooms. This was rectified, for some reason, in the lowering of the latter two to match the eighteen-foot Blue Room ceiling. Hoban's moldings were reproduced from the originals, deep coves of a simple sort but heavy in scale to suit the large rooms. The walls of each of the parlors were hung in brilliant colored silk, stretched over a linen base and a pad of cotton batting. Yellow gold, rose, and blue were used to enhance the Green Room's blue-green; the Red Room's pinkish lipstick red was varied by a pinkish white upholstery, used with red sofas and side chairs; the Blue Room was all royal blue. White wood trim contrasted sharply with the strong colors. Bare oak parquet covered the floor in the Blue Room, and a broadloom deep-pile solid red rug was in the Red Room. The Green Room rug, of green, gold, blue, and red emblazoned with the

presidential seal, had been used there since the last days of the Coolidge administration. Where furniture was concerned, the parlors contained reproductions purchased for Coolidge, Hoover, and Roosevelt, mingled with some furnishings put there by McKim.

The brilliant pale green of the State Dining Room was the biggest surprise of all. It was an icy, air-conditioning color popular during the 1950s, for all its claims to being colonial. A thousand flaws were hidden by filler and paint, deep scratches, splits, chips, patches, all forgotten in a smooth, multilayered application of the near-white green. McKim's stone mantel, which Theodore Roosevelt had ordered recarved, was gone, replaced by a heavy molding of green marble surrounding the firebox. The stone was dirty and would have looked odd with the light paneling, lost without the wood grain. Truman withdrew it in favor of a new one. The mantel with the buffaloes can be seen today in the

(Top) The basement corridor as finished by McKim in 1902. (Bottom) Lorenzo Winslow's restoration of the basement corridor. The vaulting was restored to its original appearance but imitated in plaster over lath, what was left of the original structural groining torn away.

Truman Library in Independence, Missouri.

On the ground floor, or basement level, a high wainscoting of smooth marble blocks replaced the magnificent austerity of the old, enveloping plastered vaults with a chilly monumentality. One of the grandest effects in the White House, the vaulting was always the richer for its simplicity. Winslow's idea was to relate space to the entrance hall above through the introduction of marble. This mistake has endured. Several of the ground floor rooms were fully paneled in wood cut from old joists and sills in the house, all of North Carolina pine procured by James Hoban at Elizabeth City in 1817. The 1950s craze for knotty pine found full expression in the unpainted, waxed walls of the china room, the library, and the two other official basement rooms.

An important ground-floor interior, now subdivided beyond recognition for other purposes, is the one Truman called the broadcast room. In the early days of the White House, before 1902, when it became a furnace room, this was the larger of two kitchens and the one used to prepare banquets. Even after Truman made it the radio broadcast room, situated directly beneath the entrance hall, the room kept its kitchen identity with reproductions of the two great sandstone fireplaces facing each other from east and west. Into the walls around these the president had ordered the insertion of the stones on which the Scottish stonecutters had cut their banker's marks in the 1790s, identifying portions of their work for payment. These stones Truman had had withdrawn from the stone walls. While the idea of a place for radio broadcasts seemed obvious in 1948, the broadcast room was outdated by television by the time it was finished.

The family quarters on the second floor stayed about the same. The look of an old house adapted was gone. Subtle rearrangements made possible by the reconstruction of the building had made the plan of this floor more cohesive than before. The fireplaces that had been put off center by the addition of bathrooms in the bedrooms in the central part of the floor were shifted in the rebuilding to the center of the wall. In all four corner dressing rooms the fireplaces were redesigned as corner fireplaces so each of the rooms could be divided into a bath and dressing room or sitting room. Bathrooms were placed about where McKim had put them, but they no longer appeared chopped off the corner of the room. To make closets in the president's bedroom on the south and in the bedroom across from it on the north, semicircular entrance apses were built, with ample closets behind the walls.

The most noticeable change in the second floor came with the introduction of increased functions to the eastern end of the long central hall. It had been the president's hope that the difference in floor levels between the east-end rooms and hall and the rest could be solved by making the whole floor level. As it had been, one climbed three or four steps to reach the east hall and the other rooms over the East Room. Many projects were drawn trying to satisfy Truman's request. At last it became clear that with the steel construction of the new house the area between the upper floor and the ceiling of the East Room would not have to be so thick. (It had been a large area – so large that the engineers had been able to crawl through it in their structural survey of the house, when they found that the East Room's plaster ceiling was unlocked and hanging down eighteen inches, midway, like a hammock.)

By shrinking the depth between the two stories of the house on the east, the difference in height between the east end and the central and west halls was reduced sufficiently to replace the steps with a ramp. Clearly the steps had looked better, and even the introduction of a richly detailed barrel vault over the ramped corridor did not mask its similarity to a hospital hall. Behind the side walls of this corridor were hidden a stair to the third floor on the north and a pair of closets on the south. Most of the magnificent succession of spaces, divided by tall arches and ending east and west with arched windows, prevailed; but the imposition of the narrow corridor reduced the sweep eastward to something less in effect and more complicated in resolution than it had been.

The framework, roof, and walls of the third floor were those put there by Coolidge in 1927. There was some simplification and rearrangement. It was now a huge story unto itself, divided into nine guest rooms, six servants' rooms, two sitting rooms, eight bathrooms, eight storage

Top:

The china room, in the basement. Lorenzo Winslow had the old structural timbers, some of great size, milled and made into fielded paneling for many of the basement rooms. While this paneling is painted today, it does survive. When it was made, it reflected the popular national taste for pine—and in some cases, knotty pine—paneling.

Bottom:

The broadcast room was intended as a permanent and dignified location for regular presidential radio addresses to the nation, a tradition begun by Herbert Hoover and continued by FDR in his fireside chats. Built in the restored kitchen, the room was rendered obsolete by television before it was completed and soon was subdivided for other purposes.

Opposite:

**Linen room in the third floor space
made by the pediment, 1952**

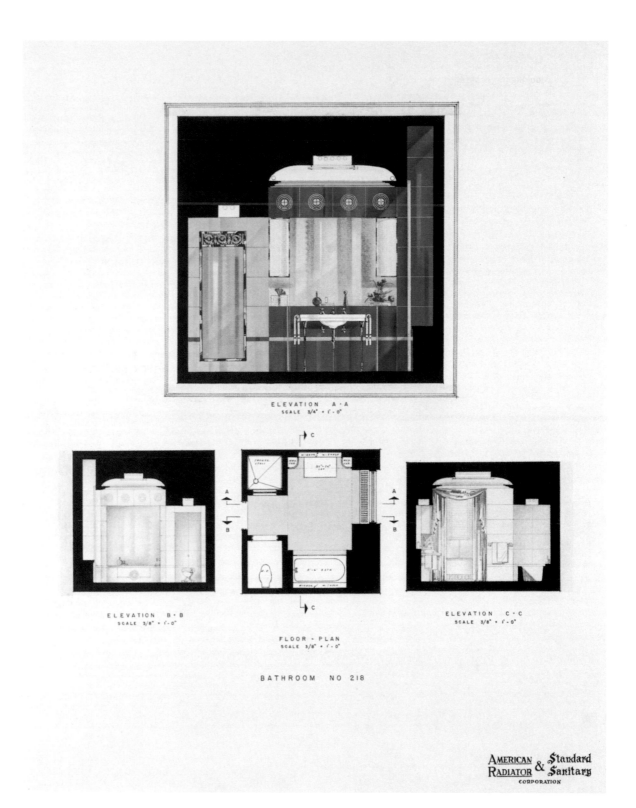

ELEVATION A·A
SCALE 3/4" · 1'-0"

ELEVATION B·B
SCALE 3/8" · 1'-0"

FLOOR·PLAN
SCALE 3/8" · 1'-0"

ELEVATION C·C
SCALE 3/8" · 1'-0"

BATHROOM NO 218

AMERICAN & Standard
RADIATOR Sanitary
CORPORATION

**Executed project for a second
floor bathroom, featuring Carrara
glass and custom-made plumbing
fixtures**

rooms, a kitchen, a great cedar closet, and a linen room, all arranged more or less around a large central corridor. Separate and apart, at the end of an upward-inclined ramp, was the rebuilt sun parlor atop the south portico. One could walk from it along the inside of the stone balustrade and see spectacular views of Washington.

Low of ceiling, simple of trim, the third floor had the finish quality of a suburban home of the time. This was a region of pine cupboards, asbestos and rubber floor tiles and linoleum, long horizontal lines of fluorescent tubing and venetian blinds, light fixtures of aluminum, and nickel-plated door hardware. The plaster walls were painted soft greens and grays. Every inch of space was used, out to the attic of the pediment of the north portico. Storage rooms and closets were in greater number than one would ever expect in a private home. The high windows, crossed by the balustrade outside, gave a foreboding cell-like feeling to the bedrooms. More than any other part of the renovated house, the third floor seems added, space that was somehow found in hiding, brought into the light, and tacked onto the rest, with no other purpose than to serve the floors below.

The commissioners, with the uneasy feeling that destruction of history was an ugly reality behind the bright progress in their work, took special pains to distribute some of the rejected materials for different worthy purposes. They adopted a general policy on January 6, 1950, as the first underjoining pits were dug to stabilize the old walls. Some material – mostly large wooden beams – was distributed to federal agencies. Twenty mantels went to museums in various parts of the country. Bricks went to several locations, including Mount Vernon, where they were used to reconstruct George Washington's orangery; some of the wood paneling and plaster ornament from the East Room went to the Smithsonian. The last category was for souvenirs. Various kinds of mementos were put in kits at Fort Myer and offered for sale. For two dollars Kit No.

Sun parlor on the south side of the third floor as replaced, 1952, sheathed in aluminum. This location atop the south portico was always a favorite spot from which to take in the prospect of the city (see page 86).

President Truman's congressional reception in the East Room to show the White House, March 23, 1952

Opposite:
Souvenirs were marketed to collectors as an official program of the restoration commission. Pieces of stone and brick—or enough for a fireplace facing—and all kinds of wood samples were packaged and offered to an eager public.

1 provided enough old pine to make a gavel; for 50 cents Kit No. 4–the most popular kit– yielded a small piece of old stone and an old square nail 2½ inches long; a brick "as nearly whole as practicable" cost $1; enough brick for a fireplace cost $100, and stone for the same purpose cost the same; two pieces of stone for bookends sold for $2.

The program brought in $50,000 but cost $40,000, and it caused tremendous trouble, even though military personnel did most of the work. Now and again one runs across a pine gavel or a fireplace facing and learns of the distinguished former service of the material. It was a strange, almost apologetic program, in the face of the destruction of a large part of the physical being of America's most historic house. But we are more antiquarian now than we were in those years after World War II, when lives torn apart by war were being rebuilt, even as new housing sprawled beyond the cities.

Winslow had gone to Williamsburg at the be-

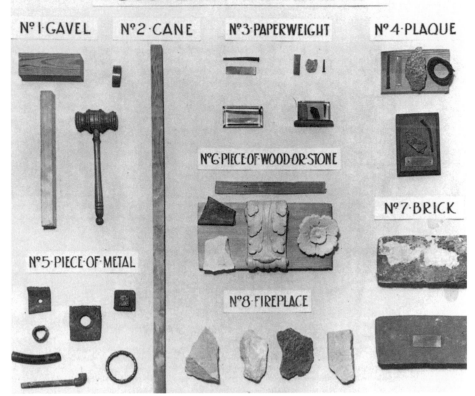

SOUVENIR MATERIAL

Nº1·GAVEL   Nº2·CANE   Nº3·PAPERWEIGHT   Nº4·PLAQUE

Nº6·PIECE·OF·WOOD·OR·STONE

Nº5·PIECE·OF·METAL

Nº7·BRICK

Nº8·FIREPLACE

275

ginning of the White House work to tour the reconstructed Governor's Palace with A. Edwin Kendrew and Bela Norton of the Williamsburg restoration project. The palace, though accurate to available historical documentation, was entirely new, built of steel and concrete concealed in an envelope of materials appropriate to the eighteenth century. The impressive structure, recreated from the historical record and archaeological exploration, had touched chords of patriotism in Depression times, as it was brought to completion in 1934. It was an image of the past, if without the substance of the original parts; it must have confirmed Winslow's feelings about the White House project, which in his view should result not only in a preserved image but also a better image, one made of original parts. The betrayal of the original, more antiquarian plan, caused by external circumstances and shortcuts, weighed heavily on Winslow. By the end of the project in 1952 he no longer had the president's ear, doubtless to some degree because of his complaining. Truman was directing the project entirely through the chief usher, Howell G. Crim, who through this involvement raised that position to a level more powerful than ever before.

President and Mrs. Truman moved back into the White House on March 27, 1952, inaugurating the renewed house. Truman was pleased to show it off in a national live television special in which he led Walter Cronkite through the main rooms, telling of events in the history of the house. In the East Room he played the great piano the Steinway company had given Franklin Roosevelt. He paused before portraits that reminded him of stories from history.

President Truman had done what he set out to do: rebuild the house for all time. His renovation was the most radical in the history of the building. Madison and Monroe had rebuilt it fairly exactly after it was burned during the War of 1812. Arthur had merely redecorated. Theodore Roosevelt's alterations were a revision of image and use, but most of the house had remained. Coolidge changed the roofline. Truman rebuilt the White House from the inside out, and it remains today, redecorated, but essentially as he left it.

Opposite:

The completed White House from the south. With the exception of the Truman balcony the view from this point, like most others, was not greatly different in 1952 than it had been fifty years before, although the inside of the house was effectively new.

U.S. Geological
Survey, Washington
West Quadrangle, 1951

8

THE HOUSE WITHIN THE HOUSE

I n the long and for the most part tranquil architectural history of the White House, the Truman renovation seems sudden and radical. Forty years' hindsight, however, makes it appear less surprising. Seen in the context of the redirection of the nation after World War II, the rebuilding of Europe, and a world in which the president of the United States was now central – a role for which there was no American precedent – the rebuilding of the White House seems in a way even appropriate. By tradition presidents can do what they please with the White House. Congress will intervene only in the matter of funding. Perhaps it can be said that President Truman did the dirty work for all those to come.

Truman saw history in broad sweeps, monumental generalities more like history as it was understood in the nineteenth century than in his own time. He took little interest in details. That the White House was edited as it was rebuilt therefore presented no problem to him, if the general picture was the same. He was no antiquarian. To him the house was returned to full use and looked about the same, with improvements; thus it was restored.

It had been more important to him from the start that the presidency remain in the White House than that the best experts contrive an antiquarian restoration. To achieve his objective he had to be fully in charge. Truman had watched commissions argue. He had listened to quarrels among experts. This work had to be carried out in a hurry, almost before anyone knew what was happening. Whether he knew or it only seems he must have known it, most of the magic of the White House is in the mystique it carries. Most of this comes from the power it represents in the world today, not from the memory of Dolley Madison's flight to safety or Lincoln's sleepless nights. Even so, history adds a flavoring.

When one enters the White House the past gives way, yet the past is there—like background music—and it gives the symbolic place its luster. One might build a new president's house, but never a new White House. Truman wished to modernize without destroying. He peeled the house back as far as he could, stopping at George Washington's original walls. Building anew from there, he kept familiar images in mind. By genius of plan, or by a result stumbled upon, or by something inbetween, the president achieved his goal of at once keeping the house and replacing it.

It is difficult from an architectural point of view to label the renovation of 1948-52 a success or a failure. As a functioning building the house works still today. This is the White House of Eisenhower, Kennedy, Johnson, Nixon, Ford, Carter, Reagan, and Bush and all who shall follow, surely well into its third century of use before it need undergo major change. The renovation was a success in the sense that it added space in which the household functions could expand and it introduced modern systems for comfort. Design was quite another matter. This feature of the project was firmly under the

Entrance hall as completed, 1952

thumb of the president, who sought advice only from those likely to agree.

The commissioners dismissed the 1902 work of McKim as an "aesthetically pleasant remodelling." Haste had made waste in the rush to honor Theodore Roosevelt's five-month schedule, although the waste of 1902 pales beside that of 1948-52. To demean McKim's transformation is to reject his reasoned concept of renovation. Structural considerations notwithstanding Truman's renovators would have profited from a study of McKim's analytical approach and of his understanding of the historic building. It was

(Top) Basement corridor and (bottom) state floor pantry, 1952

McKim, not Winslow, who showed that the White House could be preserved and still function as the home of the president. In his ability and his willingness to see through to the nut of the matter, McKim formulated a new program for using the house that allowed for the retention of its original appearance. He revised the image only insofar as the original building admitted of "improvements." To his thinking he "restored" the exterior. And to an extent this can be defended.

The weakness of the Truman renovation, by contrast, lay in the muddy concept upon which it was based. It was more akin to the ill-starred ideas of the nineteenth-century Army Corps of Engineers than to the 1902 work of McKim. Engineering matters were allowed to dominate, and little effort was made to understand the existing architecture. To the engineers the answer to all the White House problems lay in building more soundly and adding space, thus the focus on steel and concrete work and square footage. It is true that great public buildings are never large enough. A state dining room that seats 100 might as well seat 500 or 1,000, for in any case it will be crowded. In the Truman renovation advantage was taken of every inch of space that could be gained from the trim, steel-frame house built inside the old shell of stone. From hollow walls, subterranean floors, deep attic eaves, and mezzanines new space was borrowed, and the plan of the rooms was expanded. On paper there was no longer the simple arrangement of an eighteenth-century house, but instead a complex one, like a modern house, only bigger by far than any known to exist.

The old rooms of the ground, first, and second floors were situated more or less as they had always been. They were suspended, however, among a network of new secondary spaces and related to them aesthetically in much the way a stage setting relates to a cavernous backstage. Most of the new rooms do not relate to the old plan in any cohesive way. The result is a sham return to the original White House, a recognition of its more immediate images and at the same time a denial of its broader integrity as a building.

This dichotomy finds expression in the shapes and sizes of spaces, as well as in the details of

Above:
Old and new: (top) carved window detail, north front, 1790s; and (bottom) stringcourse detail, grand stair, 1952

Below:
Diplomatic reception room furnished in American antiques by Mamie Eisenhower, 1960, sparking a renewed interest in placing historic furnishings in the public areas of the White House. This idea was to make its real impact a year later, in the Kennedy administration.

Opposite:
Fireplace mantel designed by Lorenzo Winslow, diplomatic reception room

design. Where bedrooms upstairs have been reduced and redesigned to accommodate bathrooms and closets they bear no resemblance whatsoever to interiors in a late eighteenth- or early nineteenth-century house; rather they are like rooms in a hotel of the mid-twentieth century. A few steps from the embracing range of the basement's groin vaulting, a stair sneaks down into a mezzanine dressing room sleek with frosted glass, aluminum, terrazzo, and smooth Moderne wood treatments. The principal access from the ground floor to the state floor, between the East Room and the entrance hall, is a wide stair running between walls and divided into two lanes by a free-standing aluminum handrail. This stair would not be out of place in 30th Street Station in Philadelphia or in old Union Station in Omaha. The effect is institutional, durable, and hard, like a public building. McKim's White House had retained the domestic feel of a home.

McKim had taken care that his new designs, if not original to the house, embodied historical accuracy sufficient to stand alongside the original. With less caution, the renovators of 1948-52 ventured boldly into a puffy version of the Moderne, espoused since the late 1920s in government architecture and already tired out by the postwar years. This was a mode of interpreting motifs from the past by stripping them to their basics of form and line. It reaches high points at the White House in certain fetching architectural details, such as Winslow's mantelpiece in the diplomatic reception room. His design is a serene, liquid confection in which a traditional wooden mantel form flows beyond itself to take command of the whole chimney breast through white woodwork panels and tall, rounded corners that have a tambour effect. But normally the Moderne elements are out of place in the sense of the house as reflective of its origins. Particularly as the work grows older, the detailing becomes more obtrusive and odd. Yet these elements are part of the story of a building that has evolved.

There is a certain whimsical paradox to the increase in space resulting from the Truman renovation. From the time the house was first planned and throughout the nineteenth century the question of the president's occupying a "palace" had been debated. Harrison and McKinley

and to a lesser extent Cleveland had been willing to expand the White House into palace proportions. Theodore Roosevelt rather settled the issue in 1902 with his restoration of the smaller, early image from the outside. Even so, critics complained of the foreignness and imperial tenor of his revised interior. But more often than not the architectural meaning of "palace" as criticism for the president's house had simply been one of scale. The house George Washington first approved in concept was a building of enormous scale – approximately the size of the National Gallery of Art. Lesser palaces were proposed in the late nineteenth century, both as new houses and as expansions of the existing house, and all would have appeared palatial.

Theodore Roosevelt enlarged the house with extended wings, and relatively minor additions came with Taft, Coolidge, and Franklin Roosevelt. It was Truman who, within the unchanged image of the original house, at last realized the palace. His reconstruction of the building increased the room count notably. The levels went from four to six floors, and the luxuries and conveniences were multiplied many times over.

One can imagine the ghosts of legions of congressmen and senators reacting in horror. Still it was hidden behind the familiar mask. Who was to know?

An up-to-date presidential palace was built inside the old walls. If the palace idea had in a sense won out, the new house contained none of the royal visual effects that had so concerned early American politicians. As far as the settings of ceremony are concerned it was much the same house, for it was familiar and had proved its usefulness. The character that had once seemed confusingly simple and to some provincial had long since been enhanced by McKim's embellishments. This tone was maintained, with the loss of some of its quality. Where the White House is palacelike is in the level of living it provides, and such features are seen by very few people.

From the perspective of today's sensitivity toward historic landmarks, the solution reached in 1948-52 is difficult even to imagine. Except for the stone walls, no deference was paid to historical parts. The resulting White House did not feel like an old house, even though the plan was visibly much the same and most of the new

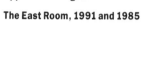

Opposite and right:
The East Room, 1991 and 1985

spaces were tucked away out of sight. Experts on the preservation of historic buildings were not consulted, and while there were few who could claim proficiency in that field just after World War II, some experts did exist. The influence of restorationists might have altered the course, at least in the reuse of architectural elements. Perhaps not, though, for in this country twenty years thereafter some so-called scholarly restorations were proceeding with little regard for original materials, an approach that is scorned today.

The new functions imposed on the old White House required more than the building had

The grand stair, (opposite) seen from the archway in the transverse hall and (above) providing a photo opportunity for President and Mrs. John F. Kennedy and guests, former President Truman and Mrs. Truman, Margaret Truman Daniels, and Clifton Daniels

space or structural stamina to provide. So the minimum was saved to maintain historical credibility and most of the building was sacrificed to contemporary needs. The climate in architectural criticism was favorable to such work. Moderne architecture had made its appearance long since, and its philosophies of building anew pervaded everything by the close of the war. The Beaux-Arts, which had limped along since World War I, was by now completely vanquished by the new ideal. Only where it rejected the past was the White House renovation at all in

step with the prevailing architectural thinking of its time.

What would the solution have been had the president, by 1948, occupied such a big house as Biltmore, in North Carolina, or White Marsh Hall, the splendid Georgian-style mansion that once stood near Philadelphia? That would have been the case had the engineers succeeded in building the mighty expansions proposed more than a half century before. In terms of space these projects might have been beneficial, but many of them would have wrought an unhappy and permanent change in the traditional exterior. It is certain, however, that no "restoration" would have been allowed that removed or reduced the monumental additions. By the end of the war requirements of security alone demanded significant alteration of the house. While at the outset the Truman rebuilding was intended to make the house safe and secure, it soon expanded its goals to making the house larger as well. Had the need for space been no consideration, would the presidential renovation have been different? Would teams of conservators have been called in to restore, while structural experts repaired and stabilized? One suspects that the answer is yes.

Had it been decided in 1948 to expand on Franklin Roosevelt's idea of a museum at the White House and to convert the entire building to that purpose, new living arrangements for the president would have followed one of several possibilities. All of these were discussed at one time or another. Blair House was never a serious contender, although it was speculated that one day the private quarters would be there, with the restored White House given over to social functions and a museum. A more likely plan would have been that broached during the Eisenhower administration, which called for a multiple-story executive structure with presidential quarters on several upper floors. Aware of the retirement comforts provided for some of his fellow officers in large apartments at hotels such as New York's Waldorf, the president warmed to the idea.

Eisenhower's ultimate waning of interest proved once again that no president was likely to want to be the one to make the decision to leave the White House. In addition to the obvious con-

Sections of the White House looking (top) east and (bottom right) west. The east view shows the north and south porticoes and, on the state floor, the entrance hall and the Blue Room, with the transverse hall between them. Above the Blue Room is the yellow oval room, and below it is the diplomatic reception room. The ramp on the third floor leads to the solarium. Under the north portico is Latrobe's vaulting system (see pages 48-52), the only original one remaining in the structure.

Opposite:
Mantelpiece, State Dining Room, a copy in marble of McKim's stone chimneypiece of 1902

straints imposed by public opinion, presidents themselves know best that the White House has functional advantages of the symbolic sort to such an extent that they outweigh nearly all consideration of moving elsewhere. The idea of relocating the president has not come up since.

Over the long view, standing apart from our standards of proper restoration today, Truman's renovation must be given some high marks. The possible, indeed obvious alternatives of the late 1940s are not appealing. As a museum alone the White House would be as empty and as dead as those state capitols that have been vacated by the legislatures and serve only as reliquaries. Even as a party pavilion or a forum for state ceremony the White House would have lost everything but its past, and that would have made it seem more distant than it is as we know it. Although in 1952 it would have been fairer to call Truman's work a reconstruction than a restoration, time has made a better fit of the word renovation, if not restoration. That the very boards Jefferson trod are no longer there, or the stairs Lincoln climbed, means very little in the overpowering sense of past one feels in the house.

Those who have followed have made few architectural alterations and none of any significance. More change has taken place in the west wing than in the residence. Truman attempted to enlarge the west wing southward with a broadcast theater and new offices. Congress would not fund this work, designed by Winslow and the president. A broadcast room was not built in the west wing until 1969, when Richard Nixon ordered the Roosevelt swimming pool floored over

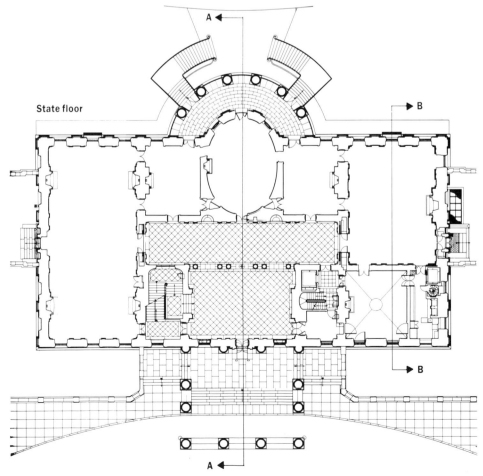

Section A–A

State floor

Section B–B

Overleaf:
State Dining Room, detail of the plaster cornice

and the present broadcast and press room put there. Partitions in the west wing are continually changed. The Oval Office and adjacent Cabinet room remain much as they were after the Roosevelt remodeling of 1934. Otherwise, partitions are moved and new ones installed quite at will. The west wing has wholly lost the sense of architectural predictability in its plan. (For security considerations the plan as it is today is not illustrated in this volume.)

Most changes in the appearance of the house have come in the form of interior decoration. Particularly with the advent of television the stage-set role of the state rooms has gained greater attention from the presidents than ever before. The theme of heritage has been favored since the 1920s. A river of antiques and traditional furnishings has flowed to the White House over the past sixty or more years. In the last half of that span the flow often became a flood. The origin of this activity goes back to Grace Coolidge in 1924 and to Lou Hoover, who succeeded her in 1929, and their interest in acquiring antiques for the house.

Eleanor Roosevelt, though involved in reproducing antiques for sale before she went to the White House, showed no interest while there, although her husband aggressively collected White House memorabilia for his east wing museum that never came to be. An interior furnishings advisory committee in 1932 supplied the Green Room with reproductions of American antiques, crowning the setting with an eighteenth-century English cut-glass chandelier. The committee furnished the Red Room later in the decade. Members of this committee had been active in building the American Wing of the

Sections of the White House looking (left) east and (top) north. The east view shows the East Room, which stretches from the front of the house to the back. Above it are, to the right, the Lincoln bedroom and, to the left, the queens' bedroom (before 1902 part of the presidential offices and later named for royal visits). The section looking north shows three tiers of transverse halls: That on the state floor extends between the East Room and the State Dining Room, passing the entrance hall with its screen of columns. In the second and third floor family quarters are the more extensive halls used as sitting rooms. Note in the basement, or ground floor, corridor the arch system that forms the east-west segment of the groin-vaulted passage.

Opposite:
Family Dining Room
on the state floor, 1999

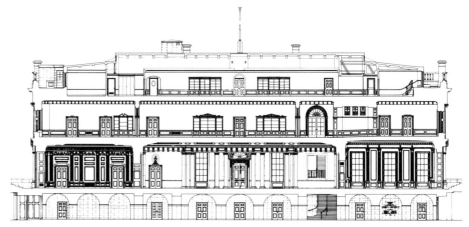

Section D–D

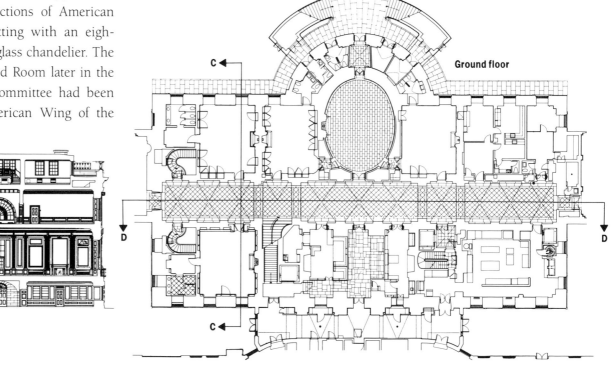

Ground floor

Section C–C

Truman administration, project by Charles Haight for redecoration, 1951

Kennedy administration

Bush administration, 1991

Metropolitan Museum of Art, opened in 1924. Relations between the White House and the committee were always difficult, the White House wanting the committee merely to raise the money and turn it over, while the committee insisted on having a major role in the decisions on decorating. Certainly the idea of imposing one's taste on some of the most famous rooms in the world has its intoxicating side.

Truman's interior decorator, Charles Haight of B. Altman and Company in New York, wished to furnish the rebuilt White House with antiques, but he had neither the money nor the support of the president, who warned him that rare antiques would receive too hard use and should not

be put in the White House rooms. The president presented a further obstacle in not concealing his personal distaste for the furnishings advisory committee. There was a chilly standoff. Few funds came from the committee, nor did their actions in any way cast doubt on the president's judgment of them.

Mamie Eisenhower thought the interiors of the Truman White House, which she inherited in 1953, looked like those in a hotel and longed for the patina of the old, such as she had known in quarters in historic houses in Europe. The president insisted that the house was virtually new and would not consent to alterations. Toward the end of the Eisenhower administration the

Above and opposite:

The Blue Room during

several administrations

American Institute of Interior Designers, under its president, Michael Greer, approached the Eisenhowers about redecorating the oval diplomatic reception room on the ground floor in period style. The President agreed. This project, completed in 1960, represented the contributions of many firms in the decorating trades in furniture, lighting, fabrics, and floor coverings.

The most highly publicized historical redecoration was launched during the brief administration of John F. Kennedy, with the participation of Jacqueline Kennedy. The project institutionalized the idea of the White House as a place to reflect American history through furnishings. The apparent renewal of the White House as a house of history contributed to the warmth the public felt toward the young family living there;

it was one of those periods, usually fleeting, when the house actually seemed like a private home. The Kennedy project was given a legal format, unlike those before. Congressional legislation designated the White House, already Reservation 1 of the National Park Service, as having interiors worthy of "preservation and interpretation," with maintenance falling to the Park Service. The White House Historical Association was established as a private nonprofit organization to enhance the interpretation of the White House to the American people. In its first years, this private arm devoted itself not only to funding the acquisition of historical furnishings but also to producing publications, among them *The White House: An Historic Guide*, which tells about the development of the building.

The Red Room, 2001 and (opposite) the Green Room, 1999

Truman administration, post-renovation

Kennedy administration

Ford administration

The second floor corridor
as living room, during several
administrations

While many antique furnishings were acquired with funds from the association and in other ways, special attention was given to documentary White House furnishings that were already there, especially the pieces bought in France by James Monroe in 1818. The definitive artistic influence on the decoration of the Blue Room was the Jansen company in Paris, represented by its principal interior decorator, Stefan Boudin; Jansen had restored such French palaces as the Grand Trianon at Versailles for official use and re-created for museum purposes Josephine's château of Malmaison. Boudin's was a rich taste, heavily antiquarian in character, although lightened by a pragmatic eye in the arrangement of objects. The design of the state rooms became dramatically historical, this Empire and that Federal. Even the then-unpopular Victorian made an appearance upstairs in the treaty room, newly named, which had served as the Cabinet meet-

Opposite:

Barrel-vaulted passage, second
floor, east end. This point in the
long second floor transverse
hallway originally led to the office
section of the house. After 1902
the space was annexed into the

family quarters. The ramp was
built in the renovations of
1948–52 to replace steps that
accommodated an incline in the
floor where it rises to a higher
level over the East Room ceiling.

ing place from 1865 until the building of the west wing in 1902.

Boudin's interiors were settings, in a sense not unlike stage scenery, meant to serve ceremony and to inspire those who experienced the rooms with the flavor of the American past. He brought to the state rooms the French taste for pageantry. The rooms were sumptuously conceived in brilliant silks and mahogany and gilt beyond anything expected from historic American houses, but in the French tradition the past was handled lightly, without American or British pedantry. Even though the obligatory advisory committee listed among its members such antiquarians and connoisseurs as Henry Francis du Pont, founder of the Winterthur Museum in Delaware, Boudin's touch was triumphant. The Kennedy Red and Green rooms knew the finest interior work since McKim's in 1902.

Little was changed in the interiors during the Lyndon B. Johnson administration. By the close of the decade of the 1960s the need for repair was evident in all the public areas. Wear is accelerated by the constant pressure of White House living, with a million tourists annually and some 40,000 invited guests. The seven-year administration of Richard Nixon saw an increase in acquisitions. Pat Nixon's participation in the project attracted both public interest and donations of money and furnishings reaching into the millions of dollars. She was determined from the outset that the effort not lag. Inspecting historic buildings contemporary with the White House, she approved decorative plaster elements to be copied to replace those installed in the state parlors during the Truman administration.

The aggressive program of collecting antiques led to the removal of all but a few of Boudin's interiors of a decade before, and those remaining were upstairs. On the state floor the parlors were entirely changed, and while they followed much the same historical period themes the results were museumlike, reflecting trends in historic house museums of the time and especially a 1970 exhibition of nineteenth-century decorative art at the Metropolitan Museum of Art. At about that time a designer was engaged who had worked on the nineteenth-century show, Edward Vason Jones of Albany, Georgia. Although not an

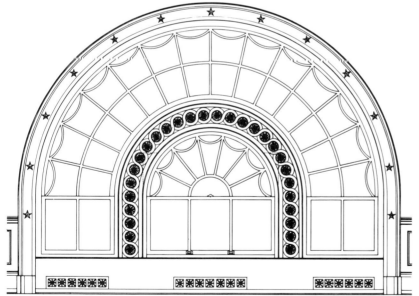

Each end of the transverse
corridor on the second floor is
lighted by fanlight windows,
which were part of Hoban's
original design. The window on
the west once lit the landing of the

grand stair; in 1869 it became the
principal feature of the west
sitting hall. (Above) On the east
end the lunette lights the hall
between the queens' bedroom
and the Lincoln bedroom.

Franklin D. Roosevelt administration

Eisenhower administration

Kennedy administration

From study to sitting room: the upstairs oval room during several administrations

architect he had designed many houses and interiors in Georgia and had developed a somewhat Beaux-Arts approach to neoclassical interior design. Many of his projects, such as the Georgia governor's mansion and the Metropolitan's nineteenth-century exhibition rooms, reflected this academic taste. His style was applied to the state parlors of the White House. Boudin's theatrical settings were replaced by interiors designed as showcases for large collections of antiques. With minor changes and some replacement of fabrics these are the interiors in place today.

Although refurnishings under Gerald R. Ford and Jimmy Carter were few, the Committee for the Preservation of the White House was active. Rosalynn Carter gave attention to increasing the collection of fine art in the house, and a substantial number of important American paintings were acquired by donation. Supporters of Ronald Reagan collected funds to redecorate the second

Northeast gate on Pennsylvania
Avenue, 1992. The stone piers
were built for James Monroe in
1818 and repositioned by Andrew
Jackson. The fencing is all of
recent date, but in outline it
copies the original. The gates of
this design installed in 1818 were
in use until 1976. The lamps were
installed in 1858 as gas fixtures.

and third floor family quarters after his inauguration in 1981. Decoration of the rooms upstairs had always been, on the whole, piecemeal; now some thirty-four rooms were finished for the first time in the history of the house. Under Los Angeles interior decorator Ted Graber all were furnished and decorated, for the most part with furnishings already in the White House or in storage in Virginia. Light colors and a strong emphasis on the central east-west corridors were combined in an attempt to reduce the inevitable sense of confinement that goes with the upper floors. George Bush has made only one notable change, the removal of Boudin's treaty room, a Victorian confection filled with memorabilia, and its conversion to the president's private study, a purpose it served from 1902 until 1928 and at shorter intervals thereafter.

The upstairs is virtually the sole domain of the president and his family at home. They generally use the state floor only ceremonially and for entertaining. Nixon liked to use the state rooms for special purposes, and private dinners were served on occasion in the Red Room. Meetings of various kinds may take place on the ground floor, always related to White House business, of course, but not necessarily involving the president or first lady. Lou Hoover introduced this use of the residence, and Mamie Eisenhower was the last to ban it.

When Truman finished his renovation the White House was too big for its job. Today it is about right. The White House employs, among many others, a head chef, a sous chef, and assistants for pastry and confections; a housekeeper supported by maids and housemen and extra workers when necessary; butlers, who serve under a maître d', who supervises the dining rooms and service; and a florist and assistants, who make daily rounds. Some thirty servants are augmented by groups of people whose tasks are not domestic. The Secret Service presence, for example, is large and constant, with guard stations within the house as well as throughout the grounds.

For the White House grounds the National Park Service has since the Kennedy era provided horticulturists and work crews who maintain groves, lawns, and gardens. The original presidential enclave, the approximately sixty acres approved by George Washington, is still officially the President's Park, including the Ellipse and Lafayette Park. Only some eighteen acres remain within the iron fence of the White House as established, with modifications, by Thomas Jefferson when he cut Washington's grand park down to size. Washington, however, had already intruded upon the botanical gardens envisioned for the grounds when he ordered the executive office buildings placed in the President's Park, to the east and west of the White House. On those same sites now stand the Greek Revival Treasury Building (1830s and 1850s) and the Second Empire State, War, and Navy – now Old Executive Office – Building (1870s), both giants, overshadowing the White House.

A fleet of cars and support vehicles, helicopters and airplanes, and the most sensitive communications devices connect the remote enclave of the White House to the outside world. For the most part the president today travels short distances by helicopter. Historically the president is not required to stop for stoplights or signs when traveling by car, and at least since the days when Ulysses Grant raced top speed in his sulky along Pennsylvania Avenue the president has been allowed to go as fast as he wishes. The presidential motorcade, which over the years has grown to some ten cars tailed by an ambulance, though not a common sight, can still be seen speeding through Washington.

The presidential complex grows constantly in subtle ways. Heretofore, Truman's White House has absorbed new needs as they arise. That time is probably coming to an end. Years of rearrangement and adjustment will postpone the problem of space needs, but the issue is already beginning to loom on the horizon, as it did first in the decade of the Civil War. West Executive Avenue was returned to the White House grounds at the beginning of World War II. East Executive Avenue was blocked off and redesigned as a pedestrian way in 1986. The closing of Pennsylvania Avenue to vehicular traffic for three blocks in front of the White House is inevitable, as is the closing of Jackson Place and Madison Place, flanking Lafayette Park. Discussions began in 1989 about possible construction of under-

Plan of the White House grounds, 1989; Pennsylvania Avenue is at the lower or north extreme. This comprises the immediate White House complex although the broader landscape, including Lafayette Park on the north and the Ellipse to the south, are still considered part of the President's Park as originally designated in the 1790s survey of the new city.

Opposite: Looking north over the lawn and out Sixteenth Street from the windows over the north entrance. From this relatively safe perspective Lincoln addressed the crowds who gathered before the White House to hear him during the Civil War.

306

ground facilities beneath the Ellipse. Reasons for these changes will be in part security, but in large measure simply the need for more room.

Restoration in the sense of preservation was never of much importance at the White House until recent years. In 1975, early in the Ford administration, an outdoor swimming pool was built behind the west wing. Before digging began, a study of historic maps and a preliminary archaeological investigation showed that this site might well be the only undisturbed ground left in the President's Park. But busy places keep busy schedules, and furious haste to build the pool precluded an orthodox archaeological dig. Archaeologists were consulted as to what to do, and though exasperated by the decision to move so fast they recommended as an emergency measure that the dirt from the pool be taken to another site for detailed study. Investigation of the great mound of dirt yielded shards of Madison china and other artifacts, confirming what documentary research had suggested in advance, that the site had been the gully filled in 1815 with debris from the basement of the burned White House.

The archaeological project of 1975-77 was watched with avid interest by those who worked at the White House. It may well have been the spark that kindled interest in historic preservation on the site by those who keep it. When in 1976 the last of Paulus Hedl's fine wrought-iron gates of 1818 was removed for security reasons, it was carefully preserved. In 1979 during the Carter administration it became clear that another repainting of the house over the thick, insecure build-up of past coats of paint was impractical. All the old layers were there, those applied in the time of Monroe, Jackson, Lincoln, and others; the paint was peeling and discolored, and the surface was quite imperfect in places. Removal of the old paint became necessary, and this was taken as an opportunity for conservation of the original stone walls.

An exhaustive search was made for an appropriate means of paint removal. The answer proved to be a combination of chemical removers, water under heavy pressure, and intricate handwork. The project, begun in 1980, was carried out in stages, beginning with the east wall.

Conservation of the walls involved plugging and recarving in many places, as well as paint removal. Concrete patches installed over the years were dug out and replaced with square-cut

Opposite:

Oval Office, east wall

The south front in protective cloth coverings during the restoration

The Historic American Buildings
Survey conducted a survey of the
White House in 1990-92, exactly
measuring it and recording it in
drawings and photographs. Field
notes, such as the one below for
the east lunette (finished drawing
on page 301), were sources for the
ink drawings seen elsewhere in
this book. While the recording
was in process, stone
conservation was under way.

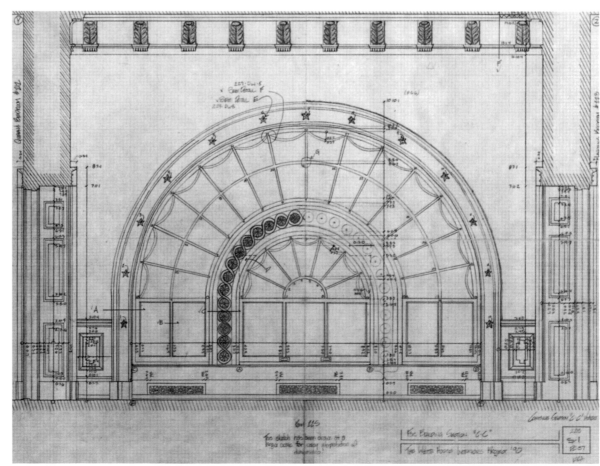

Opposite:
The north portico, stripped of
some forty layers of paint and
whitewash, is exposed to its
original stone, 1988

(Above) North front, 1978, and

(opposite) south front, 1987

inserts of limestone, perfectly fitted. Moldings and carvings, where chipped and broken, were likewise repaired or in a few cases replaced. At the conclusion of each sequence in the restoration, when the bare stone and newly restored areas had seasoned, the stone was repainted. Spray guns were used to apply the yellowish white paint at close range, thinly and evenly, approximating the whitewash sealer the Scottish stonecutters had painted on as soon as a section of wall was complete. It was the first coating that had made the White House white. The new white paint that concluded the conservation project was as smooth as the original must have

been. With the completion of the project in 1992 the house, at 200, had undergone the first scientific restoration work in its long history.

As an architectural specimen—as well as a building that must be used every day—the White House is probably unique. The replacement of materials is nearly constant. Red oak floors in the East Room, for example, have been replaced two times since Truman's renovation and those in the Blue Room once. In the general sense, however, the house is old, not new. Steeped in tradition it is a place that must function with wholly modern efficiency. Many masters are served there. Even the new house at forty raises questions of preser-

vation, as Moderne and International Style decorative parts, characteristic of the 1940s and 1950s and not unusual to the eye of that time, seem to clash with our emotional identification of the White House as a late eighteenth- and early nineteenth-century building. Checkerboard floor tiles in green and white seem today more dated than historical. Sleek molded stair rails in dressing room areas contrast with rooms filled self-consciously with period antiques; the metal shell of the rooftop solarium is reminiscent of a diner of the '40's or a streamlined aluminum trailer; and stripped-down Georgian designs in woodwork are seen practically everywhere. Will these elements survive the gradual architectural retreat of design motifs in the interiors into a purer representation of the earliest days of the house?

The White House of today has served nine presidents, from Harry Truman to George Bush, and has thus achieved a validity of its own as a historic place, even though only its walls are 200 years old. Unlike most of America's great landmarks, it has not been adapted to a substitute use. It remains the home and work place of the president. Like any building so venerable, it has had to be flexible. Such losses as it has sustained would be intolerable for Mount Vernon or Longfellow's house in Cambridge. At the White House loss has been merely part of the process.

Change at the White House proceeds according to immediate needs. Since 1964 most changes have been reviewed in advance by the Committee for the Preservation of the White House, appointed by the president; no plan definitively classifies the parts of the house as to what may or may not be altered and to what degree. And what purpose would strict rules serve? They would be an academic exercise; a plan too stringent would crowd the functions of the complex, and it would be set aside. While always carried out in the context of a certain reverence for the image the building conveys, change has often taken a ruthless course with the physical parts of the structure. Recent years have brought gentler hands, but the process must and will continue as long as the White House remains the home of the president.

Opposite:

Detail of the south portico

(Above) The north portico and (overleaf) a panorama of Washington, D.C., showing the White House in the cityscape

315

AFTERWORD

Since the publication of this book in 1992, 200 years after the cornerstone of the White House was laid, a second bicentennial has taken place. The year 2000 marked the anniversary of the first occupation of the house by President John Adams in 1800. Now into the 21st century, the White House looks back on the anniversaries of its inception as distant things, and moves into a time that will offer much more that is new. The old stone structure finds itself still the home of the president, but in circumstances no one who had built its walls stone-by-stone long ago would ever likely be able to imagine. Even President Truman, who rebuilt it for the ages, might be surprised to find that its needs far outstretch even his imaginative rescue half a century ago.

The residence itself still serves well. Ample living quarters on the second and third floors do not share the complaints of the state floor, which could always use a little more room. Tents set up on the south lawn have been used to increase the number of invited guests to the thousands. The West Wing with its two spillover buildings, the adjacent Eisenhower Executive Office Building (formerly State, War, and Navy, built in the 1870s) and the high-rise New Executive Office Building a block away (built in the 1960s) still serve in terms of space, with continual rearrangements inside to suit the nearly 3,000 members of the executive staff.

The White House lives on as it always has, because the American people and the presidents want it to. Its proclivity for adjustment, however, has been its salvation. Today more than ever, the glaring complication to continuing the White House is security.

Security here began simply as a task of locking the doors. A "porter" with his ring of keys, had his bed in the small room that is still used today as the Usher's Office to the right of the north door. The porter became "doorkeeper" July 1, 1842, attached to the Metropolitan Police newly formed in that year. Although wearing business suits, with firearms concealed, the doorkeepers were denounced in congress as a Praetorian guard protecting Caesar from the people. The issue was that the guards seemed to conflict with perceived public access to the president; congress still challenges the work of presidential guarding. Always the White House must seem open, the president available to the citizen, and although it may be largely symbolic, the importance of it cannot be overestimated in the generational adaptation of the White House.

At the outset of World War II the security line moved from the doors of the house to the outer perimeters of the grounds. The presence in the world of terrorism and the resulting attacks have changed this. Protection officials have determined it advisable to move vehicular traffic as far away from the White House as possible. President Clinton authorized the closing of Pennsylvania Avenue in 1995 and it remains closed today.

The Secret Service and the National Park Service address more extensive precautions and services, with the mandate to keep the White House the same. Where it seems to be heading is that the urban surroundings of the White House will welcome pedestrians—landscapes and historic streets retained but closed to cars and trucks. Improvements will go underground.

Interior decorating continues inside the house. Through media identification, the public associates presidents and decor. The Oval Office—ordered oval by President Taft in 1909 so it would seem less "new" and more like an official, historic White House room—once remained the same for decades but now is redecorated by administration: Style Bush yielded to Style Clinton, which stepped aside for Style Bush, Jr. Upstairs rooms are redecorated, using private funds as the particular president wishes. Mrs. Clinton directed the redecoration of the Blue Room using decorators' documents from President Monroe's 1817 rebuilding of the war-ruined White House, bringing scholarship to the changes of setting in the State Rooms.

The Blue Room work seems prophetic. It is likely that conservation, preservation, and some historical re-creation lie in the future of the White House, as the surroundings adjust ever more to modern times.

William Seale
September 1, 2001

George Washington	April 30, 1789–March 4, 1797	Benjamin Harrison	March 4, 1889–March 4, 1893
John Adams	March 4, 1797–March 4, 1801	Grover Cleveland	March 4, 1893–March 4, 1897
Thomas Jefferson	March 4, 1801–March 4, 1809	William McKinley	March 4, 1897–September 14, 1901
James Madison	March 4, 1809–March 4, 1817	Theodore Roosevelt	September 14, 1901–March 4, 1909
James Monroe	March 4, 1817–March 4, 1825	William Howard Taft	March 4, 1909 –March 4, 1913
John Quincy Adams	March 4, 1825 –March 4, 1829	Woodrow Wilson	March 4, 1913–March 4, 1921
Andrew Jackson	March 4, 1829–March 4, 1837	Warren G. Harding	March 4, 1921–August 2, 1923
Martin Van Buren	March 4, 1837–March 4, 1841	Calvin Coolidge	August 2, 1923–March 4, 1929
William H. Harrison	March 4, 1841–April 4, 1841	Herbert Hoover	March 4, 1929–March 4, 1933
John Tyler	April 4, 1841–March 4, 1845	Franklin D. Roosevelt	March 4, 1933–April 12, 1945
James K. Polk	March 4, 1845–March 4, 1849	Harry S. Truman	April 12, 1945–January 20, 1953
Zachary Taylor	March 4, 1849–July 9, 1850	Dwight D. Eisenhower	January 20, 1953–January 20, 1961
Millard Fillmore	July 9, 1850 –March 4, 1853	John F. Kennedy	January 20,1961–November 22, 1963
Franklin Pierce	March 4, 1853–March 4, 1857	Lyndon B. Johnson	November 22, 1963–January 20, 1969
James Buchanan	March 4, 1857–March 4, 1861	Richard M. Nixon	January 20, 1969–August 9, 1974
Abraham Lincoln	March 4, 1861–April 15, 1865	Gerald R. Ford	August 9, 1974–January 20, 1977
Andrew Johnson	April 15, 1865–March 4, 1869	Jimmy Carter	January 20, 1977–January 20, 1981
Ulysses S. Grant	March 4, 1869–March 4, 1877	Ronald Reagan	January 20, 1981–January 20, 1989
Rutherford B. Hayes	March 4, 1877–March 4, 1881	George Bush	January 20, 1989–January 20, 1993
James A. Garfield	March 4, 1881–September 19, 1881	William J. Clinton	January 20, 1993–January 20, 2001
Chester A. Arthur	September 19, 1881–March 4, 1885	George W. Bush	January 20, 2001–
Grover Cleveland	March 4, 1885–March 4, 1889		

SOURCES ON THE ARCHITECTURE

OF THE WHITE HOUSE

The most complete historical collection on the architecture and interiors of the White House is in the Office of the Curator of the White House, located in part of what was in early days the great kitchen of the house. Copies of visual and manuscript materials, some originals, and countless references to far-flung White House documents make this archive an outstanding resource on what might be called the material history of the place.

Most of the extant visual sources on the history of the White House as a building are represented in this book. Some items are lost—for example, the 1866 project for a new White House on Rock Creek—and others are omitted either in the interest of a balanced visual presentation or because they are easily accessible in other publications. Sources for visual materials published here are listed in the illustration credits.

Although some visual material in this volume does not pertain directly to the architecture of the house, these drawings, paintings, and photographs are used here in an architectural context. The iconography of the White House began late, with a representation on the title page of a book published in England in 1807 (see page 39) and cannot be considered extensive at any time before the Civil War. Of paintings there are few. But photographs are numerous. The first were taken in the winter and summer of 1846 (see page 103). Few have been found for the 1850s, but with the Civil War the photographic record became extensive, and it continues to the present. Most of the photographs that appear here were chosen for their usefulness to an architectural approach.

Written sources are more profuse for some periods than others, but in general the White House is a very well-documented building. The voluminous support papers of the various commissions and commissioners of public buildings, and their annual published reports regarding public buildings and grounds, are the principal sources on the physical White House. The commission papers are kept at the National Archives; most of the printed reports are at the Library of Congress, except for a few missing numbers kept in various private libraries, notably at Duke University and the Hagley Museum. Architectural material is sometimes found in the papers of the individual presidents. The Jefferson collection at the Massachusetts Historical Society is especially rich, and Madison's papers at the Library of Congress are useful for the same period. In general, presidential papers chiefly provide support of the commissioners' papers at the National Archives.

Before the telegraph and telephone, people who worked in Washington sent countless notes back and forth across town by way of messengers. Many of the letters received and sent, up to the twentieth century, survive in the records of the White House at the National Archives. Written mostly by public employees, these contain brief information about meetings, staffing, change orders, and other administrative matters and more detailed material about construction projects and the building's development and daily use. Other business papers include invoices from manufacturers, suppliers, and tradesmen, which amplify household inventories, often to a very great extent.

Throughout this book I have described features of the White House, its interiors, and its grounds that no longer exist. For the early period the sources for these descriptions lie almost entirely in business papers, supplemented by a small number of drawings and plans. Not until the later 1860s is there a body of photographs of sufficient size to assist in historical interpretation. Even when photographs are available, I have carefully gathered the written documents and synthesized the two in making my descriptions.

Papers of the architects are not plentiful. Little exists on James Hoban. His most important drawings for the house and its porticoes seem to have burned with his house soon after his death in 1831. Latrobe's drawings and letters, which are being published in ten volumes, eight now in print, by the Papers of Benjamin Henry Latrobe project at the American Philosophical Society, are an excellent source. The most useful are housed at the Maryland Historical Society and the Library of Congress. The Library of Congress also has a few unsigned drawings by Charles Bulfinch, whose services were borrowed at the White House while he was in Washington completing the Capitol. The papers of Thomas U. Walter at both the Library of Congress and the Athenaeum of Philadelphia document his work at the White House in the 1850s. The National Archives' Cartographic and Architectural Branch has drawings for renovation details by Alfred B. Mullett from Grant's time. Expansion projects by Frederick D. Owen for Harrison, Cleveland, and McKinley are also in that division of the National Archives, with additional material in the Library of Congress's geography and map division. McKim, Mead & White's papers and drawings are divided between the Avery Architectural and Fine Arts Library at Columbia University and the New-York Historical Society. A full set of the firm's photographs of the work, given by McKim to the Roosevelts, are at Sagamore Hill in Oyster Bay, New York.

All materials relating to the new third floor addition of 1927 are found at the National Archives in the records of U. S. Grant III, then the officer in charge of public buildings. Drawings for the west wing at various periods are included. Some of those for the east wing in more recent years are located in the architectural

section of the Office of White House Liaison, National Park Service, and in Lorenzo Winslow's papers at the Office of the Curator of the White House. The White House curator's office and the Franklin D. Roosevelt Library also have collections of Eric Gugler's papers. Nearly complete architectural coverage of the 1948-52 work is in the Records of the Renovation of the Executive Mansion at the National Archives, as well as in the Winslow collection. Abbie Rowe's extensive, methodically labeled photographs accompany full documentation of the Truman renovation.

Materials on current-day restoration and building projects at the White House are not generally available for security reasons. They are housed in the architectural section of the Office of White House Liaison. These sources were made available for this work, subject to restriction. Factual presentation was not impinged upon in any significant way by these limitations.

This book also draws as necessary on newspapers, published private papers, and secondary sources. By far the greater quantity of material in these categories is on life and politics at the White House, not architecture. The following published materials relate to White House architecture:

Brown, Glenn. *Memories, 1860-1930*. Washington: Press of W. F. Roberts, 1931.

Butt, Archibald. *The Letters of Archie Butt, Personal Aide to President Roosevelt*. Edited by Lawrence F. Abbot. Garden City, N. Y.: Doubleday, Page, 1924.

——.*The Letters of Archie Butt, Personal Aide to President Taft*. Edited by Lawrence F. Abbot. Garden City, N. Y.: Doubleday, Page, 1930.

Caemmerer, H. Paul. *The Life of Pierre Charles L'Enfant*. Washington: National Republic, 1950.

Carter, Edward C. II; John C. Van Horne; and Charles E. Brownell, eds. *Latrobe's View of America, 1795-1820*. New Haven: Yale University Press, 1985.

Commission for the Renovation of the Executive Mansion. *Acts and Estimates: Reconstruction of the White House, and Report*. Washington: U. S. Government Printing Office, 1952.

Crook, William H. *Memories of the White House*. Boston: Little, Brown, 1911.

Greenburg, Allan. "L'Enfant, Washington, and the Plan of the Capital." *Antiques* 140 (July 1991): 112-23.

Hamlin, Talbot. *Benjamin Henry Latrobe*. New York: Oxford University Press, 1955.

Hersey, John. "Mr. President: Ghosts in the White House." *The New Yorker* 27 (April 28, 1951): 36-38, 40, 42-50, 53-55.

Hoover, Irwin H. *Forty-Two Years in the White House*. Boston: Houghton Mifflin, 1934.

Hunt-Jones, Conover. *Dolley and the "Great Little Madison"*. Washington: American Institute of Architects Foundation, 1977.

Jeffrey, Thomas E., ed. *The Microfiche Edition of the Papers of Benjamin Henry Latrobe*. Clifton, N. J.: James T. White, 1976.

Jennings, J. L. Sibley. "Artistry as Design: L'Enfant's Extraordinary City." *Quarterly Journal of the Library of Congress* 36 (Summer 1979): 225-78.

Jensen, Amy Lafollette. *The White House and Its Thirty-five Families*. New York: McGraw-Hill, 1970.

Kimball, Fiske. "The Genesis of the White House." *Century Magazine* 95 (February 1918): 523-28.

Kimball, Marie. "The Original Furnishings of The White House." *Antiques* 15 (June-July 1929): 481-86 and 16 (July 1929): 33-37.

Kite, Elizabeth. *L'Enfant and Washington, 1791-1792*. Institut Français de Washington. Cahier III. Baltimore: Johns Hopkins University Press, 1929.

Klapthor, Margaret Brown. "Benjamin Latrobe and Dolley Madison Decorate the White House." *Contributions from the Museum of History and Technology*, Paper 49 (1965).

Koch, Robert. *Louis C. Tiffany: Rebel in Glass*. New York: Crown, 1964.

Kurjack, Dennis C. "Who Designed the President's House?" *Journal of the Society of Architectural Historians* 12 (1952): 27-28.

Leish, Kenneth W. *The White House*. New York: Newsweek Book Division, 1972.

McDaniel, James I. "Stone Walls Preserved." *White House History* 1 (1983): 38-45.

Marie, Jeanne and Alfred. *Marly*. Paris: [Pub. n. a.], 1947.

Monkman, Betty C. "The White House: 1873-1902." *Nineteenth Century* 3 (1978): 81-84.

Moore, Charles. *The Life and Times of Charles Follen McKim*. Boston: Houghton Mifflin, 1929.

Nesbitt, Henrietta. *White House Diary*. Garden City, N. Y.: Doubleday, 1948.

The Restoration of the White House, Senate Document 197, 57th Congress, 2d Session. Washington: U. S. Government Printing Office, 1903.

Sadleir, Thomas U. and Page L. Dickinson. *Georgian Mansions in Ireland*. Dublin: [Pub. n. a.], 1915.

Seale, William. *The President's House*. 2 vols. Washington: White House Historical Association, 1986.

Singleton, Esther. *The Story of The White House*. 2 vols. New York: McClure, 1907.

Smalley, E. V. "The White House." *Century Magazine* 38 (April 1884): 802-15.

Stephenson, Richard W. "The Delineation of a Grand Plan." *The Quarterly Journal of the Library of Congress* 36 (Summer 1979): 207-24.

Torres, Louis. "A Construction History of the City Hall on Wall Street, 1699-1788." Unpublished historic structure report, National Park Service, 1962.

——."Federal Hall Revisited," *Journal of the Society of Architectural Historians* 39 (1970): 327- 38.

Van Horn, John C., et al., eds. *The Correspondence and Miscellaneous Papers of Benjamin Henry Latrobe*. 3 vols. New Haven: Yale University Press, 1984-88.

Verheyen, Egon. "James Hoban's Design for the White House in the Context of the Planning of the Federal City." *Architecture* 2 (1981): 66-82.

Addendum (2001)

Monkman, Betty. *The White House: Its Historic Furnishings and First Families*. New York: Abbeville Press and Washington, D.C.: White House Historical Association, 2000.

Ryan, William and Desmond Guiness, *The White House, An Architectural History*. New York, McGraw Hill, 1980.

White House History. See issues 1–10 (1983–2001) for articles on the architecture and history of the White House. Washington, D.C.: White House Historical Association.

ILLUSTRATION CREDITS

ABBREVIATIONS

HABS = Historic American Buildings Survey, National Park Service
LC = Library of Congress
NA = National Archives
NPS = National Park Service
NPG = National Portrait Gallery, Smithsonian Institution